LA CAUSA

Civil Rights, Social Justice and the Struggle for Equality in the Midwest

LA CAUSA

Civil Rights, Social Justice and the Struggle for Equality in the Midwest

Gilberto Cárdenas, Editor
Foreword by Henry A. J. Ramos

Arte Público Press
Houston, Texas

This volume is made possible through grants from the Ewing Marion Kauffman Foundation, the Charles Stewart Mott Foundation, the National Endowment for the Arts (a federal agency), and the City of Houston through The Cultural Arts Council of Houston, Harris County.

Recovering the past, creating the future

Arte Público Press
University of Houston
452 Cullen Performance Hall
Houston, Texas 77204-2004

Jacket design by Adelaida Mendoza

Cárdenas, Gilberto.
La Causa: Civil Rights, Social Justice, and the Struggle for Equality in the Midwest / Gilberto Cárdenas, editor; foreword by Henry A. J. Ramos.
   p.   cm. — (The Hispanic civil rights series)
Includes bibliographical references.
ISBN 1-55885-425-8 (cloth : alk. paper)
   1. Hispanic Americans—Civil rights—Middle West. 2. Hispanic Americans—Middle West—Politics and government. 3. Civil rights movements—Middle West. 4. Social justice—Middle West. 5. Equality—Middle West. 6. Community life—Middle West. 7. Middle West—Social conditions. 8. Middle West—Ethnic relations. 9. Middle West—Politics and government. I. Cárdenas, Gilberto. II. Series.
F358.2.S75C38 2004
323.1168′073077—dc22   2004041078
                                                              CIP

ACC Library Services
Austin, Texas

4 5 6 7 8 9 0 1 2 3   10 9 8 7 6 5 4 3 2 1

Contents

Foreword

Many Americans, including Hispanics, are surprised to learn that the midwestern United States has been one of the nation's most dynamic population centers for Latino community organization and activism since the early 1900's. In fact, the nation's most longstanding Hispanic service and advocacy organization is the Guadalupe Center of Kansas City, which has been continuously running and growing programs since 1919. The Midwest, moreover, has been one of the most important areas as well for Hispanic laborers and union organizing—from workers in agriculture to those in the railroad, auto, and meat packing industries. It has also been a rich region for Latino policy studies, through the groundbreaking work of such scholars as the late Dr. Julián Samora and, more recently, Gilberto Cárdenas (who assembled this volume) at the University of Notre Dame.

One of my great surprises, after I first joined the professional staff of the American G.I. Forum in 1980, was the vibrancy and number of midwestern Hispanic advocates with whom I was able to meet and collaborate when I represented the Forum as its principal staffer in Washington, DC. On organizing trips to Detroit and Saginaw, Michigan, or to support leaders in Kansas City, Missouri, and Topeka, Kansas, or during state conferences in Omaha, Nebraska, and other parts of the region, I quickly became aware of the Midwest's deep history of Hispanic civil rights struggle—one that I had known nothing about prior to joining the Forum staff. But learning of this history firsthand from Latino leaders of the region, I came to appreciate what significant and essential contributions midwestern Latinos have made to the advancement of our people and our nation. I came to appreciate that the Midwest and its Latino communities have long been on the cutting edge of virtually every major advance in social justice that has involved the United States's Hispanic people, from the early struggles of César Chávez's farm worker movement, to the formation of significant anchor organizations, including not only the G.I. Forum, but also the National Council of La Raza, the Mexican American Legal Defense and Educational Fund, and the Southwest Voter Registration and Education Project (which eventually informed the development of the Midwest Voter Registration and Education Project).

While the social justice accomplishments of midwestern Latino leaders and groups have thus been many, far too few contemporary observers of U.S. civic and Hispanic community life understand this. Too little still has been written and recorded to make this history a more salient aspect of the nation's public awareness. The publication here is intended to address this problem by bringing forward in an impressive collection the historical analyses of leading Latino scholars and practitioners relative to the major individuals, organizations, and movements that have shaped midwestern (and national) history from a regional Hispanic viewpoint.

This volume, ably organized by Gilberto Cárdenas of the University of Notre Dame's Institute for Latino Studies, is part of an important series of civil rights studies being produced by Arte Público Press, with support from such leading national funders as the Rockefeller and C.S. Mott Foundations, Carnegie Corporation of New York, and the James Irvine Foundation. The series is dedicated to expanding public appreciation of post-World War II Hispanic contributions to American social justice history and the many lessons of that history, especially where younger Americans are concerned, relative to the continuing need for public leadership and advocacy on the issues.

The volume here, focused on midwestern Latino community experiences and issues, was made possible by a generous grant from the Kansas City-based Ewing Marion Kauffman Foundation. We are especially indebted to the Foundation's Andrés Dominguez and Adriana Pecina, whose programmatic leadership in the area of Youth Development made this support possible; and to Eugene R. Wilson, the Foundation's former senior vice president for strategic programs and planning, whose support was also a significant factor in securing Kauffman's involvement in this work. The Foundation, in its wisdom, understood early on that educating young people about the history of social justice leaders is an important investment in their own development as informed leaders for the future. We appreciate and applaud that perspective, and seek to use the products of the Arte Público Press Civil Rights Series as tools for youth leadership development.

The current publication, *La Causa: Civil Rights, Social Justice, and the Struggle for Equality in the Midwest*, is one that both young and more seasoned readers will find informative for its breadth in covering historical, as well as more contemporary aspects of midwestern Hispanics' articulation of the key issues of the times. We are indebted to the various contributors—some of the region's and the nation's most accomplished individuals in their respective fields—for their hard work to bring the book's important contents forward.

In addition, I am compelled to thank Stephanie Lubicz, my assistant, for her early and valuable support in the review and editorial process that led to this book's publication, as well as Arte Público's able staff in Houston for their indispensable support of series publications like the one at hand.

It is our great hope that readers of books like this one will find them a meaningful addition to their libraries, as well as their sensibilities about Hispanic contributions to the American community. As the Latino community of the United States expands to become the nation's new minority of record, with now nearly 40 million members (and projections that portend a doubling of that number in the decades to come), it is more important than ever that such books be made widely available to Americans of all backgrounds. By coming to a deeper understanding of how integrally involved Latinos have been in the nation's democratic evolution, we substantially increase our prospects to share a future based on what draws us all together as Americans, rather than what divides and separates us. Such a shared vision of our fate can only be in all of our interests, whatever racial or ethnic background we bring to the discussion.

Henry A. J. Ramos
Executive Editor
Arte Público Press
Hispanic Civil Rights Series

Introduction
La Causa: Civil Rights and Struggles for Equality in the Midwest
Gilberto Cárdenas

Activists, educators, academics, and legal experts have contributed their perspectives to this volume on the status of Latinos in the Midwest, with special attention to issues of civil rights and social justice. The authors approach the topic from a broad perspective, situating civil rights and social justice concerns in the context of the social, political and economic conditions of the Latino population in this region both past and present. While the book focuses on the Midwest, many of the issues addressed here bear a striking similarity to other regions of the United States. Nevertheless, where possible, we seek to present the specificities by which these issues have played out in a distinctively Midwestern setting.

Recognizing both the national and regional settings in which civil rights and social justice issues emerge does not ignore the role that international dynamics play in struggles to recognize and attain rights and justice. The migration and settlement of Mexicans in the Midwest have been integral components of the Mexican immigrant experience in the United States since before the advent of mass migrations in the 1910s and continuing to the present. Today, Chicago and its surrounding communities can claim the country's largest Mexican-origin population, second only to Los Angeles and surpassing both Houston and San Antonio in the 2000 census. Population growth in the city of Chicago, fueled largely by both legal and undocumented immigration, is augmented by natural growth and shaped by the internal migration to the suburbs by both foreign and native stock. In marked contrast to the past, Latinos living outside of Chicago now constitute over 51 percent of the region's Latino population. Migration and compositional changes illustrate most dramatically current trends and long-term effects in the Chicago region. They also underscore region-wide changes that will have a major impact on the current and future well-being of Latinos throughout the Midwest.

Outside of the Chicago metropolitan area, Latino migration and settlement continue to reflect a largely Mexican character. Between 1990 and 2000, influxes of Mexican workers and their families outstripped the growth of the settled Latino communities throughout the region. As in the past, the recent arrival and settlement of Mexican families throughout the Midwest can be seen as an integral component of the territorial dispersion of Mexican workers into areas previously settled by Mexican and Latino workers. But in many places, this migration serves as the foundation of entirely new settlements. If not by primacy, at least by sheer size, these settlements redefine both the physical and social identities of the communities where immigrants have settled. A Latino presence is now evident where Latinos had previously lived in relative anonymity and an entirely new identity has emerged where Latinos had not previously resided. Several examples illustrate this point. In 1970, a suburb immediately bordering the city of Chicago to the west—Cicero—reportedly had a Latino population of less than 1 percent. Thirty years later, the Latino population of Cicero surpassed 76 percent, according to the 2000 census. That same scenario has played out in countless small cities and rural areas in the Midwest. Between 1980 and 2000, Kansas and Missouri experienced nearly 100 percent growth in their Latino populations, and from 1990 to 2000 the number of Latinos in Nebraska increased 155 percent. In many areas, the overall population would have grown little or not at all but for the increase in the Latino population over the last decade.

Nationwide, from Census 2000 we know that the U.S. Hispanic population has jumped in the last decade, topping 35 million. Latinos have surpassed African Americans as the largest minority group in the nation. In the Midwest and elsewhere, it is now impossible to pass through the major thoroughfares of any small town or large city and miss the proliferation of stores with signs in Spanish and similar evidence of a burgeoning Latino population—although the physical and social presence of Latinos was entirely absent in many areas in the early 1980s. The influx of these newcomers into established communities has produced major changes and challenges. In areas where the Latino population has grown most dramatically, immigrants have arrived to fill low-skilled, badly paid (and sometimes high-risk) jobs in many industries. They typically remit wages to family members abroad, but they also spend money locally, in some cases revitalizing struggling inner city and small-town economies. In Iowa, for example, Latinos employed in the meat packing industry have strengthened a faltering economy, helping to fill the gap left by an aging workforce. Where the cost of living is low enough, some immigrants have purchased homes and settled in, changing the composition of neighborhoods and enriching the local culture. Although Latinos have generally brought economic prosperity and renewed vigor to communities, the response of some has proven to be less than welcoming. Not surprisingly, governments, longtime residents, and local school and health officials have had a mixed response to new Latino immigration. The arrival of unforeseen numbers of immigrant children has strained public school enrollments and budgets, especially in school systems with few bilingual staff. Clinics and hospitals may lack the funds and personnel to meet the health care needs of Latino families. Whether newcomers interact with social service agencies, police officers or non-Latino neighbors, the potential for misunderstanding and conflict is high. A relatively small number of community-based organizations, labor unions, and faith-based initiatives have sought to protect the civil rights of new immigrant populations. Yet despite the success stories, members of new Latino communities have little political power and influence. They face obstacles to obtaining social and economic opportunities and becoming fully integrated into American society.

Before the September 11 terrorist attacks, the political climate seemed to favor legal reforms that would have helped Latino immigrants, including the granting of amnesty to millions of undocumented persons. Presidents George W. Bush and Vicente Fox vowed to open the U.S.-Mexico border and foster a freer flow of people and commerce between their respective nations. The creation of a temporary worker program for Mexicans and others was under consideration. Since 9/11, however, the scenario has changed. Fearful of terrorism, many ordinary Americans now view immigrants with suspicion. The Midwest, and indeed the country, is divided between those who would freeze or drastically curtail immigration and those who believe that new laws must recognize the need for and contributions of Latino immigrant workers. Whether or not sweeping changes in immigration policy become permanent, tougher policing of U.S. borders has made it harder for illegal migrants to enter the country. Stricter enforcement of existing laws may have a long-term negative impact on Latino workers, and their families already in the United States.

All of these dynamics, recast in terms of the focus of this volume, must be understood first from the standpoint of pre-existing sets of relations between Latinos and the larger society; second, from the standpoint of current dynamics and situationally determined factors; and third, from the standpoint of a mix of emergent or entirely new issues. Many of these new issues grew out of very recent demographic changes, but they are likely to have a long-term impact on the future of Latino communities. They will play out in a variety of well-known arenas: the legal system, public policy venues, public opinion, organizational behavior, institutional responses, distributive resources and not the least, fiscal issues. Translated to more familiar terms, these arenas include the workplace, schools, health-care delivery services, state and local government agencies, legislative and administrative bodies, and the courts. Depending on a mix of circumstances, these dynamics will attain a level of saliency (from low to high) due to the kinds of organization and activities community organizations and faith-based initiatives mobilize to address issues affecting the well-being of Latinos throughout the Midwest.

This contextual framework outlining the importance of population dynamics, migration, natural growth an internal migration—coupled with an outline of the mix of arenas in which the particularities of issues are played out—would be incomplete if we failed to mention larger, more complex trends of both national and international scope. In particular, three very important considerations underpin the dynamics outlined above and bear very directly on an array of current and future civil rights and social justice issues in the Midwest: migration policy, economic policy, and citizenship policy.

Remarkably, "citizenship policy" would not have been a meaningful concept in the field of migration studies (U.S.-Americas) even as early as ten years ago. However, in light of a slowly evolving confluence of processes that accelerated in the late twentieth century, it is possible to argue that a dramatic reversal of citizenship rights has occurred in the United States and a select number of western industrialized nations. The notion of citizenship as an inclusive concept or principle has now shifted toward making it an exclusive concept and principle, manifested in the polity and the legal system's use of legal institutions and administrative apparatuses to exclude or greatly curtail the participation and entitlements of sectors of society deemed ineligible or undeserving. Individuals and their families face increasing restrictions, limiting their ability to enjoy the rights, privileges, benefits, and accumulated wealth of the very society that they helped to create and make thrive.

Economic and political requisites of society are at play. These requisites underscore and drive governmental policy, administrative action and public sentiment toward a decisively anti-immigrant stance, but with several significant exceptions.

The right to participate, the right not to be excluded and the right to enjoy the accumulated wealth and benefits of society—due in part to the real contributions of immigrant workers to the production process, consumption in the distribution system, and taxation in both arenas—should not be negated by the unwillingness of the polity or its legal system to establish a legitimate means commensurate with the demand and use of immigrant labor for people to enter or to be admitted, processed, or otherwise permitted to reside legally in the United States. After nearly one hundred years of institutionalized irregular migration, beginning in the early 20th century, migration flows still today are largely illegal, temporary and—despite 9/11—predominantly circulatory in nature. Nevertheless, such migration has always provided and still provides immediate benefits to employers and workers, as well as long-term benefits to society. Legal immigration, particularly from Mexico, remains largely a bi-product of both legal and illegal temporary migration.

With the exception of refugees, migration flows from the Americas historically have stemmed from the demand for work in the United States. The timing, mode of entry, destination and outcomes from the migration experience underpin the formation of new Mexican/Latino communities outside the pre-migration presence of many Mexican/Spanish communities in the Southwest. As a consequence, they shape the modalities and rates of integration, and ultimately the mobility and overall success of subsequent generations.

Translated in the present, we find the general discourse in the Midwest as well as in other areas of the United States on immigrant rights tied up in specific debates about access to health care, driver's license eligibility requirements, identification cards, admission to higher education, protection against spousal abuse and voting rights. Those debates will continue to play out in different ways around the country in the years to come, with important implications for Latinos in the Midwest and everywhere. By bringing together voices from diverse disciplines, this volume hopes to make a contribution to that discussion.

David Badillo's essay "From *La Lucha* to Latino: Ethnic Change, Political Identity, and Civil Rights in Chicago," gives a historical overview of the Latino struggle for civil rights in the Midwest's largest metropolis. His chapter focuses on key periods of transition from the early settlements of Mexican immigrants in the 1920s to the development of Chicano and Puerto Rican awareness in the 1960s and 70s, and to the emergence of new identities in the present day.

In "Latinos Struggle for Equality: A Case Study of Nebraska's Latino Communities," Miguel A. Carranza outlines the opportunities and challenges that both "old timers" and new arrivals to Nebraska face as a result of the state's increasing immigrant workforce population. The chapter also explores the degree to which Latino newcomers are being effectively and positively integrated into the economic, social and political lives and institutions of communities. The findings are particularly important since the Great Plains states would have experienced little or no population growth but for the increase of their Latino residents between 1990 and 2000.

Patricia Mendoza outlines the rise of Midwestern Hispanics as an electoral force in her chapter "Latinos and the Growth of Political Empowerment in Illinois." By 1980, Latinos were 14 percent of Chicago's total population, yet Latino representation in the Chicago city council, state legislature and U.S. Congress was close to nil. In the last twenty years, the political machine has allowed changes that include Latinos, but not without sustained struggle. Mendoza's essay highlights the critical role that the Mexican American Legal Defense and Education Fund (MALDEF) has played in advocating for Latino civil rights, particularly through litigation.

Education is another pivotal force in shaping leaders and planting the seeds for social change in the Latino community, as Judith Murphy points out in "Civil Rights and the Latino Community: Education." Focusing on Cristo Rey Jesuit High School in Chicago, this chapter demonstrates how a model institution that respects the fundamental right of education for youth is changing lives—and altering power relationships in the city's largest Latino neighborhood.

Ricardo Parra's essay, "Latinos in the Midwest: Civil Rights and Community Organization," gives a comprehensive overview of the Latino struggle for rights and inclusion. Documenting the civil rights issues that galvanized Latino immigrants in rural settings and big cities, Parra profiles the institutions and leaders that helped to change history over the last century. From the Midwest Council of La Raza to the Farm Labor Organizing Committee, and from small town community centers to Alinsky-style urban activism, very diverse types of organizations have served as engines in mobilizing Latinos in the Midwest.

A chapter by Sylvia Puente and Victor Ortiz, "The Latino Institute: Promoting Latino Progress through Policy Analysis, Leadership Development and Advocacy," analyzes one organization's contributions to promoting Latino civil rights in metropolitan Chicago. Through research and advocacy, the Latino Institute both witnessed and catalyzed improvements for the city's Latino community in its 25 years of existence (from 1974 to 1998). Looking at the successes and challenges that the Institute faced, the authors' case study draws important lessons for other civil rights organizations.

Discrimination, xenophobic laws, suspicion toward immigrants, shrinking economic opportunities—in a sense, the challenges that Latinos faced in the last hundred years remain the same as we enter the twenty-first century. Yet terrorism and heightened security concerns put a new twist on old problems. "In the Aftermath of September 11, 2001 and the Homeland Security Act of 2002: Implications for Midwest Latinos," Refugio I. Rochín and Alex Santana try to make sense of the changed scenario. While the full impact of post-9/11 reforms is still indeterminate, the authors rightly point out that the events of 9/11 dashed a historic opportunity to foster more open borders and cordial attitudes toward Latino immigrants and communities. What difference can one organization make in defending the civil rights of a vast, diverse and growing ethnic population? María de los Angeles Torres answers the question in her chapter, "In Search of Meaningful Voice and Place: The IPO and Latino Community Empowerment in Chicago." The IPO—that is, the Independent Political Organization of Little Village, located in the city's heavily Latino 22nd ward—played a major role in advocating for community services, political self-determination, and unity between the African-American and Latino communities. Torres traces its origins and rise along with that of Chicago's Mexican-American population, with particular attention to the work of such leaders as Jesús García, past successes, and the dilemmas that will continue to beset many Latino urban political organizations in the future.

Martha Zurita's essay "Mujeres Latinas en Acción: A Case Study of Latina Civil Rights," demonstrates the positive efforts of a Chicago nonprofit agency in protecting the fundamental civil rights of domestic violence survivors. Her chapter discusses the impacts of domestic violence from the perspectives of the victim, the children, and society at large, focusing on the particular situation of Latina immigrants. Mujeres Latinas en Acción, one of the first agencies in the country to advocate and provide services for Latina victims of abuse, provides an important case study for grassroots organizations that aim to shape public policies on behalf of immigrants.

It is my hope that this volume will substantially improve understanding of the Latino population nationally and to the particularities of its civil rights experience in the Midwest.

Latinos in the Midwest: Civil Rights and Community Organization
Ricardo Parra

The history of the United States is that of diverse people and their search for freedom, justice, and opportunity. The stories of various groups and their struggles for inclusion and acceptance mark milestones in the history of the U.S. This chapter briefly discusses the story of Latinos in the Midwest, how they organized to address issues of justice, fairness, and inclusion, as well as the roles that civil rights, community organizations, and social movements played in these efforts.

THE EMERGENCE OF LATINOS IN THE MIDWEST

The Midwest proved to be one of the first areas in the nation to experience the interaction among diverse groups of Latinos. In cities such as Chicago, East Chicago, Milwaukee, and Detroit, Mexican Americans and Puerto Ricans worked together on many shared issues and concerns. Mexicans, however, had arrived and settled in the region nearly sixty or seventy years before significant Puerto Rican and Cuban immigration began. They located themselves throughout the Midwest, while Puerto Ricans and Cubans tended to migrate to very specific geographical areas.[1]

The first and largest wave of Mexicans came during the Mexican Revolution, 1910-1921, when many Mexicans fled their country and settled in the industrial and railroad areas of the Midwest. These people found jobs as track hands for the railroad, in steel mills, packing houses, and industrial factories in such cities as Chicago, East Chicago, Detroit, Gary and Kansas City. Years later, from the 1940s through the 1970s, groups of Mexican American farm laborers from Texas moved to the region. Many settled out of the migrant stream into permanent occupations. Michigan became the prime state for this kind of settlement activity due to its high utilization rate of migrant farm laborers. Other states utilizing either *braceros* from Mexico or farm laborers from Texas included Illinois, Wisconsin, Ohio, Indiana, and Minnesota. The central states of Kansas, Iowa, Nebraska and Missouri used migrant farm laborers, but not to the extent of the Great Lakes States.

The Midwest is separated in two federal regions, composed of Chicago Great Lakes region, covering the states Illinois, Wisconsin, Minnesota, and Michigan; and the central states area of the Kansas City region of Kansas, Iowa, Missouri and Nebraska. There are important distinctions between these two regions. The central states are largely made up of rural communities, small and medium size cities, with only a few large cities and suburbs that include Kansas City, Missouri and Kansas City, Kansas, Wichita, Topeka, Omaha, Lincoln, Des Moines, and Davenport. The Great Lakes area is composed of large industrialized zones, including such cities as Chicago, Milwaukee, Detroit, Gary, Grand Rapids, Cleveland, Toledo, Minneapolis-St. Paul, and Indianapolis. According to the 2000 U.S. Census, approximately 3,105,843 Latinos live in these two regions.

Latino population numbers soared in the Midwest Great Lakes Region during the time period of 1990 to 2000, according the U.S. Census. Evidence shows that this is a fast-growing population with double and triple-digit growth. Illinois increased from 904,446 to 1,530,262, up 66.2 percent; Indiana increased from 98,788 to 214,536, up 117.2 percent; Michigan increased from 201,596 to 323,877, up 60.7 percent; Minnesota increased from 53,884 to 143,382, up 166 percent; Ohio increased from 139,696 to 217,123, up 55.42 percent; and Wisconsin increased from 93,194 to 192,921, up 107 percent. The Hispanic population in the six states of the Chicago Region increased from 1,491,604 to 2,622,111, up 75.8 percent.

In the central states Kansas City region from 1990 to 2000 the following occurred: Iowa increased its Latino population from 32,647 to 82,473, up 152.6 percent; Kansas increased from 93,670 to 188,252, up 100.97 percent; Missouri increased from 51,702 to 118,592, up 100.97 percent; and Nebraska increased from 36,969 to 94,425, up 155.41 percent. The Latino population in the four states of the region increased from 214,988 to 483,732, up 125.00 percent.

Illinois has the largest Latino population in the Midwest regions with 1,530,262. Chicago is now the second largest city in the United States for Mexicans and second largest for Puerto Ricans. The Latino population now makes up 26 percent of the city's population, accounting for 753,644 people.

The 2000 Census documents that Latinos are no longer live mainly in states

Hispanic Population by Type for Midwest Regions, States: 1990 and 2000

(Area	1990 Total population	1990 Hispanic population Number	1990 Percent	2000 Total population	2000 Hispanic population Number	2000 Percent	Hispanic type Mexican	Puerto Rican	Cuban	Other Hispanic
Chicago Region										
Illinois.........	11,430,602	904,446	7.9	12,419,293	1,530,262	12.3	1,144,390	157,851	18,438	209,583
Indiana.........	5,544,159	98,788	1.8	6,080,485	214,536	3.5	153,042	19,678	2,754	39,062
Michigan.......	9,295,297	201,596	2.2	9,938,444	323,877	3.3	220,769	26,941	7,219	68,948
Minnesota	4,375,099	53,884	1.2	4,919,479	143,382	2.9	95,613	6,616	2,527	38,626
Ohio	10,847,115	139,696	1.3	11,353,140	217,123	1.9	90,663	66,269	5,152	55,039
Wisconsin	4,891,769	93,194	1.9	5,363,675	192,921	3.6	126,719	30,267	2,491	33,444
Kansas City Region										
Iowa	2,776,755	32,647	1.2	2,926,324	82,473	2.8	61,154	2,690	750	17,879
Kansas..........	2,477,574	93,670	3.8	2,688,418	188,252	7.0	148,270	5,237	1,680	33,065
Missouri	5,117,073	51,702	1.2	5,595,211	118,592	2.1	77,887	6,677	3,022	31,006
Nebraska	1,578,385	36,969	2.3	1,711,263	94,425	5.5	71,030	1,993	859	20,543

such as California, Texas, Florida and New York, but also in areas such as the Midwestern states and several southern states. Nationally, according to the census, the Latino population increased by 58 percent, from 22.4 million in 1990 to 35.3 million in 2000, compared with an increase of 13.2 percent for the total U.S. population.

LATINO ORGANIZATIONS

Sociedades Mexicanas

Some of the first organizing efforts in the Midwest centered around churches and the Mexican mutual aid societies, both of which attempted to fulfill the need for fellowship, community, and identity. Particularly between the years of 1900 to 1940 during which the Mexican Revolution produced the first large wave of Mexican migration to the United States, the *mutualistas* organized as social and fraternal mutual aid societies assisting in burial insurance programs, credit unions, social events, *fiestas patrias* (patriotic celebrations), etc. The larger industrial sectors of the Midwest (Chicago, Kansas City, Detroit, East Chicago, Gary, etc.) saw many such organizations form and provide a significant social and cultural function in Mexican communities.

The membership of the *mutualistas* was largely composed of newly arrived Mexican workers with low paying, back-breaking jobs as railroad hands, laborers in the packing houses, steel mills, and other industries. The names of the organizations reflected not only the Mexican background of the membership but also the cooperative spirit of the unions. Such groups as the Sociedad Mutualista, Sociedad Unión Cultural Mexicana, Comité de Beneficiencia Mexicana, and Union Cívica Mexicana were quite active throughout the Midwest, occasionally becoming involved in social action activities. For example, the Unión Cultural Mexicana in Kansas City pressed for improved health care in the 1930s.

Some of these organizations have managed to survive to the present. Some own buildings and dance halls, some operate bars and credit unions and are an important force in the Fiestas Patrias, the annual Mexican Independence Day celebrations.[2] These early social, civic and fraternal organizations were cognizant of the discrimination Mexicans often faced and tried to ease this burden through strengthening the bonds of Mexican patriotic nationalism, culture, community service, and civic action. They were often the only groups that stood in solidarity with Mexican individuals and communities when they faced injustice, prejudice, discrimination, lack of acceptance and indifference, or when they were cast away by social structures of the dominant society as foreigners or aliens.

The Great Depression in the 1930s affected the civil rights and human rights of a number of Mexican individuals and their families, as exemplified by the forced repatriation to Mexico. Despite this history of indiscriminate deportations, many Mexican Americans served in the armed forces during World War II, some made the ultimate sacrifice for their country, some came back wounded, others fought bravely and earned medals for valor. It is estimated, that nationally, more than 500,000 Mexican Americans served in World War II.[3]

In the Midwest, as part of the war effort, many women, including many Mexican and Mexican American women, were part of the workforce in factories or other industries. For many, it was an opportunity to bring needed income into their war-era households. As men left for the service, the social infrastructure of these Midwest communities experienced fundamental changes, even if only for the duration of the war. Women were left with greater responsibilities as heads of households, wage earners, and community leaders. These women worked in various capacities in machinery , manufacturing, transportation, farm work and the medical field. They helped produce military vehicles, arms, uniforms, and communication equipment.[4] To aid the agricultural economic sector, the United States inaugurated the Bracero Program, which contracted and imported guest workers from Mexico. The Bracero Program began in August 1942 and lasted until it was eliminated by Congress in 1964.

As Mexican-American veterans returned from World War II, they were quickly reminded that conditions of discrimination and social inequality in their communities had changed very little. Some were denied membership in veterans' organizations or made to feel unwelcome; others were denied services or employment by local business and commercial establishments. Such open acts of discrimination were neither remote nor isolated but commonplace in many of their home communities in the Midwest. Confronted by such open acts of discrimination, many of these Mexican-American veterans became increasingly frustrated with the constant reminders of social inequality represented by poor schools, segregated and inadequate housing, and restrictions to certain sections of movie theaters, restaurants, parks and churches. Having served the country in World War II, these veterans were convinced that they should no longer tolerate treatment as second-class citizens. As one Mexican American put it, "We fought for the American ideals that our parents had taught us as children and we believed that our misfortune was merely a way of life. After the war, we clearly realized that these deplorable conditions only existed because of racial discrimination. We were no longer afraid, like our parents, to confront the local officials regarding these terrible problems. Our battle for eliminating social discrimination was less frightening when compared to the horrors of war we had recently experienced" (Santillán, 105). Mexican-Americans from the Midwest won at least five Congressional Medals of Honor, and others were awarded citations for valor. In the small, Illinois town of Silvis, 130 of the town's young Mexican-American men fought in World War II, Korea, and Vietnam. Eight were killed in action. During the 1940s and 1950s, discrimination in employment and promotions remained a larger reality in many Latino communities than it is today. Railroad companies, packing houses, steel plants, auto factories, and other types of assembly plants were seen as sympathetic to Latinos. Even in these industries, workers faced the prospects of dead-end jobs with little opportunity for promotion, due to discrimination. Some of these companies were unionized, and it was in there that Latinos learned about the union movement, and its importance to them.[5]

Founded in 1929, the League of United Latin American Citizens, in Corpus Christi, Texas, was one of the first and probably the most prominent Latino organization to adopt a position of assimilation or integration as a solution to improving the plight of Mexican Americans. LULAC soon found its way to the Midwest and became a prominent organization. By the 1950s, LULAC chapters were found in nearly all states of the Midwest. Originally, the organization appealed mostly to middle class Mexican Americans. Its image was that of a Mexican American social fraternal group that conducted queen contests, picnics, socials, and raised money for scholarships. However, with the advent of the Chicano Movement, LULAC members embraced the challenge to keep current with the events and issues. They kept pace with many current developments by passing resolutions in support of the farm workers, on education, and other Mexican American concerns. Today, LULAC has been in the national civil rights advocacy forefront, along with such groups as the National Council of La Raza (NCLR), and the Mexican American Legal Defense and Educational Fund (MALDEF), fighting for education, fair immigration policies, battling against English-Only policies, promoting English Plus, and other important issue facing Latino communities.

The establishment of both of these types of organizations such as the American G.I. Forum and LULAC signaled a new approach for a greater demand for inclusion as first-class citizens and a more determined effort to abolish barriers of discrimination. As a general rule, these groups tended to cautiously shy away from electoral politics, although some of these leaders were politically appointed to positions in both the Kennedy and Johnson administrations.

From the 1950s to the 1970s, other types of organizations emerged to test the waters of electoral politics in their communities. The 1960 "Viva Kennedy " campaigns served as a catalyst to involve Mexican Americans in national presidential campaigning in a direct and substantial way for the first time in U.S. history. The Kennedy effort is often described as a southwestern political phenomenon, which is historically incorrect since similar "Viva Kennedy" campaigns were conducted in the states of Illinois, Indiana, Michigan, Nebraska and Iowa (Santillán 106). The period from 1950 through 2002 was marked by remarkable change, activism, and progress. The civil rights movements raised consciousness about discrimination in public accommodations, housing, employment, and education. Some Latinos, through their churches—for example, the Catholic Committee on Inter-Racial Justice—and other organizations, lent support to this movement for civil rights and social justice. Many Latinos began to more fully comprehend issues involved in societal and institutional racism and discrimination in the South, as well as in other parts of the nation. Those involved, like their African-American counterparts, participated in freedom rides, marches, and other forms of support as individuals. Latinos embraced non-violent protest and struggle that later became a major aspect of the farm worker movement led by César Chávez.

Midwest Council of La Raza

In 1970, at a Conference of Midwest leaders and activists, the Midwest Council of La Raza was formed. The Midwest Council, an advocacy and self-determination organization, grew out of a conference sponsored by the Institute for Urban Studies of the University of Notre Dame in 1970. The meeting was called to highlight Mexican Americans in the Midwest and bring together leadership from the Southwest, Washington, D.C., and states surrounding Indiana to discuss a plan to merge all Mexican Americans into one national group. More than 200 leaders from throughout the ten Midwest states attended, including 100 student leaders. Leaders from each of the invited states presented reports on their respective states.[17] Some of the chief planners, organizers and presenters at the conference included Graciela Olivárez, Dr. Julián Samora, Dr. Ernesto Galarza, Dr. Jorge Prieto, Dr. Thomas Broden, Rubén Alfaro, among many others.

In its nearly ten years of existence, the Midwest Council pushed to give greater cohesion to the efforts of Spanish-speaking groups in advocating their own interests and focusing attention on the presence of Spanish-speaking people in the Midwest. Its activities included conferences, community development, communications, education, research, and training. Among the Midwest Council's numerous projects were major conferences, such as the political education conference called Mi Raza Primero, held in Muskegon, Michigan, in January 1972. The purpose of the conference was to promote political education and explore new political strategies and approaches in addressing issues in the Spanish-speaking communities of the Midwest. Bert Corona and José Angel Gutiérrez were the keynote speakers, raising awareness about the plight of undocumented immigrants and the importance of the immigration issue. Two philosophies emerged from this conference: one group thought Chicanos should work within the Democratic Party; another group wanted to support La Raza Unida Party. It was an indication of a new independent political movement in the Midwest (Parra 243).

The establishment of the Midwest Council of La Raza in 1970 served as the focal point for demanding greater awareness of the presence of Mexican-Americans and other Spanish-speaking groups in the ten-state region that comprises the Midwest. The Midwest Council of La Raza worked to persuade Midwest leaders and organizations to begin to see themselves as part of a larger regional community with particular local and mutual interests, and carried that same message outside the Midwest to other organizations and institutions. This regional view was further bolstered by demographic data presented in the 1970 Census, which reported that the Spanish-origin populations of Illinois, Indiana, Michigan, and Ohio were approximately equal to those of Colorado, Arizona, and New Mexico.

La Raza Unida

Unlike its southwestern counterpart, La Raza Unida in the Midwest developed organized advocacy groups rather than as a political party. Chicano leadership in the Midwest felt that La Raza Unida would be more effective in obtaining reforms and benefits in this way. A party, they felt, would risk exposing voter weaknesses among Chicanos. Later, some areas of the Midwest emerged with strategies for building a Raza Unida-type political party.

Initial Raza Unida efforts began in Michigan under the leadership of Rubén Alfaro. Because of the large farm worker population in this state, initial organizing efforts concentrated on their issues. Marches were held at the state capital to highlight the plight of the farm workers. As more and more people began to identify with Raza Unida's efforts, chapters soon spread throughout the state. State conventions were widely attended. La Raza Unida began to develop a communications network throughout the state. Demands began to be made for state agencies to provide more services to Chicano areas. Through continued advocacy, some progress was made, as various sections of state government opened up to provide more outreach and access, by including Chicano representation and staffing in important departments of state government (particularly in the key areas of education, social services and civil rights). Rubén Alfaro also encouraged others in the Midwest to organize. He introduced the Raza Unida concept in Ohio, Iowa, and Wisconsin. In Nebraska, a statewide organizing drive similar to the one conducted by La Raza Unida in Michigan, was started. This effort, headed by the Reverend Robert Navarro, was called the Nebraska Statewide La Raza Coalition (Parra 241).

Labor and Civil Rights Organizations

The Midwest has also witnessed numerous groups develop around issues related to labor, particularly farm labor, as well as around a variety of civil rights issues. The Farm Labor Organizing Committee (FLOC) was founded in 1967 by Baldemar Velásquez, and in 1979 was formally organized as a labor union of farm workers in the Midwest. In 1978, FLOC workers voted to strike all Campbell's tomato field operations in northwestern Ohio. FLOC then organized a boycott of all Campbell Soup products.

For a large number of citizens and immigrants, migrant farm labor was the main or only source of employment. It was typically harsh work, providing a minimal level of subsistence; in addition, agricultural employment was often seasonal and irregular. When the National Labor Relations Act was passed in 1935, farm labor was excluded. Consequently, farm workers have had to devise various strategies to struggle for better wages and working conditions. History was made when FLOC signed three-year labor contracts with Campbell Soup, its Ohio tomato growers, and its Michigan Vlasic pickle growers, in February 1986. The contracts gave FLOC farm workers a new set of labor rights and benefits. Finally, workers had won the right to unionize and have a voice in determining wages, benefits, and grievance procedures.[6]

Other organizations developed throughout all sections of the Midwest. However, their successes and failures were quite varied.[7] In Wisconsin organizations such as the Obreros Unidos, the United Migrant Opportunities Services (UMOS) and the Latin American Union for Civil Rights, all developed in the later 1960s to serve various needs within the Chicano/Latino communities. In Indiana, farm-labor organizing activities were sponsored by the United Mexican Americans (UMA), the Midwest Council for La Raza, and the Farm Labor Aid Committee (FLAC). United Mexican Americans was formed in South Bend, Indiana, in August 1969. The membership consisted mostly of blue-collar Chicano factory workers. An attempt was made at statewide organization, and chapters were soon established in Fort Wayne, Decatur, and Marion.

Like Raza Unida in Michigan, UMA was an advocacy organization and not a political one, but UMA was issue oriented. Marches and leafleting in support of the United Farm Workers' California strike were carried out. In South Bend, one of the projects undertaken was to gain greater participation in the El Centro Migrant Program. UMA was successful in this drive and Guadalupe González, a UMA member, became the first Chicano director of El Centro. Another effort by South Bend UMA was to advocate for a Chicano social service center to be funded by the local poverty program and to obtain a Spanish-speaking department within the Catholic diocesan structure.

Youth Organizations

At the heart of most organizational activities in the late 1960s and early 1970s were the youth. The high levels of energy and commitment displayed by these young people manifested itself in the creation of a multitude of organizations. They ranged from Brown Berets in urban areas to student organizations on many Midwest college and university campuses. Many of these student groups, inspired by the actions of the student movement in the Southwest, proliferated rapidly in the Midwest and began to make their concerns known.

Many of the once mild social and fraternal Mexican American student organizations began to change their style, tactics, and even names. For example, the Mexican American Student Association at Wichita State University (MASA) soon became Movimiento Estudiantil Chicano de Aztlán (MECHA). In Kansas City, the United Mexican American Student Association (UMAS) surfaced; in Topeka it was the Latin American Student Service Organization (LASSO); at the University of Kansas it was the Association of Mexican American Students, which eventually became MECHA; at Kansas State the organization which surfaced was MECHA; in Chicago it was the Organization of Latin American Students; in St. Paul it was the Latin Liberation Front; in Iowa it was the Chicano-Indian American Student Union; at Indiana University Northwest in Gary it was Adelante; and at the University of Notre Dame it was MECHA at the undergraduate level and the Centro de Estudios Chicanos e Investigaciones Sociales at the graduate level.

These organizations pressed for more recruitment efforts aimed at Chicanos and Latinos, employment opportunities at the staff and faculty levels, relevant cultural studies programs, and counseling and supportive services. They sponsored cultural awareness events, which sought to bring people together with leaders and activists of the Chicano Movement thereby providing important forums for giving voice and expression to the Chicano struggle. Teatro groups were particularly active in not only providing entertainment but also in providing an ideological message "between the lines" of the acts (Parra 245).

Unique among the student organizations was the Centro de Estudios Chicanos e Investigaciones Sociales at the University of Notre Dame. Established in September, 1972, to sponsor and promote social action and research within the Chicano community, the Centro began as an outgrowth of the community activities of Chicano graduate students. It was later organized into an active force for task-oriented community development. Centro de Estudios Chicanos was significant in that it was the first project of its kind to be initiated in the Midwest and indeed might have been the only such project to be initiated outside the Southwest and East Coast. The Centro aims were to benefit Chicanos in the Midwest through programmatic social action activities and scholarly research. The Centro and other Midwest centers that followed would fulfill a need for regional and national advocacy, for historical documentation and broader private, public, and scholarly attention to the plight of Latinos in the Midwest. Among the Centro's projects was the Midwest Conference on Raza Studies held in South Bend on April 23–25, 1974, and sponsored in conjunction with the Midwest Council of La Raza and the National Concilio for Chicano Studies Administrative Institute in Boulder, Colorado. The conference brought together Chicano professionals to develop strategies to cope with the issues that challenged the existence of Chicano studies as a viable, academic discipline. In August 1974, Centro completed a study of the social and economic conditions of the Spanish-origin population of South Bend. There was also a study of Chicanos in the Midwest and the Great Lakes region completed in January 1973. Another effort was made publish manuscripts based on the research studies of graduate students, including oral histories and compilation of newspaper documentation dealing with Chicano/Latino activities in the Midwest (Parra 245).

State Commissions

In the Midwest, Latino leadership was remarkably successful in convincing state legislatures to establish Latino state commissions in each of the Midwestern States. These unique commissions were initially designed to provide guidance to elected officials and appointees regarding policies and legislation affecting Latinos. The establishment of these state commissions provided Latino leadership with the benefits of access and input into state public policy. It also provided an important training ground for cultivating community leadership in the field of public policy and politics (Santillán 110–111). These commissions included the Spanish Speaking Peoples Study Commission Report (Illinois), the Governor's Council for Spanish-Speaking Peoples (Wisconsin); the Commission on Spanish-Speaking Affairs (Ohio); the Mexican American Commission (Nebraska); the Spanish-Speaking Affairs Council, later, Chicano/Latino Affairs Council (Minnesota); the Spanish-Speaking Peoples Commission, later, Iowa Latino Affairs; the Commission on the Status of Spanish Heritage People's, later the Indiana Hispanic/Latino Commission; the Commission on Spanish-Speaking Affairs (Michigan); the Governor's Advisory Council on Hispanic Affairs (Missouri); the Ohio Commission on Hispanic/Latino Affairs, and the Advisory Committee on Mexican American Affairs, later, the Kansas Advisory Committee on Hispanic Affairs.

Civic and Improvement Associations

Community civic and improvement associations focused on neighborhood issues rather than city hall's partisan power politics. Regardless of what political party or faction was in power, these organizations stood as vigilant advocates for their communities. They saw their roles as conscientious promoters and defenders of neighborhood and community interests. Past examples of these types of organizations include the former Mexican American Neighborhood Council in Kansas City and Pilsen Neighbors in Chicago. It has been neighborhood and community-based organizations that have kept and continue to keep the focus neighborhoods and communities. Saul Alinsky, one of the most famous community organizers of the 20th century, perfected a style of organizing while operating from his Chicago-based Industrial Areas Foundation, that later became a school for organizers. His strategy was based on neighborhood and community organizations, many of which were community churches or church organizations, federated into a single large organization. Saul Alinsky chose not to build around an ideology, but rather on the self-interest of communities. He believed in the primacy of the people and a free and open society. Some critics attacked the idea of an organization of organizations based on self-interest and power building, stating that they would lose their original missions or be co-opted or corrupted by the pursuit or accumulation of power, and that they would thereby lose their values and original missions.

Civil Rights Organizations and Agencies

In 1975, the Washington-based National Council of La Raza (NCLR) opened its field office in Chicago and began to build its constituency base of affiliate organizations. As a private, nonprofit, nonpartisan, tax-exempt organization, NCLR worked to reduce poverty and discrimination, and improve life opportunities for Hispanic Americans. Led by Raúl Yzaguirre, NCLR has expanded its base of affiliate organizations in the Midwest and held its popular national conference in the Midwest in such cities as Chicago, Milwaukee and Kansas City. Many of its conferences have attracted upwards of 15,000 people. Throughout the years, NCLR has been the leading national Latino civil rights organization and has provided technical assistance, well-informed advocacy and research in the fields of civil rights, education, health, employment, social services, immigration and public policy. In 1973, it adopted a pioneering policy that required half of its board of directors be comprised of women.

The Mexican American Legal Defense and Educational Fund (MALDEF), founded in 1968 in San Antonio, Texas, is the leading nonprofit Latino litigation, advocacy and educational outreach institution in the United States. Headquartered in Los Angeles, MALDEF has regional offices in Atlanta, Los Angeles, San Antonio, Chicago, and Washington, D.C., with a satellite office in Sacramento and program offices in Phoenix, Albuquerque, and Houston. In 1980, MALDEF opened a regional office in Chicago, Illinois. It is a legal advocacy organization dedicated to the specific gamut of civil rights issues that affect the Latino community both regionally and nationally. During the early 1980s, the Midwest offices of MALDEF, the Puerto Rican Legal Defense and Educational Fund, along with Latino community groups, were in the spearhead of the redistricting battles. These local and state reapportionment efforts took place in Detroit, Milwaukee and Chicago.[8] The Latino community prevailed, and new district boundaries were drawn and special elections held. As a result, two Latino candidates were elected to the Chicago city council, and the mayor, clearly aware of the importance of the Latino vote in his 1987 reelection bid, appointed several Latinos to his administration. In 2001, MALDEF argued in Chicago that the Lake County Board had passed a redistricting plan with the intent and effect of diluting the voting strength of Latinos in Lake County. MALDEF filed a voting rights lawsuit against the Lake County Board on behalf of Latino residents of Lake County.

Research Efforts

The Midwest has begun to develop partnerships between Universities and communities by supporting research centers. In the early 1990s, more research organizations began to appear. Some of the research centers in the Midwest now include the Julián Samora Research Institute at Michigan State University, the Institute for Latino Studies at the University of Notre Dame, and the national Inter-University Program for Latino Research (IUPLR).

CHICAGO'S LATINO COMMUNITY

Influenced in part by new ideas and experiences, Chicago saw a new generation of Latino leadership and organizations emerge in the 1970s. The result was a dramatic rise in the level of organizing within the Pilsen community. These community leaders included Juan Velásquez, Felipe "Phil" Ayala, Linda Coronado, Arturo Vásquez, Danny Solís, Felipe Aguirre, and Rudy Lozano. Some of the organizations established during this era include Centro de La Causa, Casa Aztlán, Hogar de Niños, Mujeres Latinas en Acción, CASA, Latino Youth, Asociación Pro Derechos Obreros, and others.[9]

Centro de Acción Social Autónomo (CASA), formerly Illinois Raza Unida party or El Enfoque, promoted political education and awareness. Leaders con-

ducted popular forums to involve the community in political dialogue and discussion groups (Parra 246). One of the leaders of CASA was Rudy Lozano, who
was both dedicated and charismatic, as well as instrumental in the formation of
the Midwest Commission for Defense of the Undocumented. In addition to
being a community activist, he was a primary organizer of the Near Westside
Branch of the Independent Political Organization and the Midwest Director of
the International Ladies Garment Workers Union. As a member of Harold
Washington's transition team, Lozano had been instrumental in uniting African
American and Latino groups. He had also been a key ally within the Mexican
community in the election of Harold Washington. In 1983, he lost a close race
for alderman of the 22nd ward. Shortly after the election, he was shot to death
in his Pilsen home. The Rudy Lozano branch of the Chicago Public Library,
named in honor of this fallen community leader, opened in 1989.[10]

LATINO INFLUENCE IN CHICAGO

According to Brian Rogal, writing in "Latinos Emerge as Force in Politics,
Economy,"[11] for the Chicago Community News Project, Latinos are transform-
ing the look and feel of Chicago and surrounding areas. As Rogal points out, they
are increasingly set to grasp real influence over politics, culture, and economy.

It is ironic in a sense that Chicago's Latino community turned out to be a rising center of social change. At the height of the Chicano Movement in the Midwest, most ideas of social change seemed to be coming from California, Texas,
or Colorado and other southwestern states. How could Chicago, a city of
machine politics, offer lessons and models for social change, self-determination
and independence? A closer look and analysis of the history and dynamism of
Chicago provides many answers to these questions.

Chicago is where the labor movement started and was nurtured. It is the
home of Saul Alinsky's Industrial Areas Foundation (IAF) and mass-based community organizations. Most importantly, however, it is a city of ethnicity and
ethnic neighborhoods, the Midwestern city with the largest Latino population,
the second largest U.S. city of Mexican population outside of Mexico. Experiencing sharp growth since 1980, Chicago's Latino population increased from (a
79 percent increase since the prior census count of 753,644). Cook County's
Latino population increased a dramatic 115 percent. Much of this is a result of
growth in the Mexican population, with an unknown portion attributed to the
undocumented Mexican immigrants. According to the 2000 Census, Latinos
make-up 27% of Chicago's population and 12.5 percent of the suburban population (Rogal). The census further showed that Mexicans are the largest of all
Latino-origin groups in Chicago, comprising 75 percent of the Latino-origin

population; followed by Puerto Ricans, representing 11 percent; and Central and South Americans, making up 14 percent of the remaining portion of Latino-origin population.

Chicago, once the port of entry for Latino immigrants, has seen many newcomers immigrate directly to its suburbs. As a result, Latinos in suburban Chicago increased from 291,653 in 1990 to 651,473 in 2000. For example, in the city of Elgin, forty miles from Chicago, the Latino population grew from 28% in 1998 to 34% in 2000. Cicero, a city once comprised of a population predominantly Italian and East European, grew from 37% Latino in 1990 to 77% today. Latino population growth in towns and cities has generally led to conflicts between these municipalities and the newly arrived residents. Many towns have pushed to restrict the number of persons residing in houses, a setback to Latinos with large families. In November 2000, the U.S. Department of Housing and Urban Development asked the U.S. Department of Justice to investigate allegations that the city inspectors applied tougher standards to Latino homes. In 2002, the city of Elgin agreed to settle and pay families that had suffered discrimination.

In the push for increased political representation on behalf of Latinos, several challenges remain in the sphere of Latino politics. Currently, political leaders can cast aside Latinos because of their relatively low voter turnout, in part due to non-citizenship status. With over 900,000 Latinos of voting-age, Latinos could have a significant voice in politics, but only 350,000 are registered. Juan Andrade, president of the United States Hispanic Leadership Institute and Chicago *Sun-Times* columnist, notes that 35 percent of Latinos are under 18, and 300,000 are undocumented. Latinos in the 2000 election cast only 4 percent of the votes in Illinois. Among several Chicago organizations that have made efforts to register Latinos has been the United Neighborhood Organization (UNO), previously headed by Daniel Solís, the current 25th ward alderman. The organization, currently led by executive director Juan Rangel, has held naturalization and registration drives and emphasized home ownership.

To address this same concern, Congressman Luis Gutiérrez organized workshops, attracting hundreds of individuals, in order to aid them in becoming citizens. An active leader in immigration reform, adept at building coalitions among diverse groups, Congressman Luis Gutiérrez, a Puerto Rican, won the 2002 primary for the 4th district congressional seat by a 3-to-1 margin by the Mexican-American supported by Mayor Daley. The law mandates redistricting occur every ten years, following the taking of the census in order to adjust congressional districts to population changes. A 2001 state commission voted to raise the number of mostly Latino districts in the 118-member General Assembly from four to eight.

Over the years, Chicago's Latinos have been active in organizing grassroots organizations, such as the Little Village Community Development Corporation. Typical of their actions was the 2001 campaign that forced the Chicago school district to construct a long-promised school in Pilsen. The Pilsen Neighbors Community Council, another grass roots organization, has fought gentrification and rising property taxes in Pilsen. It has also successfully sponsored Fiesta del Sol, the biggest summer street festival in the Midwest.

Future Trends

A potential void in leadership is projected for the future. According to some experts, many of today's current community leaders are not sufficiently nurturing enough young Latinos. Other observers disagree, stating that Latino leadership is becoming more ideologically diverse, with the appearance of liberals, moderates and conservatives. A number of factors may be contributing to this, such as varying levels or speed of political, economic, and social integration. A new trend in politics has many Latino leaders moving into politics from business or nonprofit work. This is very different from the 1970s and 1980s, when activists emerged from universities and community groups.

Many of the above trends will test the skills and sophistication of civil rights and community leaders as they seek to organize and build agendas on a wide range of issues, while, at the same time building unity in the midst of a growing and diverse population. Midwestern approaches to civil rights and community organizations in Latino communities demonstrate an amalgamation of many diverse ideas, philosophies, ideologies, theories, and strategies. To look at Midwest Latino communities is to see communities with unique experiences, including the levels of acculturation, old or continuing immigration, differences in history and length of the U.S. experience, the mix of various Latino cultures and also the extent of the dominant culture. All are evolving. It is a dynamic process occurring with different pushes and pulls. These are creative and adaptive actions, creating changes at different degrees.

In the Midwest, each community has its own political culture. Each locality is unique and requires the development of strategies that take into account their own political, economic, and cultural environments. As a result, Latino leaders in the Midwest have had to be more creative in confronting and negotiating with power structures in their respective areas. They have learned how to build alliances and coalitions, organize and reorganize, as well as build new organizations and community institutions. As Midwest Latino leaders continue to organize for civil rights and social progress, they will develop new styles of organizing, new leaders and organizations, setting an example for the rest of the nation.

Notes

[1]Richard Santillán, "Latino Politics in the Midwestern United States: 1915–1986," *Latinos and the Political System*, edited by F. Chris García (Notre Dame: University of Notre Dame Press, 1988), p.101.

[2]Ricardo Parra, Víctor Ríos and Armando Gutiérrez, "Chicano Organizations in the Midwest: Past, Present and Possibilities," *Aztlán* 7/2 (1978), p. 238.

[3]Richard Santillán, "Saving Private José: Midwestern Mexican American Men during World War II, 1941–1945," *The Journal of Interdisciplinary Studies: A Journal of Research and Innovative Activities*, 14 (Fall 2001), p. 19.

[4]Richard Santillán, "Rosita the Riveter: Midwest Mexican American Women During World War II, 1941–1945," *Perspectives in Mexican American Studies: Mexicans in the Midwest* 2 (Mexican American Studies and Research Center, University of Arizona, 1989), pp. 115–116.

[5]According to Dr. Richard Santillán: "Historically, the union movement in the Midwest has resisted the participation of Mexican Americans, Puerto Ricans, and blacks, often ignoring the social and economic needs of its minority rank-and-file members. The history of exclusion by labor unions was based largely on racial and ethnic discrimination, job competition, and the fact that minority workers were unwittingly recruited as strikebreakers. Currently, the discriminatory, union practices have gradually decreased with the establishment of aggressive minority caucuses within the labor movement." In Richard Santillán, "Latino Political Development in the Southwest and Midwest Regions: A Comparative Overview, 1915–1989," *Latinos and Political Coalitions, Political Empowerment for the 1990's*, edited by Roberto E. Villarreal and Norma G. Hernandez (Greenwood Press, 1991), p. 121. The exceptions to the above are labor unions that consisted of minority workers and immigrants and had a more open international perspective of organizing all working people. Examples of such unions are the International Ladies Garments Workers Union, now organized as UNITE (Union of Needletrades and Textiles Employees, AFL-CIO) and the Service Employees Union (SEU).

[6]W.K. Barger and Ernesto Reza, *The Farm Labor Movements in the Midwest: Social Change and Adaptations Among Migrant Farmworkers* (Austin: The University of Texas Press, 1994).

[7]The history of labor organizations and Latinos in the Midwest shows the formation and development of such organizations as the Latin American Labor Advisory Committee, the Labor Council for Latin American Advancement (LACLA), Latin American Labor Council, the Chicago Area Hispanic Labor Council, and the Latin American Committee on Labor Action. Some of the

Latino labor leaders in the Midwest have included Hank Lacayo of the United Auto Workers, Percy Ramíez of the United Auto Workers, Hank "Babe" Gómez and Jesse Arredondo of local 1010 of the United Steel Workers, Lee Silva of the United Steel Workers in Michigan, Mary Rivera Ruiz of the Amalgamated Meat Cutters and Butcher Workmen, and Baldemar Velásquez of the Farm Labor Organizing Committee (FLOC), AFL-CIO.

[8]"The Latino communities were successful in convincing the judicial system that both the Milwaukee and Chicago reapportionment plans violated their civil rights by diluting their voting power. The courts, therefore, ordered both the redrawing of new district boundaries and special elections. This historical outcome in Chicago was the stunning election of two Latino candidates favored heavily by Mayor Harold Washington, a black, which literally broke the political stalemate between Mayor Washington and the former majority on the Chicago City Council. Mayor Washington, clearly aware of the political importance of the Latino vote in his 1987 reelection bid, added several key Latino appointments to his administration." (Santillán 112)

[9]*Rudy Lozano: His Life, His People* (Chicago: Taller de Estudios Comunitarios, s.d.), p. 29.

[10]June Skinner Sawyers, *Chicago Portraits: Biographies of 250 Famous Chicagoans* (Chicago: Loyola University Press, 1991).

[11]Brian Rogal, "Latinos Emerge as a Force in Politics, Economy," *Community News Project* (Chicago: Community Media Workshop, 2002).

Latinos[1] and the Growth of Political Empowerment in Illinois
Patricia Mendoza

During World War I, the first wave of Latinos (Mexicans) arrived in Illinois lured by the prospect of employment with the higher paying railroad and other nonagricultural jobs (Padilla 20). Mexicans were followed in the late 1940's by a second group of Latinos: Puerto Ricans (Padilla 23). Throughout the subsequent years, the Latino population continued to grow until 1980 when Latinos represented 14% of Chicago's total population and 5.56% of Illinois' population.[2] Yet, Illinois' election history showed that *not one* Hispanic had been elected to a Chicago city council seat since 1915,[3] and no Hispanic from Illinois had ever been elected to the state general assembly or the United States Congress.

Prior to 1980, Latinos had made attempts to obtain political empowerment.

In 1972, the Puerto Rican Organization for Political Action filed suit to force the Chicago Board of Election Commissioners to provide Spanish-speaking voters with instructions and assistance in the Spanish language.[4] They wanted voting instruction, ballots and ballot labels on voting machines to be printed in Spanish as well as English, and they wanted election judges in heavily Latino precincts to be bilingual in both English and Spanish. The Board of Elections maintained it had no legal obligation to provide these things. However, faced with litigation, it offered to provide the requested assistance during the impending November 1972 election. The judge found the Board of Election's failure to take steps to provide election assistance in Spanish prior to the commencement of the lawsuit significant granted and a preliminary injunction stating: "The enforcement of important rights of the plaintiff class should not depend, however, upon

19

the voluntary acts of the defendants or upon my prediction that defendants will do what they say they intend, but will not agree, to do (Puerto Rican Organization 611)."

Less successful was the Latino community's first attempt to have representation in Chicago's aldermanic ward redistricting plans. In 1970, a group of individuals, including one Puerto Rican, challenged the ward map adopted by the City Council alleging that the ward boundaries had been drawn "to avoid having any ward in which the majority would be Puerto Rican."[5] The evidence clearly established that the principal map drawer had considered the location of predominantly black and Puerto Rican areas in formulating the new ward boundaries. The court stated that although no minority racial or ethnic group was entitled "to have any particular voting strength reflected in the [city] council . . . such strength must not be purposefully minimized on account of their race or ethnic origin (Cousins 843)." However, despite the evidence presented, the court concluded that it was "unable to say that plaintiff's evidence so clearly established that the ward boundaries were the product of purposeful discrimination" (843). Nevertheless, the court ordered a new trial (844). On retrial, the district court held "that the considerations for the shape and boundaries of the 31st Ward [the ward in question], were primarily political and that the failure to include certain areas of blacks or Puerto Ricans caused them no discernible loss of voting strength."[6]

It was against this backdrop that the Mexican American Legal Defense and Educational Fund (MALDEF) came to Chicago. MALDEF, a civil rights organization, had been founded in San Antonio, Texas, in 1968 to address the discrimination and violation of the civil rights of Mexican Americans.[7] Ten years later, MALDEF came to Chicago at the urging of several prominent Latino leaders, who included members of the Mexican American Lawyers Association (MALA), Judge David Cerda (the first Latino judge in Illinois) and Virginia Martínez, an attorney who had interned at MALDEF"s San Francisco office and who ultimately became the Chicago office's first associate counsel. Their plea was simple: the Latino population in the Midwest was growing, and access and opportunities for this growing constituency were not forthcoming.

MALDEF first came to Chicago for the limited purpose of conducting a census educational outreach campaign, the goal of which was to educate the growing Latino population on the importance of participating in the census. The message to the Latino community was that the census was the basis for everything from allocations of federal funds to redistricting and that Hispanics had to participate fully in the census if they were to benefit. The office had a small and simple beginning. The individuals hired to run the census project, first Mario

Moreno and then Eva Vera, worked out of the office of Virginia Martínez, then an attorney in private practice. However, the success of the census project in identifying the growing and diverse Latino population in the Midwest convinced the leadership of MALDEF to establish a full service regional office to serve the Midwest.

The Midwest Regional Office officially opened in Chicago in October, 1980. Since that time, MALDEF has been at the forefront of civil rights litigation in the Midwest, setting precedent in many cases.[8] But without a doubt, MALDEF"s greatest impact has been in the area of political empowerment for Latinos.

The dramatic demographic changes revealed by the 1980 census ushered in a new era for Hispanics. The white population of Chicago had decreased while the black and Hispanic population increased.[9] State law required the city council to redistrict the city on the basis of new census data by December 1 of the year following the taking of a national census (Ketchum 1400). MALDEF wasted no time in using those changing demographics to advocate for the creation of wards that provided Latinos with fair representation. In fact, in 1981, the City Council adopted a ward map that provided for four Hispanic majority wards (Ketchum 1401). At first glance this might have appeared to be a victory for the Hispanic community, which had never before had a majority ward. However, Hispanic voters were unsatisfied with the adopted map because it identified a "Hispanic majority ward" as a ward with a "Hispanic *total* population of more than 50%," that is to say, a simple majority. Hispanic voters argued that a simple majority of the total Hispanic population in a ward was insufficient to allow Hispanics to elect a candidate of their choice.

As a result, in the summer of 1982, MALDEF and the Puerto Rican Legal Defense and Education Fund (PRLDEF) filed suit on behalf of six Hispanic voters ("the Velasco plaintiffs").[10] The suit charged that the map adopted by the City Council intentionally manipulated boundaries and "fractured"[11] the Hispanic population in order to minimize Hispanic voting strength.[12]

The District Court found a violation of Section 2 of the Voting Rights Act[13] and ordered the defendants to create a new map using "voting age population" instead of "total population" in determining the relative racial composition of a ward. However, the Court agreed with the City Council that a simple majority was adequate to permit a minority group to elect a candidate of its choice (Ketchum 1402).

Dissatisfied with this decision, the plaintiffs appealed to the Appellate Court to order the District Court to devise a new map adopting a 65% minority population guideline in creating minority majority wards (Ketchum 1402). The Court of

Appeals agreed with the plaintiffs and sent the case back to the District Court with certain guidelines to aid the court in fashioning a new ward map (Ketchum 1412). The Court of Appeals criticized the District Court's holding that a simple majority provided minority groups with a reasonable opportunity of electing a candidate of their choice. In devising a remedy, the Appellate Court instructed the District Court to consider the usually lower voter registration and turn-out patterns of certain minority population groups (Ketchum 1413) as well as their "younger-than-average population" and citizenship status.[14] The Court noted that "there [was] simply no point in providing minorities with a "remedy" for the illegal deprivation of their representational rights in a form which [would] not in fact provide them with a realistic opportunity to elect a representative of their choice."[15]

After providing the District Court with a framework for creating a remedy, the Court of Appeals directed the District Court to re-examine those wards with significant Hispanic populations and determine whether four wards could be created, each with a sufficiently large majority of Hispanics to provide them with a reasonable opportunity to elect candidates of their choice (Ketchum 1418).

In 1985, the parties presented a settlement map to the court for approval, which created four majority Hispanic wards with greater percentages of Hispanic voting age population than the originally challenged map.[16] The court approved the map noting that "while the population of Hispanics in absolute numbers may seem to support a greater number of Hispanic wards, the dispersion of Hispanics makes creation of more than four majority Hispanic wards virtually impossible" (Ketchum 557).

The litigation did not end there, however. The plaintiffs also petitioned the court for special elections in the wards that were redrawn under the settlement plan. The court granted the request, concluding that "legal and equitable considerations in this case support special elections" (Ketchum 568). These special elections took place on March 18, 1986, and resulted in the number of Hispanic aldermen increasing from one to four: Miguel Santiago,[17] Jesus Garcia, Juan Solis and Luis Gutierrez.[18] Thus began a new era for the Latino community in Chicago. But the victory extended beyond the Latino community. It gave a one-vote majority in the city council to the new black mayor, Harold Washington.[19]

The struggle for Latino representation at the state level was no less contentious. The state legislature had failed to adopt a redistricting plan by June 30, 1981, as mandated under the 1970 Illinois Constitution.[20] As a result, in July 1981, the Legislative Redistricting Commission ("Commission") was established. From the outset there was concern among the Latino community because the Commission had no Hispanic representation. During public hearings held in Chicago to obtain public input regarding the redistricting plan, "Hispanics pointed out that they had no representation in the General Assembly and urgently requested an opportunity to secure such representation" (Rybicki 1087). Despite these pleas, the Commission adopted a new redistricting plan in October, 1981, which failed to adequately address those concerns. Instead, the plan split up the two largest Hispanic concentrations in Chicago among several house and senate districts, resulting in no majority Hispanic districts (Rybicki 1095).

In 1982, Hispanic voters (the Del Valle plaintiffs) and two other groups challenged the redistricting plan adopted by the Commission.[21] The Del Valle plaintiffs alleged that although those responsible for drawing district lines for Chicago "were aware of these sizable Hispanic population centers,[22] [they] intentionally fractured [split up] both Hispanic communities by dividing each community among four separate legislative districts" (Rybicki 1123).

The Commission justified the decision to fracture the Hispanic community by arguing that the districts were designed to accommodate future growth and migration patterns that were characteristic of these Hispanic communities (Rybicki 1123). One member of the Commission analogized this justification to "buying a snowsuit for a young child—purchasing a suit several sizes larger than the growing child's present dimensions . . . in order to allow the child to grow into the suit and thus prolong its use" (Rybicki 1123). The DelValle plaintiffs challenged this explanation by noting that "no other racial, ethnic or political group was fitted to 'snowsuit' districts and that the Commission's actions served to exacerbate existing underrepresentation of Hispanic interests in the General Assembly" (Rybicki 1123).

The parties reached a settlement on January 7, 1982.[23] Under the terms of the Settlement Agreement, Hispanics constituted approximately 71% of the population in Commission House District 20, 63% of the population in Commission House District 9 and 50% of the population in Commission House District 10 (574 F. Supp. 1123). Moreover, Commission Senate District 5, which encompassed House Districts 9 and 10, contained an Hispanic population of approximately 56%" (Rybicki 1124).

The court held that "under all the circumstances, . . . the Hispanic Settlement Agreement [was] fair, adequate and reasonable to Hispanics and afford[ed] them a fair opportunity to elect candidates of their choice to the General Assembly" (Rybicki 1124). Thus were established the first Hispanic state legislative districts. The first legislative election that followed the entry of the settlement agreement was for the 1983-1985 legislative term. The first Latino State Representative elected after the settlement was Joseph Berríos in the 9th District.[24] The

1984 election added Juan M. Soliz in the 20th District. The first Latino Senator, Miguel Del Valle, was elected in 1987.

While the 1980 census provided the Hispanic community with its first opportunity to create city wards and legislative districts that afforded them an opening to elect candidates of their choice, it would not be the last. By 1990 the Hispanic population had increased to 19.6% of the city of Chicago's population and 7.9% of the State of Illinois' population (U.S. Census Bureau 1990 Race Data). As a result, Hispanic representation at both the city and state levels increased yet again. In addition, Latinos were successful in creating the first Latino majority congressional district in Illinois: the Fourth Congressional District. However, as in the 1980 redistricting, these increases in Latino representation came about as a result of litigation. In Chicago, as sure as night follows day, litigation follows redistricting.

The Chicago City Council failed to redistrict Chicago's fifty wards using the 1990 census data by December 1, 1991, as required by law. As a result, Illinois law provided that *any ten* aldermen could propose a redistricting ordinance and have it put before the voters at a popular referendum.[25] All four Hispanic aldermen proposed a redistricting ordinance that would have provided for *nine* majority Hispanic wards.[26] However, they were unable to secure the requisite ten aldermen in support of their ordinance; thus their ordinance was not placed on the ballot. Two alternative redistricting ordinances were placed on the ballot and the ordinance that was ultimately selected by the voters on March 17, 1992, provided for seven majority Hispanic wards (14% of the total number of wards in Chicago).

In April of 1992, MALDEF filed suit on behalf of a group of Hispanic registered voters challenging the map.[27] Plaintiffs argued that while the Latino population in the city of Chicago had experienced tremendous growth, the population of both African Americans and whites had declined from 1980 to 1990. Yet Latinos were able to elect representatives of their choice in only 7 out of 50 wards, with whites still controlling the city council, despite a loss in population of approximately 250,000 people. The suit alleged that the aldermanic ward map should have provided Latinos with the opportunity to elect representatives of their choice in nine out of 50 wards. The suit further alleged that in limiting the number of Latino-majority wards, the white aldermen in control of the remap process intentionally diluted Latino voting strength to protect white incumbencies. The litigation was long and protracted. Finally, five years later, on June 9, 1997 the district court held that the plaintiffs had failed to show that Latinos did not have equal access to the political process.[28] The plaintiffs appealed this decision.[29]

On April 1, 1998, the Appellate Court upheld the lower court's decision but also found that the relevant population for calculating majority wards was a "citizen voting age population standard," (Bonilla 704). Since the Latino population in Chicago is overwhelmingly young and a large percentage is comprised of immigrants who have not yet become citizens, using "citizen voting age population" as the appropriate standard to determine Latino majority wards reduced the eligible Latino population. As a result, the Appellate Court found that Latinos were overrepresented in the city council. Nonetheless, it allowed the seven wards to stand.

Meanwhile, political foot-dragging was occurring on the state legislative side as well. Governor Jim Edgar vetoed the Illinois Legislature's statewide redistricting plans for the state house and the state senate on June 30, 1991. As a result, state law delegated the task of redistricting to the Illinois Redistricting Commission. The Commission held a number of public hearings at which MALDEF provided testimony and maps protecting the voting rights of Latinos. On October 4, 1991, the Commission introduced a plan that contained many, but not all, of MALDEF's recommendations. A week later that plan was challenged in the Illinois Supreme Court.[30] MALDEF intervened in the matter claiming that the map diluted Hispanic voting strength.[31] The Court sent the matter back to the Commission, which held additional hearings, in which MALDEF participated, and thereafter adopted an amended redistricting plan. That plan provided for four Hispanic super-majority districts in the House and two in the Senate.[32] MALDEF remained dissatisfied with the adopted plan because it believed that the Commission could have created an additional Senate district on the north side of Chicago, which could have been an additional majority Latino district (or at least a strong Latino "influence"[33] district). As a result, MALDEF, on behalf of a group of Hispanic voters (the "Méndez counter-plaintiffs") joined a lawsuit, which challenged the adopted map and alleged among other things that the Hispanic community on the Northwest side of Chicago had been fractured (split up).[34] In a decision entered on March 11, 1992, the Court rejected the claim and held that "the plan approved by the Illinois Legislative Redistricting Committee provided a meaningful opportunity for minority voters to elect candidates of their choice in areas where this opportunity [was] warranted by their population numbers, and [did] not intentionally discriminate along racial lines" (Illinois Legislative Redistricting 717). Despite this loss, the Hispanic community had gained additional representation in the legislature, going from two supermajority house seats and one simple majority house seat under the 1980 census, to four supermajority house seats. In addition, on the senate side, representation increased from one senate seat with a 56% Latino majority in 1980 to two senate seats with Latino supermajorities.

The 1990 census ushered in a victory as well with respect to Latino representation in the United States Congress. Prior to 1990, Illinois had never had a Latino majority congressional district. That changed in 1992.

The 1990 census revealed that Illinois' population increased in smaller proportion than the United States as a whole, necessitating a reduction in the number of congressional seats apportioned to Illinois from 22 to 20.[35] Under the Illinois Constitution, the Illinois General Assembly was required to "implement a constitutionally sound Congressional redistricting plan" by June 30, 1991 (Hasket 638) – a mandate the Illinois General Assembly failed to meet. As a result, five separate lawsuits were filed, including a challenge on behalf of Latino voters (the Nieves plaintiffs) in Cook County.[36] The Latino plaintiffs sought the creation of a Latino majority Congressional District which, they argued, was mandated under the Voting Rights Act because of demographic and population changes reflected in the 1990 census (Hastert 638).

Not only did all parties to the litigation agree that population and demographic changes within the City of Chicago from 1980 to 1990 mandated the creation of an Hispanic majority district, but they also reached an agreement prior to trial as to the configuration of the proposed Hispanic majority district.[37]

On November 6, 1991, the court issued an order reapportioning Illinois' twenty congressional seats.[38] Through this order, the court created a "majority-minority" Hispanic Congressional District, the Fourth Congressional District, for the first time in Illinois history. The first Congressional election to take place under the newly created map in 1992 sent a Hispanic representative, Luis Gutiérrez, to Congress. He was re-elected in 1994.

In February 1995, James R. King, a white resident of the Fourth Congressional District, filed a lawsuit challenging the constitutionality of the Hispanic majority district. King contended that the district was drawn predominantly on the basis of race and violated the Equal Protection Clause of the Fourteenth Amendment.[39]

The outcome of this litigation hinged in large part on whether the Mexican and Puerto Rican communities that had been joined in this district were politically cohesive.[40] King maintained that they were not. The premise of his argument was that the Puerto Rican and Mexican-American communities, which together account for an overwhelming majority of Chicago's Hispanic community have different cultural, social, political and economic concerns that serve to separate rather that unify the Latino community. King further contended that these differences manifested themselves in ethnically polarized bloc voting: Mexican-Americans predominately vote for Mexican-American candidates while Puerto Ricans predominately vote for Puerto Rican candidates.

To support these propositions, King presented the testimony of three witnesses: Jorge Custodio, a Puerto Rican and a purported expert on the similarities and differences between the Mexican and Puerto Rican residents of the City of Chicago;[41] Javier Galindo, a Mexican American owner of a small business and resident of the 4th Congressional District[42] and Manuel Torres, a Puerto Rican who unsuccessfully ran for alderman in 1986.[43]

The Court found the testimony of these witnesses unpersuasive, concluding that "the lay opinion elicited by King at trial to demonstrate and substantiate the claimed lack of cohesion [among Mexicans and Puerto Ricans] was mainly anecdotal, often incredible, and wholly insufficient to support the inferences and conclusions King seeks to draw." To the contrary, the Court found the record "replete with testimony establishing the political and social cohesiveness of the Hispanic community."[44] The two state senators at the time, Jesús García (Mexican-American) and Miguel de Valle (Puerto Rican), both testified about the common political concerns of Mexican-Americans and Puerto Ricans and their joint efforts to represent the entire Latino community in the Illinois General Assembly.[45]

Congressman Luis Gutiérrez, whose district was in jeopardy, likewise identified common political, economic and social concerns that affected both Mexican Americans and Puerto Ricans.[46] Dr. Félix Padilla (also Puerto Rican), a respected sociologist and ethnographer, also testified at length about the historical as well as present-day solidarity and cohesiveness of the Chicago Latino community.[47]

The court concluded that the Fourth Congressional District was limited in size to the minimum number of Hispanic residents generally believed necessary to counteract the effects of racial bloc voting and ensure that the Hispanic electorate had a reasonable opportunity to elect a candidate of its choice. It further determined that the district's extraordinary configuration was required to preserve "shared communities of interest."[48] Accordingly, the Court held that the Fourth Congressional District was constitutional.[49]

The Latino population continued to increase throughout the 1990's so that by the 2000 U.S. Census, the Latino population in the city of Chicago had increased to 26% of the city's total population and the State's Latino population had increased to 12.3% of the State's total population. This steady increase allowed for the creation of additional Latino majority city wards and state districts.

At the city level, the city's proposed plan purported to create eleven Latino majority wards. Although MALDEF was not completely satisfied with the city's proposed plan (MALDEF had submitted a compromise plan which provided for twelve Latino majority wards, many with slightly stronger percentages of Latino population),[50] MALDEF decided against filing a challenge. Instead

MALDEF found itself in the position of asking the U.S. District Court for permission to become a party to and help defend the City against a lawsuit filed by the Polish American Congress.[51] The suit challenged the city's newly created 30th aldermanic ward, alleging that it unfairly diluted Polish American voting strength. The district in dispute was a Latino majority district, and MALDEF wanted to insure that the interests of Latino voters were protected. While the Court denied MALDEF's motion to intervene, it allowed MALDEF to participate in the litigation, which has not yet been resolved.

Most dramatic, however, was the growth of Latino representation at the state level where Latino representation doubled! As a result of MALDEF's advocacy efforts, the Illinois Redistricting Commission adopted a map that contained eight Latino majority house districts and four Latino majority senate districts.[52] This growth allowed for the creation, for the first time in history, of the Illinois Latino Legislative Caucus. The goal of the Caucus is to further the legislative agenda of Latinos in Illinois. Membership is open to any members or members-elect of the Illinois General Assembly who are Latino or who represent a legislative district that has a majority Latino population.

Already in its first year, the Illinois Latino Legislative Caucus has been instrumental in securing legislation of significance to the Latino community.[53] The future growth and success of the Illinois Latino Legislative Caucus is limited only by the Latino community's ability to become citizens and their ability and willingness to participate in the electoral process. If those two things can be overcome, Latinos have the potential to become a political powerhouse in Illinois.

Notes

[1] The terms Latino and Hispanic will be used interchangeably.

[2] See BUREAU OF THE CENSUS, U.S. DEPT. OF COMMERCE, STATISTICAL ABSTRACT OF THE UNITED STATES: 1981, 3 (1981).

[3] William E. Rodríguez was elected in 1915 to a one year term which ended in 1918. *Centennial List of Mayors and Aldermen and Other Elected Officials of the City of Chicago 1837–193, p. 23.* In 1981 Mayor Jane Byrne appointed Joseph Anthony Martínez to fill a vacancy created in the 31st Ward by the resignation of Alderman Chester Kuta. See *Response of Plaintiffs and Intervenors In Compliance With Final Pre-Trial Order,* filed in *Ketchum v. Byrne* on October 7, 1982.

[4] *Puerto Rican Organization for Political Action v. Kusper*, 350 F.Supp. 606 (1972).

[5] *Cousins v. City Council of Chicago*, 466 F.2d 830 (7th Cir. 1972), 833.

[6] See *Cousins v. City Council of Chicago*, 361 F.Supp. 530, 533 (N.D. Ill. 1973). This decision was affirmed on appeal. See *Cousins v. City Council of Chica-*

*go,*503 F.2d 912 (7th Cir. 1974).

[7]At the time of its creation, MALDEF's jurisdiction included Texas, California, New Mexico, Arizona and Colorado.

[8]MALDEF practices in five program areas: Education, Immigrant Rights, Employment, Public Resource Equity and Political Access.

[9]

	1970	1980
Non-Hispanic White	65.5%	43.2%
Black	32.7%	39.8%
Hispanic	7.3%	14.0%

Ketchum v. Byrne, 740 F.2d 1398, 1400, fn 1 (7th Cir. 1984) citing BUREAU OF THE CENSUS, U.S. DEPT. OF COMMERCE, STATISTICAL ABSTRACT OF THE UNITED STATES: 1981, 3 (1981).

[10]*Velasco v. Byrne,* 82 C, 4431. Two other groups of plaintiffs also filed suit and the *Velasco* suit was consolidated with those cases and referred to as the *Ketchum* litigation. See *Ketchum v. Byrne,* 740 F.2d 1398 (7th Cir. 1984).

[11]In voting rights terminology "fracturing" is the process by which a minority group that could form a sizeable majority in one district is split into two or more districts in which the minorities constitute an ineffective political grouping. *Ketchum* at 1408, ftnt 8.

[12]The Northwest side Hispanic community was split among six wards (the 26th, 30th, 31st, 32nd, 33rd and 35th wards) with Hispanic populations in these various wards ranging from 24.1% to 57.3%. On the Southwest Side, the Hispanic community of Pilsen was split into two wards (the 1st with 30.7% and the 25th with 52.6% Hispanic population) instead of being left intact, as it might have been, as one ward with an Hispanic population of 72.9%. In addition, the Little Village community, which could have been left entirely within the 22nd Ward with an Hispanic population of 78.8%, was split between the 12th and 22nd Wards with 32% and 64.3% of the total population respectively. *Ketchum* at 1409.

[13]Section 2 of the Voting Rights Act of 1965, 42 U.S.C. § 1973, as amended, prohibits any practice that has the intent or the result of denying a citizen of the United States the right to vote on account of race, color or stuatus as a language minority. Section 2 states in pertinent part:

(a) No voting qualification or prerequisite to voting or standard, practice or procedure shall be imposed or applied by any State or political subdivision in a manner which results in a denial or abridgement of the right of any citizen of the United States to vote on account of race or color, or in contravention of the guarantees set forth in section 4(f)(2), as provided in subsection (b).

(b) A violation of subsection (a) is established if, based on the totality of circumstances, it is shown that the political processes leading to nomination
or election in the State or political subdivision are not equally open to participation by member of a class of citizens protected by subsection (a) in
that its members have less opportunity than other members of the electorate to participate in the political process and to elect representatives of
their choice.

[14]The Appellate Court cited the District Court trial transcript in noting that "the
Chicago Hispanic population on the near southwest side is composed of a significant proportion of Mexicans who have not yet had an opportunity to
become citizens" (*Ketchum* 1414). The Appellate Court went on to approve the
trial court's directive that there be a "corrective" for non-citizenship (*Ketchum,*
1415, n. 19). In its opinion, the Court of Appeals cited the following statistics:
"According to the 1980 census statistics, 69.7% of whites, 60% of blacks and
57% of Hispanics are of voting age. The percentages of individuals reporting
that they were registered to vote in 1980 are: whites 68.6%, blacks 60.0%, Hispanics 36.3%. The percentage of individuals reporting that they had actually
voted in 1980 was: whites 60.9%, blacks 50.5%, Hispanics 29.9%" (*Ketchum*
1413).

[15]*Ketchum,* 1413. The Appellate Court further observed that a "guideline of 65%
of total population has been adopted and maintained for years by the Department of Justice and . . . the Supreme Court . . . as representing the proportion
of minority population reasonable required to ensure minorities a fair opportunity to elect a candidate of their choice, (*Ketchum* at 1415).

[16]The court described the settlement agreement as follows:

[t]he Hispanic communities of Little Village and Pilsen were fractured
under the City Council and [district] court-approved maps among the 1st,
12th, 22nd, and 25th Wards. These adjoining communities, however, possess
sufficient populations to create two compact majority Hispanic wards. The
settlement plan creates a 72.9% Hispanic total population in the 25th Ward
in Pilsen, and a 78.1% Hispanic population in the 22nd Ward in Little Village. Likewise the West Town/Humboldt Park neighborhood was fractured
among the 26th, 30th, 31st, 32nd, 33rd, and 35th Wards, effectively diluting
Hispanic voting strength. By redrawing the ward boundaries to contain primarily the West Town/ Humboldt Park geographic area, the compromise map
creates two majority Hispanic wards in the 26th (64.2% Hispanic total population) and the 31st Ward (59.6% Hispanic total population). The 32nd and
33rd Wards, which neighbor the 26th and 31st Wards to the North and East,
retain significant, albeit minority, Hispanic populations (44.8% and 35.9%

Hispanic population respectively). Thus, the compromise map creates four majority Hispanic wards, restores the existing Hispanic communities, and ends the dilution of Hispanic voting strength through fracturing. 630 F. Supp. at 558.

[17]The only incumbent—elected in 1983 from the 31st Ward which had been redrawn by the District Court in 1982 as part of its initial remedy. He defeated Joseph J. Martinez who had been appointed by Mayor Jane Byrne in 1981 to a vacancy created by the resignation of Alderman Chester Kuta.

[18]Luis Gutierrez subsequently became Illinois's first and to date only Latino Congressman.

[19]Harold Washington had been elected Chicago's first Black mayor in 1982. After his election, the city council divided primarily along racial lines, with the white aldermen holding a twenty-nine to twenty-one advantage. After the special elections, the city council was evenly divided, permitting the mayor to cast the deciding vote.

[20]Under the 1970 Illinois Constitution, the Illinois legislature is mandated to redistrict "all legislative seats in the Illinois House and Senate in a manner such that an equal share of the population, under the most recent census, resides in each district" [*Rybicki v. State Bd. of Elections of Ill.*, 574 F. Supp. 1082, 1085 (N.D. Ill. 1982)]. If the legislature fails to approve a legislative district plan "by June 30 of the first year following the census, an eight-member Legislative Redistricting Commission must be formed" (574 F. Supp. at 1085).

[21]*Del Valle v. State Board of Elections*, 82 C, consolidated by the court with *Rybicki v. State Bd. of Elections of Ill.*, 574 F. Supp. 1082 (N.D. Ill. 1982).

[22]At least two major Hispanic aggregations are easily identified in Chicago, one on the Northwest Side (the West Town and Humboldt Park neighborhoods consisting primarily of Puerto Ricans) and the other on the Southwest Side (the Pilsen and Little Village neighborhoods consisting primarily of Mexicans and Mexican-Americans). (574 F. Supp. at 1089).

[23]The court in a footnote provided an excerpt from the Hispanic Settlement Agreement, which reads in part as follows: "the Hispanic plaintiffs believe that Senate Districts 3, 4, 5, 6, 10, 11, and 18, and House Districts 5, 6, 7, 8, 9, 10, 11, 12, 20, 21, 22 and 35, as constituted in the [Settlement Agreement], fairly and reasonably provide Hispanics in those districts with the right to participate and vote in electing representatives from those districts to the Illinois General Assembly without fear of dilution of their vote considering the 1980 Census data and the geographic location of concentrations Hispanic population," (574 F. Supp. at 1124, n.104).

[24]See Illinois Blue Book, 2001–2002. Legislative Roster, 1818–2002, Represen-

tatives, p. 489.

[25]See Ill. Rev. Stat. ch. 24, 21–40.

[26]See *Bonilla v. City Council of City of Chicago*, 809 F.Supp. 590, 591 (N.D. Ill. 1992).

[27]*Bonilla v. City of Chicago,* No. 92-C-2666 (U.S. Dist. Ct., N.D. Ill.). This case was subsequently consolidated with *Barnett v. City of Chicago,* No. 92-C-1693 and *Smith v. City of Chicago,* No. 92-C-2104, two additional challenges to the 1990 city of Chicago ward map.

[28]*Barnett v. City of Chicago,* 969 F. Supp. 1359, 1371 (N.D. Ill. 1997).

[29]See *Bonilla v. City of Chicago,* 141 F. 3d 699 (7th Cir. 1998).

[30]See *The People of the State of Illinois ex rel Burris v. Ryan.*

[31]See *Martinez v. Illinois Redistricting Commission,* No. 72662 (Illinois Supreme Court).

[32]See *Illinois Legislative Redistricting v. LaPaille,* 786 F.Supp. 704, 707 (N.D. Ill. 1992).

[33]An "influence district" is a district that includes a large number of racial or linguistic minority voters but less than the number or proportion that would allow voters from the minority group to control the result of the election in which they agreed on an issue or candidate. In the case of "influence districts," a sizable minority group can be said to be able to "influence" the outcomes of elections, but not control them. *The Impact of Redistricting in Your Community, A Guide to Redistricting,* Sponsored by MALDEF, LDF and NAPALC., 18–19.

[34]*Illinois Legislative Redistricting v. LaPaille,* 786 F. Supp. 704 (N.D. Ill. 1992), 708.

[35]See *Hastert v. State Board of Elections,* 777 F.Supp. 634, 637 (N.D. Ill. 1991).

[36]See *Nieves v. Illinois State Board of Elections,* No. 91 C4154. *Nieves* and three other challenges, *Rosebrook v. State Board of Elections,* No. 91 C 4656; *Collins v. State Board of Elections,* No. 91 C 4643 and *Chicago Urban League v. State Board of Elections,* No. 91 C 5472, were consolidated with *Hastert v. State Board of_Elections et al.,* 777 F.Supp. 634 (N.D. Ill. 1991).

[37]The Court took note of the "extraordinary configuration" of the proposed Hispanic district, likening it to "a Rorschach blot turned on its side" (Hastert 648, fn 24). The Court recognized, however, that the Chicago Hispanic community resides principally in two dense enclaves, one on Chicago's near northwest side and one on the near southwest side. The plan connects these enclaves by creating a C shaped configuration. Nevertheless, the court recognized that "the separation of the clusters is not indicative of the existence of two distinct communities, but appears to have occurred as a result of exogenous physical and institutional barriers" (Hastert 649).

[38]See *King v. State Board of Elections*, 979 F. Supp. 582, 586 (N.D. Ill. 1996).

[39]Id.

[40]See *King v. State Board of Elections*, 979 F, Supp. 582, 596 (N.D> Ill. 1996).

[41]Mr. Custodio was only a five year resident of the City of Chicago. Prior to coming to Chicago, Custodio resided in Texas and before that he lived in Puerto Rico. Custodio's highest educational degree was a Bachelor of Arts in Education. Throughout his professional life he had been a photographer, educator and communications director. He did not have training in the field of sociology, political science or history. Nevertheless, he testified that Mexicans and Puerto Ricans have different cultural holidays and different spending habits (Mexicans send money to Mexico, while Puerto Ricans never send money to Puerto Rico). Moreover, he believed that naturalized United States citizens who are of Mexican ancestry were not entitled to the same benefits as Puerto Ricans. *King v. Illinois State Board of Elections*, trial transcript.

[42]The issues important to Galindo as a Mexican-American citizen were immigration and NAFTA. He has no opinion about Puerto Rican statehood or whether there should be special tax incentives for the island of Puerto Rico. *King v. Illinois State Board of Elections*, trial transcript.

[43]Torres testified that the issue affecting Puerto Ricans is statehood whereas for other Hispanics the issue is immigration. In his opinion, Mexicans would vote for the Mexicans and the Puerto Ricans would vote for the Puerto Ricans. *King v. Illinois State Board of Elections*, trial transcript.

[44]*King* 979 F. Supp. 582, 613 (N.D. Ill. 1996).

[45]Senator García testified as to the common concerns of the Latino community affecting education, health, crime, and economic development, all of which form the basis for a common political agenda. The lack of English-language proficiency was also a common issue for Latinos, affecting their daily life and political participation. Senator Del Valle testified that elected officials often worked together on issues affecting areas of the community that might not be in their district. Both senators stated that they worked closely on various issues of interest to the Latino community (*King v. Illinois State Board of Elections*, trial transcript).

[46]Congressman Gutiérrez testified that since the 1980's he had worked on a number of coalition efforts by Latinos of different nationalities. The issues included immigration/citizenship workshops, working against school overcrowding, supporting bilingual education, adequate health care and anti-crime efforts, and working to assist Latin American countries devastated by natural disasters. All of these coalition efforts were addressed from a Latino perspective, based on a common history, culture and language of the residents of both

the north and south sides of Chicago that form the core of District Four (*King v. Illinois State Board of Elections*, trial transcript).

[47]*King* at 979 F. Supp. 582, 613 (N.D. Ill. 1996).

[48]*King* at 616, 617.

[49]Subsequently, King sought review from the Supreme Court. See *King v. Illinois State Board of Elections*, 519 U.S. 978 (1996). The Supreme Court sent the case back to the District Court for further consideration in light of two cases the Court had decided in the interim. The District Court reconsidered its decision in light of those decisions and again found the 4th Congressional District constitutional [*King v. State Board of Elections*, 979 F. Supp. 619 (N.D. Ill. 1997)]. King again appealed the decision to the Supreme Court, which declined to review the decision, thus upholding the constitutionality of the 4th Congressional District [*King v. Illinois Board of Elections*, 522 U.S. 1087 (1998)].

[50]Comparison of City Plan with MALDEF Compromise Plan
(Based on Latino Voting-Age Population)

NORTHSIDE: [as close to 60% as possible, could provide an opportunity for Latinos to elect candidates as of their choice].

WARD	CITY PLAN	MALDEF PLAN
1	48%	50%
26	68%	71%
30	60%	62%
31	63%	65%
33	50%	54%
35	59%	59%

SOUTHSIDE: [as close to 65% as possible, could provide opportunity for Latinos to elect candidates of their choice].

WARD	CITY PLAN	MALDEF PLAN
11	29%	64%
12	61%	73%
14	70%	73%
22	90%	83%
25	65%	64%
10	53%	53%

This comparison was distributed by MALDEF at city council hearings on the proposed map.

[51]*Polish American Congress v. City of Chicago*, No. 02 C 1477 (U.S. Dist. Ct.,

N.D. Ill.).

[52]MALDEF subsequently successfully defended this map against a legal challenge. See *Campuzano v. Illinois State Board of Elections,* No. 01 C 50376 (U.S. Dist. Ct., N.D. Ill.).

[53]In-State Tuition for Undocumented Students (HB60) guarantees in-state tuition to undocumented immigrant students who have attended school in the state for at least 3 years; Health Care/Language Assistance Services Act (SB0061) provides a definition of a medical interpreter; provides a means for immigrants and refugees to file a complaint; and describes the responsibilities of the health care institution for the provision of interpreter services; Language Rights in the Workplace (SB679) makes it a civil rights violation for any employer to adopt or enforce a policy that limits or prohibits the use of any language in any workplace unless the language restriction is justified as a business necessity. In addition, SB0680 created the Office of Immigration Assistance within the Office of the Attorney General and HJR021 created a joint legislative task force on immigrants and refugees.

From *La Lucha* to Latino: Ethnic Change, Political Identity, and Civil Rights in Chicago
David A. Badillo

Chicago Latinos for much of the twentieth century have been engaged in a search for leadership. The issues facing their communities, especially among Mexican Americans and Puerto Ricans, comprise a broad range of civil rights concerns depending on the particular group, the era, and local and national conditions. This chapter focuses on key periods of transition, from the early settlements of Mexican immigrants in the 1920s to contemporary struggles in the metropolis. This includes the distinct national or "ethnic" circumstances prior to 1965, the development of Chicano and Puerto Rican awareness during the 1960s, the melting pot phenomenon of the 1970s and 1980s, through current trajectories or urban politics and suburban growth, accompanied by new historical identities.

Chicago's Mexican-American and Puerto Rican Communities before 1965

Flourishing Mexican-American settlements arose in Chicago's Near West Side, as well as in Back of the Yards and in South Chicago during the 1920s. They were comprised mostly of immigrants and Texas Mexicans who had lived elsewhere in the Midwest or in the Southwest before arriving in the city; there were also immigrants coming directly from across the border. Most Mexican nationals chose not to pursue citizenship and wanted to return to the homeland, making it necessary for the Mexican consul, and gradually other organizations, to offer community leadership. The Immigrants' Protection League (IPL), an advocacy group that had worked since 1908 on behalf of Chicago-area immigrants, during the 1930s protested that "innocent people, citizens and aliens alike," were "swept up [in] indiscriminate raids [and] restrained of their liberty against their consent."[1] No forcible, organized repatriation disrupted Mexicans in the city of Chicago during the 1930s. This owed to the support of sympathetic non-Mexican organizations, such as the IPL and social settlements such as Hull House, the famous settlement house on the Near West Side originally established for European immigrants in the 1880s. Another favorable factor was the diverse economy of Chicago, which was able to absorb unemployed workers more easily than did company towns elsewhere in the Midwest (including neighboring Gary and East Chicago in northwest Indiana).

Chicago's Mexican population declined modestly, from about 19,000 to 16,000 during the Depression decade (the latter figure included some 9,000 born in the U.S.). Between 1942 and 1945, many Mexicans took advantage of the need for wartime labor to work in the Bracero Program. After 1945 many braceros broke their contracts and attempted to remain permanently, blending into small *colonias*, where they found factory work, and the number of Mexican immigrants and Mexican Americans in the city kept growing. The IPL continued to provide bilingual assistance with naturalization, as more Mexicans sought citizenship for themselves and their families; this required documented proof of entry into the United States. The League also helped Mexicans obtain reentry permits after returning home.

Gradually, other groups appeared. In 1944, Mexican Americans formed the Mexican Civic Committee, to avoid ethnic friction and riots, such as had occurred against Los Angeles youths (the so-called *pachucos*) during June 1943. Ceremonies in 1945 were dedicated the Mexican Social Center to the memory of Manuel Pérez, a Chicago-born Congressional Medal of Honor winner who died in battle in the Philippines. The Center tackled problems of high infant mortality, lack of educational opportunities, rising delinquency, and substandard housing and health conditions. Veterans' organizations offered an opportunity for a greater voice in improving local conditions in neighborhoods and workplaces. Labor unions, moreover, also began to pay greater attention to Mexicans, and by the early 1950s five Mexican Americans presided over A.F.L. or C.I.O. shop locals in Chicago.

The Mexican American Council of Chicago emerged from a citywide conference held in May 1949 on "The Status of the Mexican American in Chicago." The Council, a non-profit agency housed in Hull House, established committees on housing, employment, labor relations, education, and youth, all of which provided linkages with city agencies. The Council assisted Mexican nationals married to American citizens in securing permanent residence in the U.S. and defended "wetbacks" at a time when some three hundred undocumented aliens were being apprehended monthly in Chicago and returned to Mexico.[2] One member of the Council noted in 1952 that even citizens were arrested in immigration sweeps without even having "a chance to get their clothes or money together, and taken to a terribly overcrowded jail." In front of workplaces and churches, deportees were "forced into trucks on the first lap of the journey to the border where they are dumped."[3]

By 1950, the Mexican-American community in the Chicago metropolis had grown to 35,000 (with 24,000 in the city); it included many Texas Mexican migrants who came north to Chicago in the late 1940s and early 1950s. Often the father came first before resettling the family; he would work several jobs before finally settling down on one establishment or trade. These families often lived in mixed ethnic neighborhoods; their grandparents and other family members in Texas made occasional trips north. Members of *tejano* extended families who lived across the Rio Grande also arrived, but they tended to speak less English. In either case, savings often went to land and property in the South, an historical pattern that often withered following migration north. By 1960, Chicago's Mexican community—composed of immigrants, "legal" and "illegal," *tejanos*, and other Mexican-Americans, had grown to 56,000.[4]

During the 1950s the Mexican American Council extended its outreach to include all Spanish-speaking persons in the Chicago area to augment leadership in that widely dispersed community. With the influx of thousands of Puerto Ricans to Chicago and its immediate area, a closer working relationship developed with the local office of the Commonwealth of Puerto Rico, whose director served on the Council's board of directors. From 8,000 for the entire Midwest in 1950, the Puerto Rican population grew to 32,000 for Chicago alone in 1960. The Chicago *Sun-Times* noted in the mid-1950s that the predominantly rural Puerto Rican migrants "found Chicago a strange and frightening place." Few spoke English well, nor were they "well educated in their own mother tongue," since they customarily reached only the fourth or fifth grade.[5]

The IPL also helped deal with contracts of Puerto Rican laborers in the late 1940s and 1950s. Other organizations, including the Puerto Rico Employment Association and the Welfare Council of Metropolitan Chicago, came to the defense of migrants. Among U.S. cities, Chicago soon became second to New York in Puerto Rican population. In 1956 Cardinal Samuel Stritch, the Archbishop of Chicago from 1940 to 1958, formed the Cardinal's Committee for the Spanish Speaking (CCSS) under the direction of diocesan clergy. The Catholic Church perceived the complexity of cultural differences among successive waves of the Spanish-speaking earlier than most other local institutions. Beginning in 1964 the Chicago Archdiocese, in conjunction with federal authorities, helped re-settle Cuban exiles arriving in Miami to the Chicago area.

In the 1950s and early 1960s Los Caballeros de San Juan (The Knights of St. John) facilitated Puerto Ricans organizing. The organization, founded by the Catholic Church and Puerto Rican laypersons, relied on *concilios* (councils); by 1960 there were 12 *concilios* serving Puerto Ricans throughout the city of Chicago, each representing a parish community. Los Caballeros offered referrals to city agencies and helped with employment and housing. The primary function was the provision of social activities that culminated in the celebration of El Día de San Juan between 1956 until 1966. In 1960, Los Caballeros organized Puerto Rican voters in support of the "Viva Kennedy" Democratic campaign.[6]

La Lucha and Division Street: Beyond 1960s Radicalism

The beacon for the Mexican American in Chicago, as in the Southwest, was farm worker activism in California and Texas beginning in 1965 and 1966, respectively. In 1968, the United Farm Workers Organizing Committee conducted a boycott of California table grapes, with the help of Catholic, Protestant, and Jewish groups, the Chicago Federation of Labor, and numerous Mexican-American community organizations. They led letter-writing campaigns aimed at growers, such as Guimarra and Balsamo, collected funds, and pressured chain stores not to stock grapes. Strikers from Texas also journeyed to Chicago, while Chicago organizers went to Michigan and other Midwestern venues to march and dramatize the farm worker's plight.

Jorge Prieto, born in 1918 in Mexico City, came to the United States in 1950 to work as an intern for a year in Chicago, where he was befriended by Bishop Sheil. Dr. Prieto's wife helped motivate his civic participation and persuaded him to join the Christian Family Movement, [whose monthly meetings] led, almost directly, to involvement in the civil rights struggles of the late 1950s and early 1960s. He also joined the Catholic Interracial Council of Chicago to oppose housing discrimination in Chicago and later became active in the budding Chicano Movement. In April of 1966, Prieto marched with César Chávez and striking grape pickers (who had been on strike since the previous September) on the final days of their 300-mile march from Delano to Sacramento, along with several Chicago priests and a handful of others from the Illinois delegation.[7]

Many other Chicagoans of diverse religious and cultural backgrounds joined the Chicano Movement. Howell Settlement House, a Protestant-supported social service mission aimed at Bohemian immigrants, was transformed in 1970 into Casa Aztlán, a nonsectarian, Chicano-operated center. Casa Aztlán came to house Compañía Trucha, a political street theater group modeled after the California-based El Teatro Campesino that grew out of the United Farm Workers struggle and traveled throughout the Midwest. The center also housed a health clinic and displays of murals; in the mid-1970s, local activists met to picket retailers selling non-union produce. In 1975, a law in California forced growers to hold union recognition elections, but the struggle for good union contracts, as well as against child labor, pesticides, and other abuses, continued. Even in 1980, well after the heyday of the Chicano Movement, Chicago boycotts continued against the Jewel supermarket chain through demonstrations, phone banks and donation drives, this time against certain brands of lettuce.[8]

Between 1960 and 1970, some 9,000 of the 16,000 Mexican Americans who had lived in the Near West Side were displaced by the Eisenhower Expressway and urban renewal projects related to the construction of the University of Illinois campus in Chicago. By 1970, the Pilsen area had replaced the Near West Side as the largest and most diverse of the Chicago settlements in the city. Many refugees from the Near West Side in the following decade replaced eastern European ethnics. A new generation transformed the politics of Pilsen and Chicago during the 1970s as the Immigration and Naturalization Service, *la migra*, aggressively raided factories, movie theaters and parks in search of undocumented immigrants. Many of the immigrants worked in hotels, sweatshops, restaurants and other businesses. During those years, few labor unions sought to organize the immigrant worker. Defense of the undocumented workers and their political representation would be the most important Mexican movement from 1975 to 1983. In the mid-1970s, several parishes in the Pilsen area signed a document declaring themselves sanctuaries against the Immigration and Naturalization Service. One priest noted, "The Immigration officials used to show up outside of churches and wait for people to go outside. . . . The people just left the church and . . . forced [them] to leave. [St. Vitus] church was very militantly against the way the Immigration Department would make raids in the community and would violently harass and terrorize people. Other parishes slowly but surely all took that position."[9]

In 1973 community activist Rudy Lozano formed a chapter of the Partido de la Raza Unida and later participated in the formation of CASA, an organization based in California that focused on defending the rights of undocumented workers. In 1979, Lozano became an organizer for the ILGWU. Community organizations, such as Centro de la Causa, Asociación Pro Derechos Obreros, Mujeres Latinas en Acción, Latino Youth, and others, aimed to alleviate the problems in Pilsen and, increasingly, in North Side barrios, where Mexican immigrants mixed with Puerto Ricans. Pilsen Neighbors was an Alinsky-style group whose organizers lobbied the Chicago Board of Education for the construction of a new neighborhood high school. Benito Juárez High School opened in 1977 as an alternative to distant high schools with high dropout rates.[10]

By 1970, the city's Puerto Rican population had grown to 78,000, including a sizable cohort born in Chicago. Regardless of their origins, however, Puerto Ricans during the 1960s suffered from housing discrimination and faced displacement from urban renewal in core neighborhoods, such as Lincoln Park and Hyde Park (as had Mexicans in the Pilsen neighborhood). In June of 1966, Chicago experienced a civil disturbance, along the heavily Puerto Rican area on Division Street in the Humboldt Park neighborhood. The Division Street Riot was one of the many episodes of urban unrest reported nationally, but the first among Puerto Ricans. The riot began on June 12, 1966, when a policeman shot and wounded a young Puerto Rican man, Arcelis Cruz. For three days and nights, a Puerto Rican crowd demonstrated against police brutality. By the time order was finally restored, 49 were arrested and more than 50 buildings were destroyed. The following month, at hearings held by the Chicago Commission on Human Relations, language differences, employment, housing problems, and relations with law enforcement surfaced. A Puerto Rican ethnic consciousness began to develop as a Spanish Action Committee, under the direction of a former member of Los Caballeros de San Juan, formed "to enable local residents to identify in an organized manner the physical and social problems of the community, to interpret these needs to city agencies, and work toward implementing some community-based programs."[11]

Decades later, one long-time resident, José Acevedo, cited problems going back to the late 1950s and the "wetback" apprehensions, when police had pulled suspects out of their cars, violated their civil rights with unwarranted searches, and hit or otherwise harassed them. That "ongoing situation with the police [indicated that] we were not welcome in the city." The riots resulted in an enhanced presence among Puerto Ricans in Chicago after the city called together community leaders. A new Puerto Rican identity emerged in an effort to improve conditions on Division Street, which had become the main commercial and cultural center of Puerto Rican Chicago. Subsequently the city established a "War on Poverty" office on Division Street. The disturbances also helped propel the organizing of the Young Lords Party.

Puerto Ricans jealously came to guard their turf on the near North Side against intrusion and control by outsiders. Similarly, many community leaders began to call for revolutionary nationalism liberating the island of Puerto Rico from U.S. colonial rule. These sentiments were stoked by the activities of the Fuerzas Armadas de Liberación Nacional (FALN), a radical group operating out of barrios in Chicago and New York, which took credit for bombings. FALN targeted "reactionary corporate executives" in retaliation for what they claimed was an earlier CIA-ordered assassination of two Puerto Rican nationalists. The FBI canvassed the Puerto Rican communities in Chicago and New York in attempts to identify and capture the bombers, but the tightly structured group evaded its reach and carried out further attacks, even after several key members were forced underground in 1976. The FALN offered a plan for striking back against the alleged indignities of U.S. imperialism and in the process served to bolster the distinctive identity of a generation of Puerto Ricans growing up on the continent. Strong support emerged during the 1990s for the release of FALN political prisoners, led by Puerto Rican Congressman Luis Gutiérrez, who represented Chicago's largely Latino Fourth Congressional District.[12]

Beginning in the early 1970s, Puerto Ricans and Mexicans began to form a wider Latino ethnic unit distinct from their respective national identities. One of the first "Latino" responses was the creation of a coalition of community organizations to pressure such firms as Illinois Bell, Jewel Tea, and Sears to open up employment opportunities for the Spanish-speaking working class of the city. Using protests, demonstrations, and other tactics of La Lucha, the coalition sought to implement affirmative action policies for the hire of Puerto Rican and Mexican workers. Another important attempt on the part of Puerto Ricans and Mexicans in Chicago to build a Latino framework came through the establishment of the Latino Institute, founded in 1974, whose more "traditional integrationist" program eschewed protest or coercion.[13]

Urban Coalitions in the 1980s

By 1980 the Chicago SMSA had grown to include 581,000 Latinos, fourth behind L.A., N.Y., and Miami, and ahead of San Antonio. Within the city, 422,000 Latinos were counted, including 256,000 Mexicans and 112,000 Puerto Ricans, in a distribution closer to the national norm at the time than any other city. By 1980 Latinos remained far below the rest of the population in their level of educational attainment. Among Latinos ages 25 or over, 68 percent had not graduated from high school, compared with 46 percent for blacks, and 41 percent for whites. Mexicans had the lowest educational attainment of all the Latino sub-groups, with only 31% of their population having graduated from high school. Puerto Ricans; however, faced very high dropout rates, especially at Roberto Clemente High School. This situation in 1984 precipitated a candlelit procession in front of St. Mark's Church bearing an empty casket symbolizing Latino youth's educational aspirations.

Cubans remained the most educated Latino group with 57 percent of their population having a high school diploma. Many Cubans had settled in the North Side neighborhoods of Uptown, Edgewater, and Rogers Park in the 1960s. In the early 1970s Chicago's Cuban community stood at about 45,000; by 1980 their numbers had dropped to about 12,000, as many residents moved elsewhere, especially to South Florida.[14]

Chicago's Democratic Machine—dating back to the 1930s—survived intact for many decades, through the reign of Richard J. Daley, who ran the city from 1955 to 1977. The interlude between the demise of the elder Daley and the ascension of his son, Richard M. Daley, proved to be a key juncture for Latino political empowerment. Especially noteworthy was the impact of legal challenges to decennial redistricting based on the 1975 Amendments to the Voting Rights Act. The midwestern office of the Mexican American Legal Defense and Educational Fund (MALDEF), along with Chicago Latino community groups, led redistricting battles during the early 1980s to enhance Latino representation in city hall, as well as in Springfield and Washington. In 1982, a U.S. District Judge ordered the Hispanic-majority wards increased from 2 to 4. The following year, Chicago elected its first black mayor, Harold Washington, who drew significant support from Latinos (two-thirds of whom favored him), winning by 46,000 votes out of about 1.3 million cast. Washington's election heralded the beginning of Council Wars led by Ed Vrdolyak, chairman of the Cook County Democratic Party. Vrdolyak promptly reorganized the council and his 29 aldermen mobilized against the 21 under Washington's control.

Mayor Washington favored affirmative action policies and channeled jobs toward his core constituency as the city's investment boom continued. Washington, clearly aware of the political importance of the Latino vote in his 1987 reelection bid, added several key Latino appointments to his administration. In 1985, he appointed Dr. Prieto (former head of the Department of Family Practice at Cook County Hospital) as President of the Chicago Board of Health. The 1980s saw the first significant electoral involvement of Cuban Americans in the Midwest, especially among second-generation exiles and several Cuban Americans worked for the election of Mayor Washington in 1983. He also opened the process of awarding city contracts for greater minority participation and imposed affirmative action standards on contractors and developers working on city-sponsored projects.[15]

Chicago Latinos demonstrated their sophistication in playing the much sought after role of "swing vote" in the largest city in the Midwest and the third largest city in the nation. Latinos finally helped swing the council's power to Washington in 1986 in court-ordered elections. The heavily Latino 26th Ward decided the outcome of "Council Wars" in the March 1986 aldermanic election as Washington's candidate, Luis Gutiérrez, narrowly defeated a Vrdolyak-backed candidate. Gutiérrez, born in Chicago of Puerto Rican parents, later became Chicago's first

Latino Congressman. Washington's 1987 reelection confirmed the dominance of the Washington coalition over the machine (Benett 266).

Mayor Washington was sympathetic to the Sanctuary Movement in opposing U.S. foreign policy in Central America and endorsing the granting of political asylum for refugees, although the movement was created and perpetuated by non-governmental activists. As the task of creating a Sanctuary Movement grew, the Chicago Religious Task Force on Central America became involved. Organized in 1980 in response to the four churchwomen's deaths in El Salvador, it had focused on ending U.S. support there. Lay and religious leaders in Chicago tried to coordinate a national protest movement as part of a growing coalition of movements opposed to U.S. foreign policies. An obstacle deterring Catholic groups from more openly declaring sanctuary was the archdiocese's position. Cardinal Joseph Bernardin supported existing legislation, maintaining that parishes may discreetly assist undocumented refugees but not publicize or politicize their situation.[16]

By the mid-1960s, the Cardinal's Committee for the Spanish-Speaking had dissolved, and the Caballeros de San Juan and Los Hermanos in la Familia de Dios had lost sway as Catholic lay leadership organizations. Soon after his arrival in 1982, Bernardin created the Office of the Hispanic Apostolate, under Claretian Father Pedro Rodríguez. The purpose of the office was to promote a Latino ministry and integrate the concerns of the caucus into archdiocesan organizations. The church remained actively involved in the hodgepodge of leadership strategies and approaches to politics and civil rights that had developed.

Barrios and the Contemporary Metropolis

A decade of surging immigration has helped Chicago vault past Houston and San Antonio to make its Mexican community the second largest in the nation after Los Angeles. The Mexican population of Chicago actually grew by a larger number than the Mexican population of Los Angeles over the last decade. Statewide, the Latino population grew from 904,000 to 1,530,000 over the decade, with Mexicans making up 75% of the total. The state is now home to 1,140,000 Mexican-Americans and Mexican immigrants. The Puerto Rican population in Illinois stands at 158,000 while the Cuban population grew 1% to 18,000 in the 2000 Census. Chicago is the fastest growing Latino market in the United States and has the second highest percentage of Spanish-dominant households (behind Miami, 69%), and followed by Los Angeles (56%), New York (55%) and San Antonio (28%), with Univisión the prime source of news and information for Chicago-area Latinos.[17]

Service and small-manufacturing jobs drew people away from traditional enclaves on the West Side and Far South Side to outlying municipalities, although population changes are not uniform from suburb to suburb. Blue-collar jobs that once made up the economic backbone of cities have either vanished or moved to the developing suburbs, if not overseas. In addition, neighborhood retail businesses that served the middle class have also largely relocated to the suburbs. In some locales, both the white and minority populations are increasing; in older suburbs, whites have moved out as Mexicans entered. Latinos in the suburbs tend to be concentrated in a small number of older satellite cities, such as Aurora, Joliet, and Chicago Heights, cities with weak economic bases.

The predominantly Mexican suburb of Cicero, Chicago's largest inner-ring suburb, has been the object of several civil lawsuits for discriminatory housing and employment policies. Its Latino influx has challenged the politics of a township once reliably Republican. In suburban Cook and the collar counties, small influxes of Latinos have not coincided with the departure of existing residents, and largely white suburbs in DuPage County are also taking on Mexican immigrants. Meanwhile, the Puerto Rican migration of former rural and smaller town dwellers to the Midwest that peaked in the 1950s and 1960s and leveled off in the 1970s and 1980s has been followed in the 1990s by a white-collar influx, most of whom settle in the suburbs.[18]

Elgin, located on the Fox River some thirty-five miles west of downtown Chicago, during the 1990s settled a federal fair-housing complaint by establishing a $200,000 fund to compensate Hispanic families who had accused city workers of unfairly targeting them for housing inspections. The discrimination complaint arose in 1998 when seven Hispanic families filed a complaint with the U.S. Department of Housing and Urban Development, contending Elgin inspectors focused on their property because of their ethnic background. In June 2002, a family in one western suburb charged discrimination against Latino residents by authorities enforcing building codes that set occupancy limits for local homes and by inspectors and police officers acting improperly when searching for evidence that the house was overpopulated.[19]

An estimated $8 billion annually is returned to Mexico from the paychecks of emigrants working in the United States. Some $1 billion in these *remesas* (immigrant remittances) may come from the Chicago area alone. A Mexican government official at the consulate, who helps organize and coordinate the town clubs here, points out the Mexican government's increasing efforts to work with the clubs in bringing private cash to public works in Mexico. Many towns there lack transportation, paved highways, even phone service and have poor medical care. Mexicans throughout the metropolis are becoming increasingly drawn into transnational cultural and financial arrangements, torn between sending money home and accepting permanence up north. Many, however, are able to buy houses in suburbs, especially in Cicero and Aurora. La Federación de Clubes Jaliscienses offers services to people from the Mexican state of Jalisco, including discounts on airlines, expedited contacts with the Mexican consulate, legal advice on imports and exports, facilitation of commercial links with the Jalisco state government, identification cards, and the like.[20]

In Mexico, government officials are often seen as outsiders, interlopers in community affairs, and interested only in milking the village of its resources. Despite these complications, Frank Aguilar of Cicero, a strong advocate of getting rid of street gangs, was recently elected to the General Assembly (the first Latino Republican). Further, one Latino former town trustee, Ramiro González, has been elected Town President of Cicero (after his predecessor was sentenced to an eight-year jail sentence for racketeering). Latino and Latina lawmakers, executives, even judges—mostly Mexican Americans and Puerto Ricans—continue to make tangible gains in several cities and suburbs, including the Aurora City Council.[21]

The 1980s were characterized by the substantial increase in family and female migration. Migrants from one rancho in Michoacán first arrived in suburban Chicago around 1968, a chain migration. The pioneers from that town who arrived were all men. Some had gone to California and other western states during the Bracero Program. The majority, however, were young and single. The tendency has been to locate away from the Southwest since the 1970s and towards Chicago. This migration includes mostly undocumented persons. The Amnesty of 1986 reinforced the practice of the head of the family, with documentation, bringing his undocumented family and soliciting their legal residence.[22]

In these diverse areas, Latinos struggle to develop a political identity to match local circumstances. In the city, by contrast, whereas the black-Latino alliance of the Harold Washington years has largely evaporated, coalitions among Latinos have persisted. In the past, Puerto Ricans enjoyed a disproportional share of the political representation among Latinos. In the mid-1990s, roughly half of the 25 Latino elected officials in Cook County were Puerto Rican, even though Mexicans predominated numerically. The 4th Congressional District, whose representative is Luis Gutiérrez, has a Latino population over two-thirds Mexican and about one-quarter Puerto Rican. Gutiérrez has shown a strong interest in issues dealing with Puerto Rico as well as with those facing Mexican undocumented workers, such as immigration, naturalization, and citizenship issues. In 2001, he served as Chairman of the Immigration Task Force of the Congressional Hispanic Caucus, and was detained with other protesters opposed to the U.S. Navy bombing range on Puerto Rico's Vieques Island.

Gutiérrez, who worked for Harold Washington during the mayor's first term, served as alderman from 1986 until 1993, when he was elected to the U.S. House in a special "butterfly" district encompassing non-contiguous, heavily Latino areas in the North and South Sides.

Cities and their surrounding metropolitan areas have their own tempos, problems, structures, and imperatives than those in the southwest. The lack of cohesion and unity in Midwestern Latino colonies is reflected in many ways. City and suburban areas changed before the immigrants arrived, and economic paths often override cultural considerations. Mexicans integrate by marriage and through other relational and community links like Poles, Italians, and others, as well as with other Latinos (resulting in "MexiRicans" on the North Side). Latinos stand at the forefront of contemporary urban history, and their cultural and political diversity has given them valuable and unique tools for realizing long-held civil rights goals.

A Puerto Rican Perspective on Latino Chicago

In the early 1990s, early on in my Chicago experience, while attending a concert of Puerto Rican musicians in Humboldt Park, a colleague introduced me to Carlos Flores, a long-time resident of Chicago. I soon learned that he had been involved in his youth as a member of the Young Lords, a group that later branched out to New York. Carlos and I met at subsequent concerts and events and he demonstrated considerable expertise in Puerto Rican and other Afro-Caribbean musical forms. Indeed, I have benefited considerably from our intermittent conversations and have admired his generosity of spirit and lifelong dedication to addressing the problems that have divided Latinos, while at the same time remaining true to his Puerto Rican heritage.[23]

The experiences of Carlos, a native of Guayama, Puerto Rico, provide glimpses of the city's cultural and political history from a Puerto Rican perspective. Yet it is fully a Latino perspective, having been seasoned by decades of shared struggles in neighborhoods, in political coalitions (Mr. Flores served on Harold Washington's Advisory Commission on Latino Affairs and in numerous other community endeavors), and in the cultural arena as a generous sponsor of the arts. He also has accumulated a unique photographic collection on Puerto Rican Chicago covering a thirty-year span that during much of 2003 has been displayed downtown at the Water Tower. His perspective, moreover, overlaps with many of the themes of this essay. There are, of course, numerous other possible interpretations of Chicago's Latino history, but the issues herein mentioned offer a useful starting point in exploring the city's often hidden ethnic dynamics. Carlos was in fact briefly a member of the radical Young Lords organization during the late 1960s and early 1970s, and he later became a community and civil rights activist who worked enforcing federal Affirmative Action guidelines. He has also worked to educate younger generations about the importance of their cultural heritage at the Center for Black Music Research at Columbia College in Chicago, organizing musical events and scholarly lectures, and discussing the widespread impact of Afro-Caribbean culture and music.

Carlos has lived in Chicago since 1959, where he arrived at the age of 10. His family went through the experience that most Puerto Ricans of that era shared. First came his father, then his mother and several of the children. Later, two of the siblings remaining with their grandparents in Puerto Rico were also brought north. The family settled on the North Side, near Chicago Avenue and La Salle; they later moved to the Puerto Rican barrio on Armitage Avenue. He remembers, "My dad, my mom, my grandparents, they were just hard working people." His father worked in the cafeteria of the Hawthorne Company in Cicero.

During the 1960s there was no specific "Latino identity" and the system was tailored to immigrant assimilation at all costs. As Carlos recalls, "When I came here there was no bilingual education. I remember what they used to do was to put you in the back of the room, they'd give you Crayolas and you'd spend the whole day coloring. Then you learned English, and struggled the best you [could]." It was while attending St. Michael's Catholic School in the Old Town neighborhood, he notes, that his "whole consciousness about racism and discrimination began [after hearing Italian-American kids say] that Puerto Ricans had run down the neighborhood." Living in an immigrant neighborhood he also became aware of "the whole concept of slumlords." Seeking to make sense of the mean streets, he joined the Boys Club, the Y.M.C.A., and baseball leagues, and also tasted life as a member of various "clubs," including the Continentals, and grew up among other clubs like the Paragons, Black Eagles, Latin Kings, and Young Lords (before the latter had become widely visible and politically active). The Lords later staged numerous protests to call attention to the need for community services. Their grievances included calling for systemic changes in the U.S. political and social system and they even set as one of their goals the independence of Puerto Rico. Significantly, they looked to their often distant cultural roots as Puerto Ricans in continental barrios as well as on the island.

After leaving high school, Carlos discontinued his association with the Continentals. As he entered various training programs and college he joined the Young Lords as a political organization. He always had to choose between divergent paths, but fortunately he "took the right [one]." He is self-taught in Puerto Rican history, and studied independence leaders such as Harvard-trained lawyer Pedro Albizú Campos, the former head of the Nationalist Party—"an educated

Puerto Rican" who challenged the system's norms. Carlos observed firsthand the Puerto Rican riots of 1977 in Humboldt Park, an episode, he notes, that was born of the frustration of the people clashing with overzealous law enforcement officials. During the outbreak he remembered "seeing the police lining up to sweep the park from south to north." People were thinking, "Hey, this is our day, it's Puerto Rican Day." These gatherings customarily occurred immediately after the annual Puerto Rican Day Parade in downtown Chicago; people would then gather in the neighborhood to celebrate without any official festivities. Yet the police, in that instance, took charge "and actually killed two people, right by the section of California and Division. [They] wanted to take control." As a result of the earlier 1966 riot, local government had become more receptive to recommendations from the community: "That was the waking of the community." Later, under the first Mayor Daley [and] Jane Byrne there was a lot of activism." By contrast, present-day marching and activism have become "forgotten pastimes."

Unprecedented positive outcomes in the civil rights arena occurred during the six years of Harold Washington's tenure, including the mayor's establishment of the Commission on Latino Affairs, comprised of men and women from the Mexican, Puerto Rican, and Cuban communities, where leaders including present State Senator Miguel Del Valle were groomed. Mayor Washington "had some sharp people that he drew on. It was very helpful [especially] on the issue of infant mortality [and] jobs." The mayor's impact on the overall social climate was limited, notes Flores, and short-lived, as he "didn't [even] really win the Council Wars" and there were never really any concrete "electoral solutions" formulated for political grievances. Thereafter, even with the emergence of the "wishbone" Latino Congressional district, activist Latino voices have remained muffled.

Carlos made a conscious decision not to "mix nationalism with mainstream politics; it's a whole different agenda, a movement of struggle, a movement to survive." He believes that many people mistakenly relied on elected officials. For example, the movement for Paz en Vieques (Peace in Vieques, i.e., the evacuation of the U.S. Navy from a base in Puerto Rico long used for bombing and target practice) "has become an issue of the masses, a mainstream issue, [though] it might have been spearheaded by the socialist and independence movement people." Other campaigns, such as the release of political prisoners, involve more fundamental questions of political purpose and tactics that often conflict with practical politics. For these reasons, he observes, the nationalist FALN, an "underground organization" with which he has had no direct or indirect involvement, has distanced itself from coordination and cooperation with community groups.

Flores' coordination and cooperation with community groups has always been based on maintaining a separate political agenda and aimed at cultural preservation. Concerning the question of Latino identity, Carlos observed that in the 1960s and 1970s Puerto Ricans had a more politically active voice than Mexicans, at least until Mexican-American migration and settlement jumped dramatically. Thereafter Mexican newcomers began to assimilate and participate to a greater extent. Referring to the surging influx of Mexicans at a time when Puerto Rican migration had stabilized, he reflected, chuckling, "around 1970 all hell broke loose." Puerto Ricans, due to the unique circumstances of their arrival and reception (as well as the fact that they often return to the island to raise their children, to work, or to retire), maintained their culture and traditions even more than in the homeland. By contrast, Carlos observes, after Mexicans first arrived after World War I they tended to assimilate more over time and move to the suburbs, Anglicize their names, or otherwise embrace a "Mexican-American" identity which never required that they specifically identify with their country. In the post-World War II context, by contrast, Mexicans increasingly adopted a totally different approach—maintaining their culture, language, and identity. He notes some divisions emerging in the contemporary Mexican community, however, between undocumented workers and others. Carlos sees the evolving approach towards a common Latino identity as one sometimes dictated by practical concerns, especially in job situations: "Basically it's a matter of convenience—to create survival for your family" you sometimes have to become more of a Latino.

During the confrontational 1970s, Flores was always involved in some sort of movement to bring together Puerto Ricans and other Latinos, though he concedes the existence among contemporary activists of a compromising attitude towards the seemingly impenetrable "powers that be." While attending the University of Illinois's Chicago Circle Campus as an undergraduate he was one of about forty students arrested for occupying the chancellor's office in a movement for greater representation for Latino students, faculty, and staff. While later working for the federal Equal Employment Opportunities Commission, he observed a lack of seriousness in pursuing genuine equality and found that "young blacks [and] Latinos [didn't] want to be associated with Affirmative Action," despite their debt to such programs. "People used to chain themselves to the Chicago Transit Authority so that the CTA would give more jobs to Latinos. A lot of people don't realize that police officers, bus drivers, and others [were] out there [fighting]." [They think] they made it on their own [but] they don't know that there were some struggles that took place so that they could get their jobs." He pointed out that the police department was forced to abolish its height requirement only after numerous lawsuits had presented previously ignored demands as civil rights issues.

Carlos believes that contemporary Chicago has lost some of its earlier ethnic flavor as a result of the gentrification of former Puerto Rican barrios such as Lincoln Park and Old Town, and also because of excessive cultural assimilation. He remains concerned also with the lingering effects of racism both within the Latino community and in the larger society, and particularly of media portrayals of Latinos ("We don't all look like Julio Iglesias, Gloria Estefan, and Ricky Martin"). Always articulate and candid, he argues that African Americans, too, need to be educated about their Latin American background and ties with Latinos, especially the historical factors that connect African slavery to the Caribbean and Latin America, as against the evolution of slavery in this country. He remains proud of the African heritage of Puerto Rico and is fully aware of the factors that have diluted Latino political strength.

In conclusion, Chicago Latinos, not surprisingly, offer a wide range of different perspectives on issues, such as whether their political identity is one of a "racial" or "ethnic" minority, whether discrimination has diminished appreciably in recent decades, and where the most glaring civil rights inequities lie—not to mention questions of culture and nationality. Most, however, find that Latino political unity is necessary to bridge ethnic diversity. Latinos have integrated economically, politically, and socially and compete with Poles, Italians, African Americans and others. Their cultural and political diversity has given them valuable and unique tools for realizing long-held goals. Greater internal cohesion among the various national subgroups might culminate in a more sophisticated and perhaps cohesive identity, reshaping their ethnicity beyond the "rainbow coalition" legacy of the Harold Washington era. Latinos of various backgrounds have most readily adopted the "umbrella ethnicity" when challenging inequities, suggesting an historical convergence of interests within the realm of civil rights.

Notes

[1]Abel Davis, President, IPL, to William N. Doak, Secretary, U.S. Department of Labor, Washington, D.C., November 2, 1931: IPL Supplement II, Box 4:

[2]Frank X. Paz, "Mexican-Americans in Chicago: A General Survey." [Chairman, Committee on Mexican-American Interests, Council of Social Agencies of Chicago] January, 1948. Welfare Council, Box 147, Folder 4, Chicago Historical Society.

[3]Mrs. Frank X. Paz to Chicago *Sun-Times* (March 14, 1952): 12.

[4]Louise Año Nuevo Kerr, "The Chicano Experience in Chicago: 1920–1970," Ph.D. Dissertation, University of Illinois at Chicago Circle, 1976. 148, 151.

[5]Chicago *Sun-Times* (February 3, 1954): 60.

[6]Félix M. Padilla, *Puerto Rican Chicago* (Notre Dame: University of Notre

Dame Press, 1987), 130.

[7]Jorge Prieto, *Harvest of Hope: The Pilgrimage of a Mexican-American Physician* (Notre Dame: University of Notre Dame Press, 1989) 95, 105.

[8]"Stand With Us Now," *¡Sí Se Puede!* [Chicago Boycott News] UFW of America, AFL-CIO, Chicago, (August 22, 1975): 1, 2.

[9]Robert Starks, quoted in Taller de Estudios Comunitarios, *Rudy Lozano: His Life, His People* (Chicago: Taller de Estudios Comunitarios, 1991) 106.

[10]"Report of the Commission for Justice for Rudy Lozano" [February 25, 1985] Taller de Estudios Comunitarios, 79.

[11]Félix M. Padilla, "Puerto Rican Chicago" 208; quoted in Mervin Méndez, "The 1966 Division Street Riots," *Diálogo* [Center for Latino Research, DePaul University] 2 (1997): 30, 31.

[12]"Terrorism on Trial: Justice and the FALN," Chicago *Tribune Magazine* (October 22, 1995): 29–31.

[13]Padilla, *Puerto Rican Chicago* 126.

[14]María Torres, "Just Asking" Chicago *Tribune Magazine* (February 3, 2002): 14.

[15]Larry Bennett, "The Dilemmas of Building a Progressive Urban Coalition: The Linked Development Debate in Chicago," *Journal of Urban Affairs* 9 (1987): 263, 2.

[16]Robin Lorentzen, *Women in the Sanctuary Movement* (Philadelphia: Temple University Press, 1991) 15–25.

[17]"Diversity Is Gaining in 'White' Suburbs," Chicago *Tribune* (April 8, 2001) [web version].

[18]Latino Institute, "Latinos in Metropolitan Chicago: A Study of Housing and Employment" (Chicago: Latino Institute, 1983), 51.

[19]"Elgin Fund to Pay Hispanics Facing City Bias," Chicago *Sun-Times* (August 21, 2002).

[20]Patricia Zamudio, "*Huejuquillense* Immigrants in Chicago: Culture, Gender, and Community in the Shaping of Consciousness." (Ph.D. dissertation, Northwestern University, 1999) 145, 278.

[21]"Minorities Gain Seats in Legislature," Chicago *Sun-Times* (February 3, 2003): 3.

[22]Jennifer S. Hirsch, "En el Norte la Mujer Manda: Gender, Generation, and Geography in a Mexican Transnational Community," *American Behavioral Scientist* 42 (June/July 1999):1346–1348.

[23]I am grateful to Carlos Flores for sharing his time and his thoughts during a recorded lunch interview, amid clanking plates and lively voices, at the Café Central—one of Chicago's oldest Puerto Rican restaurants—in May 2003.

The Latino Institute: Promoting Latino Progress through Policy Analysis, Leadership Development and Advocacy

Sylvia Puente and Víctor Ortiz

This chapter is an analytical overview of the Latino Institute's work to promote civil rights for the Latino community of the Chicago metropolitan area. It describes the organizational structure of the Latino Institute and its research, public policy, and advocacy efforts during its 25 years of existence, from 1974 to 1998. It analyzes these efforts to draw insights for future initiatives.

The Creation of a Latino Identity

"Who should have the power to control and determine their [Latinos'] future? If the central objectives are self-determination, equity, and independence, how can the necessary resources and skills be obtained with which to translate these goals into realities? The ability to influence change is directly tied to economic and political power. This influence is magnified through the effective use of information and the media. There is a pressing need to develop a unified and responsive Hispanic strategy that articulates the economic, education, political, social and employment concerns and goals on a short, medium and long-range basis."[1]

This quote from one of its first publications clearly expressed the goals that guided the Latino Institute during its 25 years of operation. Created in 1974 out of the momentum reached by intense grass-root-community organizing of the time, the Institute was forged as a vehicle for "equity, self-determination, and independence." This chapter traces the strategies and accomplishments that sustained such commitment and draws some organizing lessons from the Institute's inception, maturation period, and eventual termination in 1998. Building on a synoptic overview of the programs and organizational transformations, the chapter aims to highlight the strengths and eventual limitations of this staunch commitment, given the changes in the political climate in Chicago and its Latino groups though the years of existence of the Institute. The persistent commitment provided a horizon to steer many of its decisions. At the same time, it circumscribed its capacity to expand its bases of support to meet the increasing expectations it generated.

A common explanation for the Institute's demise is that it came about from insurmountable fiscal deficits. In this view, the Institute borrowed funds from its different programs, expecting future revenues to come in to close the internal financial gaps incurred. However, these gaps spiraled over time, increasing to the point where operation of the Institute was no longer sustainable. From another perspective, the Institute ceased its operations due to deeper factors. From this perspective, beyond its fiscal problems, the Institute became a victim of its own success. In other words, the competence level of the institution was pushed to a breaking point and became unable to meet the demand for its services with the level of available human and financial resources.

This second explanation points to the discrepant magnitude between the needs addressed by the Institute to promote Latino civil rights and the limited resources at its disposal. Aside from differences in the managerial styles of its various subsequent directors and the ebbs and flows of funding availability, this chapter evaluates this miss-match between resources and responsibilities as they concern the political underpinnings of the Institute's goals and strategies. The central point of this account is that the Institute's demise came about from its failure to expand the leadership base among its original community base at the same rate that the demands imposed on the organization grew. This failure was derived from the unwanted yet progressive distance between the Institute and the grassroots organizations that created it. As it became more sophisticated in its eventual focus on public policy analysis, it did not fully develop the community leadership required to share the demands and distribute the workload of the technical aspects of impacting the public policy making process. Hence, the technical skills required to conduct policy analysis were never fully transferred through its leadership development. At the same time, it did not relieve itself of the demands of responding to community inquiries or advocacy efforts. Precisely because of its intense commitment to the community, it attempted to meet virtually all of its requests.

This resulted in a paradox: in some ways the Institute grew increasingly distant from the community while also remaining actively engaged with it. This unwanted yet gradual distance between the Institute and its community base was propelled by an inherent tension among the Institute's three goals: equity, self-determination, and independence. Obtaining equity was in constant tension with obtaining self-determination and independence. Equity was understood as enhanced access to resources and participation in leadership positions. However, this access was defined by mainstream standards and appealed to power networks in which Latinos had little control. Therefore, maintaining the goals for self-determination and independence required a careful articulation of strategies in the Institute's programs so as to not be subordinated in the process of obtaining equity.

A prominent strategy of the Institute was to enhance the visibility of Latinos as legitimate and long-standing members of society at large. This enhanced visibility was accomplished through linking all Latinos under a common political identifier.

This challenge of bridging the diverse communities as a means to channel demands for greater resources, opportunities and recognition was clearly understood by the founders of the Institute. It was evident in the choice of the Institute's name. When the Latino Institute was created, the notion of "Latino" was novel. The various groups identified themselves by their ancestral country of origin, e.g. Mexican, Puerto Rican, or Cuban, and the collective term, if used at all, was "Spanish-Speaking."

The adoption of the term "Latino" to name the Latino Institute in order to unify the diverse Latino groups in working for common goals was groundbreaking. In practical terms, the emergence of this Latino political identity responded to the composition of Chicago's Latino population, which was unique in the nation.[2] Chicago was the only major city in the United States that had a significant presence of the three largest Latino groups: Mexicans, Puerto Ricans and to a lesser extent Cubans. It is estimated that in 1970, Mexicans were about 54%, Puerto Ricans about 32%, Cubans about 6%, and other Latinos about 9% of the city's nearly quarter of a million Latinos.[3] In contrast, major cities such as Los Angeles, New York, and Miami were characterized by the prominence of one of these three groups .

In his groundbreaking book, *Latino Ethnic Consciousness: The Case of Mexican Americans and Puerto Ricans in Chicago*, Félix Padilla notes the political significance of the new term:

> Latino ethnic-conscious behavior, rather, represents a collective-generated behavior which transcends the boundaries of the individual, national and cultural identities of the different Spanish-speaking populations and emerges as a distinct and separate group identification and consciousness.[4]

The use of the term Latino was a means of fostering a group identity. It allowed individuals to maintain their ethnic identify such as Mexican or Puerto Rican, but provided the framework for the various Spanish-speaking groups to unite in the pursuit of social, political, and economic equality (Padilla 61). Members of various Spanish-speaking groups, who understood that the social and economic reality that they experienced in the city was similar, chose the term to define themselves. Based on this shared recognition, they constructed a new political identity to add potency to their demands for civil rights. In actuality, this new term created the possibility for the development of a Latino civil rights agenda that previously did not exist.

In addition, the Latino Institute adopted an expansive vision of civil rights. It was not a strict legal definition, such as prohibiting or eliminating discrimination, but rather one that sought to reduce the gap that existed between the Latino community and greater society. Padilla states:

> . . . the establishment of the Latino Institute in 1974 was viewed as the creation of a highly systematic and orchestrated effort meant to eliminate the obstacles that had frustrated the attempts of the Spanish-speaking in improving the quality of their life in the city (Latino Institute: History and Philosophy).The Latino Institute was formed to seek economic and social progress, self-determination, and to impact those institutions and agencies that stood in the way of the progress of the various Spanish-speaking communities (126).

This commitment to equity was worded in the mission statement:

> *The mission of the Latino Institute shall be to empower committed individuals and groups to obtain, for the Latino community, a fair share of public and private resources to improve the quality of life for the Latino community in the Chicago metropolitan area.*

The new political identity was, therefore, instrumentally rooted in this shared commitment for equality of opportunity. As previously mentioned, however, this commitment was underscored by a tension over independence and self-determination. This tension manifested itself vividly in discussions over the location of the Institute's offices. For many, the Institute should be housed in a Latino neighborhood. Having been forged out of community involvement, it was argued that the Institute belonged in the midst of the community in order to serve its needs and be supported by it. Others saw two serious problems with this reasoning. A significant problem was presented by the residential concentration of the Mexican and Puerto Rican communities. Placing the Institute in one or the other community risked the instrumental balance of the emerging coalition. This perception was widespread. One staff member is quoted by Padilla saying that: "We would not have been a Latino Institute over in Pilsen because we would have faced the problem favoring Mexicans. How can we profess to be a Latino Institute in Pilsen or Westtown? (123)"

Based on these accounts, Padilla notes that the dilemma was resolved by establishing the office in downtown Chicago:

> *It was determined that a neutral location would prevent identification with a particular community, as well as demonstrate the commitment to not compete with existing community organizations. This choice praised by many, nevertheless has been perceived and criticized by some community members as a non-community oriented location.* (123)

Establishing the Institute downtown served two important purposes. At the time, Mexican neighborhoods were concentrated mostly on the south side of the city and Puerto Rican neighborhoods were on the north side. Therefore, a downtown location placed the Institute practically within the same distance of both communities. The response to the spatial dilemma underscored a second important dilemma, which related to the criticism reported in the last quote from Padilla regarding "a non-community oriented location." This dilemma related not to its geographical proximity to Latino groups but to its logistic immediacy to dominant centers of power. Symbolically speaking, a downtown location meant a solid step in asserting the inclusion into mainstream society that the Institute aimed to promote. In addition, logistically, such location offered the Institute greater proximity to city government and the financial district. María Cerda, the first Executive Director of the Latino Institute, explicitly stated this logistical consideration:

> *Our efforts could only come out of downtown because we wanted not only to tap the (communities') internal leadership but also the leadership of the city: the power-makers and policy-makers.* (Padilla 124)

The dilemmas on the location of the Institute brought to the surface the tension between the goal for equity and the goals for self-determination and independence. This tension caused a complex predicament that persisted during the entire existence of the Institute. The downtown location of the Institute established an orientation to carve a space into mainstream power centers as a means of enhancing access to resources and opportunities. This orientation set the Institute on a long process over 25 years of adapting its strategies to the increasing demands generated by its own accomplishments as well as the constant growth of the Latino community.

Strategies For Progress[5]

The Latino Institute employed a variety of strategies that evolved over time with the development of the agency. The formulation of these strategies responded closely to conditions in the Latino communities and in response to the overall political climate of the city, state, and country. The formulation of strategies responded to requests from the community and, in turn, the strategies guided the institutional structure of the Institute. For example, its first programs focused on leadership development and eventually laid the foundations for its Division of Training and Management Assistance. However, as trainees applied their new or enhanced skills in a variety of efforts, they and others began to request information on the Latino population and on a variety of issues pertaining to it, such as bilingual education, housing, and employment. The Institute undertook the task of providing such information, viewing this as a vital part of leadership development. This work laid the foundation for the growth of Institute's Division of Research and Documentation.

Afterward, armed with both skills and information, community advocates began the task of shaking loose from the establishment resources that neighborhoods needed. The number of battles to be fought, however, was great, and the community once again looked to the Institute for assistance. In response, the Institute stood shoulder to shoulder with these early advocates in negotiating with, confronting, and otherwise influencing a variety of power structures. This work laid the foundation for the Institutes' Advocacy Division.

Over their lifetimes, the Institute's three programmatic divisions did extensive work. The Training Division organized and trained members of bilingual education advisory councils, and trained staff and volunteer leadership of organizations serving Latinos, as well as a variety of other individuals and groups. The Research Division provided basic demographic data as well as sophisticated analysis of Latino political empowerment. The Advocacy Division, among other activities, incubated and/or supported community organizations and coalitions, analyzed legislation and policy, testified in courts, and provided advocacy skills coaching.

The Institute's responsiveness to existing community needs, coupled with its ability to anticipate new needs, led it to pioneer efforts in a variety of areas. These areas included community organizing, health, business, and the use of census data. The Institute's efforts in these areas opened doors through which many Latinos have been able to walk. In turn, the work of these Latinos, together with the exponential growth of the Latino population, paved the way for numerous organizations now serving the community. The Latino Institute incubated numerous organizations, often providing space and technical assistance.

The Institute also engaged in formal and regular planning processes. Driven by a desire to make the best use of the Institute's unique strengths in order to accomplish its mission, this process produced goals and objectives that provided the structure for the Institute's work, a structure from which the Institute was able to respond to issues as they emerged.

The Latino Institute is perhaps best known for its research on the Chicago area Latino community. This model for research developed over the years and eventually matured into the Latino Institute's ability to conduct policy analysis and impact the public policy making process. This evolution is illustrated below.

LATINO INSTITUTE
MODEL OF DEVELOPMENT OF RESEARCH DIVISION TO THE
LATINO POLICY CENTER

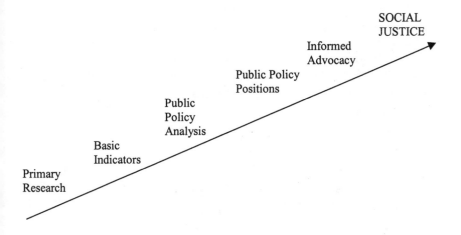

This model of development represents the growth and maturation of the Latino Institute research work. From its first research publications in the late 1970's until the mid 1980's, the Institute conducted mostly primary research. For example, the Latino Institute conducted a survey of 135 Latino-owned businesses in Chicago. The survey determined their characteristics and identified barriers to their economic development. While this type of new information was greatly needed, the expense and other resources it required were not the most efficient use of the Institute's resource capabilities.

As a result, the Institute shifted its emphasis to secondary research for collecting and analyzing basic data, primarily from federal sources. The Institute pioneered the ability to aggregate census and other data in a way that uniquely illuminated the characteristics of neighborhoods in Chicago and suburbs of the metropolitan Chicago area. This data was released in Latino profiles and "Lat-Stat's: Latino Statistics and Data."

With a substantial body of basic data and indicators, the Institute began to conduct public policy analysis. From the production of primary research, its emphasis shifted to the community impacts and demands of taking public policy positions in areas such as education, political empowerment, poverty, the North American Free Trade Agreement, and immigration. While the Institute had a long history of undertaking advocacy efforts, this evolution armed the Institute's advocacy with irrefutable data to substantiate its demands.

In 1992, the Latino Institute adopted the following definition of public policy: "Public Policy is any legislation, regulation, rule, program or practice and its interpretation, created or implemented by the public or private sectors to improve the quality of life for an individual, group, or society."

The Institute's studies enabled its Board of Directors to adopt formal public policy positions. These policy positions provided the base of support for the Latino Institute to conduct informed advocacy. For example, public policy decision-makers were informed about the impacts on given measures on the Latino community. These policy makers came to have a high regard for the Institute's analyses and recommendations, given the reliability of information and soundness of the studies.

The public policy and advocacy strategies employed in this process are presented below.

Techniques for Policy Analysis and Advocacy Strategies, Latino Institute	
Policy Analysis and Advocacy Strategies	**Techniques**
Monitor Policy Developments	Review Literature Track Legislation Track Regulations Manage Relationships
Advocacy with Policy Makers	Conduct Power Analysis Write Correspondence Hold Meetings Provide Testimony Implement Advocacy Campaigns
Interaction with Community	Organize Provide Issue Education Provide Technical Assistance
Applied Policy Analysis	Conduct Research Conduct Data Analysis Write Fact Sheets Publish Research Notes Publish Publications Adopt Public Policy Positions
Capacity Building	Provide Technical Assistance Conduct Training Implement Leadership Development
Influence Media	Maintain Media Relations Disseminate News Releases Hold Press Conferences

All the strategies of this model were considered and a plan was developed whenever the Institute adopted a public policy position.[6] The six strategies included the monitoring of policy developments to understand the effects of policy shifts, completing applied policy analysis to document the effects of policy, and conducting advocacy with policy makers to ensure the adoption and implementation of equitable policies. The strategies also included interaction with community leaders (to ground analysis and advocacy in the expressed needs of the community), leadership capacity building (to develop a larger cohort of community leaders engaged in policy), and media relations (to incorporate Latino concerns in the news making process).

The development of these public policy techniques, definition, and a public policy and advocacy training reflect a level of maturation and sophistication in the organizational development of the Latino Institute.

Highlights Of Accomplishments

The Latino Institute's accomplishments encompassed both issue areas as well as strategies for impacting these areas. In all cases, these strategies were utilized to promote progress on a given issue area. This section is organized, accordingly, around a discussion of the Institute's issues work in education, political empowerment, immigration, and its strategic work and accomplishments in leadership development, research and data analysis, and public policy advocacy.

Education

The Institute's reports on education and particularly overcrowding helped the community make its case, along with all the grassroots work, and make its case for new schools to be built in Latino communities. The best case is five new schools in Little Village between 1995 and 1997. Other schools have been built in other communities as well. Without those publications there would have been more debate, more delay and more resistance.

Jesús García
Former State Senator
Executive Director, Little Village Development Corporation

From its inception, the Latino Institute established itself as a major stakeholder in education. One of the Institute's first programs, beginning in 1975, was Parent Leadership Training. The "goal of this program was to facilitate the development of functional bilingual councils that would relate in an on-going basis to issues and situations related to the education of the Latino community in Chicago."[7] These councils were mandated by the Illinois Office of Education at each school with a bilingual program.[8] The Program promoted parental involvement in schools and trained parent advocates in a "learning by doing" so they could contribute to their children's educational progress. The program was highly regarded by the Chicago Board of Education as well as by teachers and administrators.

The Parent Leadership Program set the model for much of the Institute's future education work. The hallmarks of this model included parental participation, dialogue with education stakeholders, and advocacy with policy makers. The Institute undertook several extensive public policy and advocacy campaigns to promote bilingual early childhood education in addition to regular bilingual education. These campaigns were wide-scale community organizing efforts that mobilized hundreds of parents. During this time period (the late 1970's), the Latino Institute also facilitated several trips to the Illinois State Capital so that parents could voice their concerns to the state legislature and the Board of Education to prevent a reduction in funding for bilingual education (*Annual Report 1977* 5, 13).

At the initiation of Chicago's historic school reform, in which each school was given the authority to elect its own governing body, the Institute's central goal was the active participation of parents and residents of Latino communities in education reform activities. Therefore, it focused its work on the approximately 100 public schools with a majority of Latino students.[9] In these schools, it developed a sample training curriculum for local school councils and provided training on the new school reform act and the central role of the new local school councils. In addition, the Institute commented on issues such as the CPS financial crisis, equitable school funding, charter schools, vouchers, and the use of Chapter I funds. In particular, the Institute researched conditions of overcrowding. The seriousness of the problem was documented in a report that showed that two out of every three Latino children attending a public elementary school in Chicago were in overcrowded classrooms. The Institute conducted extensive advocacy and provided testimony on this issue during several legislative hearings. Eventually, it was invited to participate as a member of the Blue Ribbon Advisory Committee on Capital Improvements, a multi-billion dollar effort to rehabilitate the infrastructure of schools and build new schools.

Political Empowerment and Redistricting

According to Jesús García, former state senator and a major political figure during many of the years of operations of the Latino Institute, "*The publications (on demographics and political empowerment) helped set the stage for the creation of more Latino super majority wards and districts. Their (Latino Institute) publications had the credibility and standing that established the baseline for the community numbers.*"

The Latino Institute conducted data analysis on the political empowerment of the Latino electorate in Chicago. Some of the studies on the topic were: *Al Filo/at the Cutting Edge: The Empowerment of Chicago's Latino Electorate* (September 1986); *Latino Perspectives for 1990: New Numbers, New Leverage* (Latino Institute: May 1998); *LATSTAT, Latino Statistics and Data Series, Voting* (Latino Institute, Chicago, Illinois, 1994); *Total Voters, Registered Voters, Voter Turnout and Votes for Latino Federal and State-Level Elected Officials in the November, 1992 Elections by Chicago Voting Precinct* (Latino Institute, 1993). These publications drew the link between Chicago's growing Latino community and its potential for political power. Accordingly, they also documented election results in various electoral districts.

The Institute also published analyses of numerous local election results. In particular, it closely monitored the 1986 special aldermanic election and the 1990 redistricting processes. The 1986 election resulted in the first ever Latino majority wards in the city of Chicago. Its publication, *Al Filo/At the Cutting Edge: The Empowerment of Chicago's Latino Electorate,* emphasized the historical importance of this election: "These elections also afforded City government the opportunity to emerge from a deadlock that had polarized it along racial lines."[10] This deadlock had embroiled city government upon the election of Harold Washington, the first African American mayor of the city, who was brought to power through a broad coalition of progressive and voters of color.

The Latino Institute also worked with the Illinois Latino Coalition for Fair Redistricting in the early 1990's. The Institute prepared and presented testimony before the city council on the aldermanic ward remap, as well as testimony on the state reapportionment process. The resulting reapportionment process increased the aldermanic districts in the city of Chicago represented by Latinos from four to seven. In addition, it also created the first ever Illinois congressional district from which a Latino was elected.

As part of the aldermanic ward effort of the 1990 redistricting process, the Latino Institute developed a map based on census block data that showed the maximum number of Latino majority wards that could be created. It highlighted the districts in which Latino influence could be enhanced, the number of which surprised many political observes. This effort allowed the Institute to contribute to early negotiations with elected officials on the ward remap process. It gave Latino elected officials the data and analysis they needed to participate in informed negotiation efforts. [11] Furthermore, it demonstrated that the Latino community had the technical capacity and knowledge to participate in redistricting and ensured that a Latino perspective was integrated into the behind the scenes negotiating process.

Immigration

In 1996, the Personal Responsibility and Work Opportunity Act denied vital benefits to most non-citizens and barred legal immigrants who entered the United States since August of 1996 from medical and welfare assistance.[12] This legislation resulted in program cuts to Supplemental Security Insurance, Medicaid, Food Stamps, and Temporary Assistance to Needy Families. Latino Institute research showed that up to 22,000 elderly and disabled individuals in Illinois would lose SSI benefits and 38,000 would lose food stamp benefits. It was estimated that the total amount of benefits lost would be $130 million. Immigrant communities were going to be particularly hurt by this legislation.

The Institute worked with a coalition of organizations involving an unprecedented number and variety of ethnic communities in a campaign to develop state programs to address the impact of the cuts in federal benefits.[13] This effort led by the Institute resulted in a $10 million allocation from the Illinois General Assembly to develop new state programs to provide services to immigrants. This legislation made Illinois the first state with a large enough number of immigrants to pass legislation that would restore SSI benefits to senior citizens and the disabled.[14]

Part of what made this public policy and advocacy campaign so successful was its collaboration with the Jewish Federation of Metropolitan Chicago in forming the Illinois Immigrant Policy Project to research Illinois' immigrant communities. Six publications came out of this project.[15] This research lifted the visibility, credibility and expertise of the immigrant coalition effort to the public at large and to Illinois policy makers. The allocation of $10 million and its reauthorization in subsequent years was perhaps the most significant and tangible immigration victory that the Latino Institute achieved. While it was done in partnership with many other groups, the coalition was strengthened by the research and publications that had been produced as well as the Latino Institute's unique capacity to estimate the costs and number of individuals who would be impacted by this legislation.

Leadership Development

It (The Springfield Public Policy Workgroup) gave me an understanding of how legislation happens, that I frankly did not have before that.

Jessie Ruiz
SPPW Participant
Chairman of the Hispanic Lawyers Scholarship Fund of Illinois

The Latino Institute sponsored several opportunities for community members to become acquainted with the legislative process. One of the most successful of these programs was the *Springfield Public Policy Workgroup* in 1997, in partnership with MALDEF (the Mexican American Legal Defense and Education Fund.) The guiding principles of the Springfield Public Policy Workgroup were to:

1. Maximize access to state programs and services to immigrants
2. Ensure non-discrimination in ascertaining citizenship/immigration status on impacted state program
3. Increase funding for schools
4. Equally distribute resources that are resulting from block granting to the state
5. Ensure equitable access in the State Human Service reorganization

The overall purpose of the collaboration was to create and implement a nonpartisan coordinated effort to minimize the negative impact of proposed legislation and, in turn, propose initiatives beneficial to the Latino community. The workgroup, composed of twenty Latino professionals received on-site training on the legislative, public policy, and advocacy process.

The training brought together state policy makers and their staff members with Latino community members. The workgroup was designed to create an understanding of the Springfield legislative process. Members met during the Spring of 1997 to review pending legislation in the areas of employment and workforce, school finance reform, human service restructuring, and immigration. They analyzed this legislation, determined its impact on the Latino community and made recommendations to elected officials. This training allowed for a dialogue between community members and elected officials. It exposed community members to first-hand knowledge of legislative work and provided the members of the Illinois General Assembly direct input from community representatives. Ultimately, it set an important precedent for future efforts that led to a greater understanding of the legislative policy making and promoted a greater Latino presence in Springfield.

Another example of leadership development through training was the Latino Institute's role in the State Legalization Impact Assistance Grant Program (SLIAG). The Institute provided on-going technical assistance to numerous organizations providing adult education classes to persons legalized under the Immigration Reform and Control Act of 1986. Consultation and workshops were provided in such areas as proposal writing, planning and managing contracts, public relations, and accessing public and private resources for adult education.[16]

The Latino Institute also assisted in the development of several organizations that have each worked to advance the Latino community.[17] In some cases the Institute provided physical space as the organization was being created, served as fiscal agent, and/or provided technical assistance. A few of these organizations are:

HACIA—The Hispanic American Construction Industry Association, a 24-year old business member organization whose mission is to promote the participation of its members in public and private construction projects throughout the Chicago land area. HACIA was founded to prevent discriminatory practices in the construction industry."[18]

UNO—The United Neighborhood Organization works to build power for Latino communities within the public arena, with an overall directive of enfranchising the Hispanic local and national social frameworks.[19]

HACE—The Hispanic Alliance for Career Enhancement provides linkage and access for Hispanic professionals to private and public organizations, thereby strengthening the foundation for the professional and economic advancement of the Hispanic community.[20]

Latinos United—Latinos United is a metropolitan-area housing advocacy organization whose mission is to achieve equitable participation in housing, housing-related employment and economic development opportunities for Latinos by effecting change in public and private policies and practices through community empowerment, capacity building, monitoring, research, education, negotiation, confrontation, and litigation.[21]

Research and Data Analysis

The Latino Institute provided the refined demography data necessary to analyze housing, labor and education patterns for Hispanics. In so doing it helped establish the sense of a Latino community that could often be overlooked or lost in the sprawling complex metro Chicago regional area.

Melita Garza
Chicago Tribune Reporter

As previously mentioned, the Latino Institute expanded from its initial training and leadership development emphasis. In the early 1980s, the Institute began to produce research reports that documented the Latino growth in the Chicago metropolitan area and the overall status of Latinos in areas such as housing, employment, income, and other measures of social and economic well-being. These reports provided basic demographic and social indicators on the status of the Latino community in Chicago. Such data was useful for a myriad of purposes to both Latinos and non-Latinos.

The Latino Institute was recognized as the go-to place for research on any situation within the Latino community.

Fred Siegman
Fred Siegman Consulting Service
(active in Jewish community relations)

Aquí Estamos: Hispanics in Chicago, (Latino Institute, 1982) is considered the first of these publications. It provided an economic and historic overview on Mexican, Puerto Rican, and Cuban initial settlements in the Chicago area as well as the neighborhoods and suburban communities. This report also provided the first analysis of the Latino population in the areas of employment, education, housing and health. It examined factors, such a bilingual and higher education, attrition rates, racial composition of schools in Chicago, as well as an overview of the housing conditions and health status of Latinos. Among its many findings it stated that:

1. "Hispanics are currently the fastest growing population group in the city of Chicago, having registered a population increase of nearly 70% between 1970 and 1980."
2. "Hispanics in Chicago are among the lowest paid, most poorly housed, and least educated of all ethnic minority groups."
3. Latinos in Chicago are excluded from the decision-making process and they are seriously under-represented in business, industry, and government, as well as in professional occupations.
4. "The availability, accessibility, affordability, quality and continuity of services to Hispanics are serious problems that continue to threaten a productive and creative force within the city of Chicago." [22]

The report coined the refrain for future Latino Institute research and policy analysis. This refrain documented the status of the Latino community, defined the extent of existing disparities and inequality, and set the direction for redress. This refrain also established the framework for virtually all of the Latino Institute publications throughout its existence. Some of these were: *Latinos in Metropolitan Chicago: A Study of Housing and Employment* (Latino Institute, 1983); *Latino/Non Latino Profiles* (Latino Institute: March 1993); *The Changing Economic Standing of Minorities and Women in the Chicago Metropolitan Area: 1970 – 1990, Interim Report, 1992* (Chicago Urban League, Latino Institute and Northern Illinois University, 1994); *The LatStat Series: Latino Statistics and Data on Poverty, Income, and Housing; Latinos Face to Face/Latinos Cara a Cara* (Latino Institute, 1994); and *Toward a Latino Urban Policy Agenda: Lati-*

no Growth, Diversity and Education Status (Latino Institute: May 1996).

The Latino Institute established collaborative research projects with the Chicago Urban League and Northern Illinois University, two other noted area research institutions. One of the findings of this collaboration was published under the title of *The Changing Economic Standing of Minorities and Women in the Chicago Metropolitan Area: 1970-1990, Final Report 1994*. This report, a comprehensive economic analysis of census data, found a widening gap in the economic standing among White, Latino and African–American families during this time period. It reported that income levels for African Americans families were only half (52.7%) those of Whites in 1990, down from 62.9% in 1970. It also showed that Latino family income dropped from 68.5 percent of White family income in 1970 to 58.8 percent in 1990.

Responding to the publication of these findings in the Latino Institute report, one newspaper headline noted, "Latinos and Blacks are on an economic treadmill."

The collaboration with the Chicago Urban League and Northern Illinois University also yielded seven additional Latino Institute publications. These reports were part of a Working Poor Series that documented the status of Latinos, African Americans, Asians and Whites in the labor market. One of the salient findings of these analyses was that a disproportionate number of Latinos and African Americans work but remain poor, dispelling the myth that work is a path out of poverty. While this is now widely known, this series of publications was the first to make this argument for minority populations in the Chicago metropolitan area. The findings were reported in the following manner:

1. Racial and ethnic minorities are disproportionately represented among working poor families, in metropolitan Chicago; 33.4% were African-American and 28.6% were Latino.[23]
2. One out of every three persons who are working poor holds a full-time/full-year job. Almost one out of every three African-American adults (32.3%) work full time and are working poor.[24]
3. Latino working poor adults are most likely to be full-time workers; 42.9 percent of working poor Latino adults work full-time.

These findings were particularly timely, given that they were released between 1993 and 1997, when welfare reform at the federal level was being radically restructured, placing a five-year life-time cap on the receipt of benefits. These analyses clearly posed a warning that full-time employment would not necessarily mitigate poverty, even as welfare recipients became employed.

The series also offered a number of policy recommendations to mitigate the plight of the working poor in the area of tax policy, training, incentives and service provision.

Latinas

The Latino Institute also published at least three reports with an emphasis on women.[25] They documented the challenges and strengths that Latinas face, among them: "A set of three different pressures converge on the Latina working woman: Lower socioeconomic status in a nation stratified by class, gender in a patriarchal system and ethnicity in a race conscious society."[26] Yet, another message was that Latinas are resilient and express a strong commitment to strengthening and improving their communities. As motivation for their involvement, they cited the need to expand opportunities for youth, to leave the world a better place for their children, and to make the political process more accountable."[27]

The *Latinas in Chicago* report was commissioned be a local agency, Mujeres Latinas en Acción, which used the report to fill a critical void in information about Latinas and use the data to "ensure that a Latina perspective is voiced on critical issues impacting this community" (8). Interestingly, the status of Latinas did not change much between 1980 and 1990: Latinas participated in the labor force as much as all other women, 53% in 1980 and 57.2% in 1990, compared to 51.6% and 56.6% for all women respectively. Latinas are most likely to work in manufacturing, 35.7% in 1980 and 28.5% in 1990, and sales and clerical positions, 35.3% in 1980 and 38.8% in 1990, and least likely to work as professionals, 9.4% in 1980 and 13.8% in 1990.[28]

Latino Urban Policy Agenda[29]

The Latino Urban Policy Agenda (LUPA) was a collaboration with other Latino focused policy institute's around the country.[30] The project offered a powerful solution to the vexing problem of obtaining reliable and accurate data about the urban Latino experience in the United States. Each consortium member had the capacity to analyze data from a community-based perspective. In 1996, LUPA shared the findings with national policymakers at a two-day conference in Washington, D.C. The findings looked at such factors as Latino growth, race, ethnicity, age, citizenship, education, labor force participation, and poverty for Latinos living in Chicago, Houston, Los Angeles, Miami, and New York City. Thus, it allowed a preliminary determination of how much of Latino socio-economic status was a function of location, ethnicity or citizenship. For example, did the economic status of Puerto Ricans in Chicago look more like that of Puerto Ricans in New York or like that of Mexicans in Chicago? Likewise, the study also distinguished between the data on immigrant and native-born Latino status? The findings confirmed established assumptions:

1. Immigrant Latinos have lower median family incomes than native born Latinos.
2. Immigrant Latino families are more likely to be poor than U.S.-born Latino families.
3. The socio-economic status of Mexicans in Chicago is more likely to resemble that of Mexicans in other parts of the country than it is to resemble Puerto Ricans who reside in Chicago.
4. The socio-economic status of Puerto Ricans in Chicago is more likely to resemble that of Puerto Ricans in other parts of the country than it is to resemble Mexicans who live in Chicago.[31]

Public Policy and Advocacy

Thus by engaging in the research and policy, and in creating an advocacy agenda, the Latino Institute helped move the community toward action on that agenda. This resulted in the advancement of the community as it relates to education, affordable housing, employment and other areas of civil rights that are essential toward equal opportunity.

Jesús García
Former State Senator
Executive Director, Little Village Development Corporation

Many of the Institute's publications established the foundation for its public policy work. Advocacy was enhanced with the data and analyses of the Latino growth and lingering inequities in education, employment, housing, income, and poverty.

There are countless examples of advocacy that the Latino Institute undertook during its 25-year history. Sometime these positions were grounded in analyses that the Latino Institute had conducted, such as was the case with the North American Free Trade Agreement, progressive taxation, school funding or affirmative action. Other times, it was a gathering of the facts to write a letter stating the Latino Institute perspective on an issue such as casino gambling, literacy or the alleged discrimination by the Boy Scouts of America.

The Latino Institute provided countless testimony on varied issues. For example, the Institute supported more effective participation in government by granting citizens the right to view and copy public records[32] and testified on pay equity to the House Labor and Commerce Committee.[33] The Institute also had a track record of testifying when appropriate on all of the issues that it worked on: education, immigration, workforce development, housing and health.

The Institute also conducted advocacy by promoting citizenship. In the mid 1980's, it was among the first organizations to conduct outreach to encourage Latinos to become citizens. This effort was conducted with staff and volunteers at various community locations and paved the way for other Latino organizations to undertake this effort.[34]

As an example of an advocacy initiative outside of the Latino Institute's traditional areas, in 1990, the organization convened the Coalition in Defense of Access to Channel 44, an alliance of more than 110 Latino organizations, businesses, elected officials and groups representative of all the Latino nationalities in Chicago. The coalition was concerned with preserving access to WSNS-TV, at the time, Chicago's only full-time Spanish-language television station. The station had been denied a license renewal by the Federal Communications Commission. This license loss represented a potential loss of access to information and cultural benefits to the Latino population on issues that the Institute cared about, such as school reform, legalization, the census, voter registration, and health. Among the numerous activities of the coalition were press conferences, meetings with decision-makers, public meetings, a petition drive, collection of affidavits and a media campaign.[35]

Civic Participation and Interethnic Relationships

At the time . . . they were the only organization that explicitly had inter-group relationships on their agenda, to build relationships between the Latino community and other communities.

Fred Siegman
Fred Siegman Consulting Service

Through many of its research endeavors, coalitions, and participation on boards and commissions, the Latino Institute forged relationships with representatives of Chicago's diverse communities. Relationships with the African-American community were key during redistricting, and relationships with other immigrant communities were important during work on immigration issues.

In addition, because the Latino Institute was located downtown and because it was perceived as a credible organization, Latino Institute staff were asked to serve on countless committee's and task forces, and to make presentations to innumerable groups. In many ways, the Latino Institute fulfilled the realization expressed by its first executive director, María Cerda, and was widely sought after to provide a Latino perspective for key decision-making bodies.

Conclusion

Who should have the power to control and determine their [Latino] future?
This is the opening question of the Latino Institute publication cited at the
beginning of this chapter. This chapter enumerated some of the Institute's
impressive array of contributions in response to this fundamental question. Its
contributions encompass data, training, leadership development, advocacy, and
policy analyses, all of which supported community efforts to learn and enforce
civil rights. Throughout its 25 years of operations, the Institute brought visibility to the community and highlighted its strength and challenges in numerous
vital areas that range from education, political empowerment, and immigration,
to housing and media representation.

The chapter notes two important constants in the Institute's operation
throughout the years. The Institute maintained a staunch commitment to fostering equity, self-determination, and independence for the Latino community.
Likewise, it maintained alert attention to this community's needs and input.
Along with celebrating the accomplishments of the Institute, the aim of this
chapter is to gain a deeper understanding of these persistent commitments as
they were negotiated in the development of the Institute. As previously indicated, the Institute faced a never resolved tension. The mandate for the Institute was
to generate programs and initiatives to remedy inequality on a wide-range of
issues. However, this mandate required negotiating with traditional power structures, such as city hall, the board of education, and major corporations for
resources to finance the programs. These negotiations qualified the goals for
self-determination and independence in the search for equality. The inherent
tension among the Institute's stated goals was clearly manifested in the decision
to establish the offices of the Institute in downtown Chicago, closer to the mainstream network of power than Latino neighborhoods.

Despite its relative geographical distance, the Institute sought to remain loyal
to its advocacy of self-determination and independence by dynamically articu-
lating its programs to respond to the needs of the community. Its initial program
provided leadership training among grassroots organizations, some of which
had been involved in the creation of the Institute and made explicit requests for
this training. Gradually, these requests extended to address the need for better
information to advocate for employment or educational improvements in more
effective and sophisticated manners. This in turn required the development of
research capabilities at the Institute. Soon, data production allowed the Institute
to publish position papers and directly intervene in legislative processes through
testimony and electoral campaigns. Finally, a significant amount of the Insti-

tute's resources were also dedicated to policy analysis.

The level of sophistication and the public standing of the Institute steadily increased. In its last years, it was regarded as a "think tank" for Latinos, and its analyses were widely read. It also carried out ambitious research and advocacy projects. Sometimes, these projects were conducted in collaboration with other advocacy and research institutions, such as MALDEF, the Jewish Federation, and Northern Illinois University. However, the demand for the Institute's work stretched thin its human and capital resources. Driven by the magnitude of Latino community needs as well as by the interest that its growth generated in the public at large and among public officials, the Institute faced an overwhelming degree of "success."

A salient case of this overriding success concerns the relationship of the Institute with local and national media. By the 1990's, virtually all of the Institute's publications received wide spread media coverage, all of the Institute's press conferences were well attended, and members of the media called on the Latino Institute on a frequent basis. In fact, in its last year of operation, the Latino Institute was responding to media requests on a daily basis. Taxing as this attention may have been, it was difficult to turn down.

To a large extent, the Latino Institute, especially during the 1990's, had an ally in local and national media. This attention intensified the visibility of the Latino community that the Institute was set to enhance in its initial years. In its later years, staff members of the Latino Institute were often quoted in the *Chicago Tribune* and *Sun-Times* and were frequent guests of local public radio. As such, these interviews were valuable opportunities to disseminate information and analyses that promoted a constructive understanding of Latinos among themselves as well as in the public at large.

The public visibility and the well established reputation of the Institute self-propelled it to its own demise. Mounting demand for data, analyses, and opinions not only from the media but legislators, educators, and the public at large, pushed it beyond its capacity to function properly. Administrative complications eventually evolved into chaos and eroded its fiscal solvency. Yet, explaining the termination of the Institute's operation on pure administrative terms overlooks crucial political underpinnings that may alert us to similar problems in other valuable public institutions advocating for civil rights.

Two important insights can be gained from the case of the Latino Institute for other civil right institutions. One is the overriding imbalance between the demand on information and services of Latino communities and the capacity of non-profit organizations to address such overwhelming demand. The Latino Institute skillfully expanded to address the demand. Yet, such capacity was eventually overridden. Its case alerts us to the need for careful administration in order to avoid the pitfall of significant growth that leads to the undermining of financial or human resources.

The second insight suggested by the case of the Latino Institute concerns precisely a way to avoid or address this pitfall. Perhaps a way to avoid the Institute's demise could have been in paying closer attention to the expanding leadership among grass root groups. Unfortunately, this attention was fatefully undermined by the accelerated momentum of demands for services made on the Institute.

Overtaken by the spiral of ever more sophisticated projects, the Latino Institute lacked the resources to fully develop its leadership program and to fully cultivate expertise among its original constituencies. Given limited resources and funding opportunities, its research and public policy capacity was more fully developed while its leadership program struggled for funding. While it is unfortunate that these two program areas did not develop at a parallel pace, it was a direct response to the external environment's overwhelming demand and requests for data and the need to impact public policy. Also, the effervescence of community activism of the seventies had greatly diminished by the mid 1990s. Ultimately, however, it could also be argued that the seed for the Institute's end was ingrained in the inherent tension between the search for equity through participation in mainstream networks at the expense of grass root contact.

The Institute generated an impressive array of data, analysis, and publications. Yet it also provided us with a salient case study for civil rights organizations to remind themselves of the need to administer their growth by attending to the symbiotic connection with the community that brought them into existence.

Notes

[1] Latino Institute Research Division, *Aquí Estamos: Hispanics in Chicago*. Submitted to: The Illinois Continental Bank (Reston, Virginia: Latino Institute, October 1982), p 63.

[2] The author believes that currently, the term "Latino" can be used to describe the unique circumstances of growing up in the United States with a strong Latino identity and can be used to describe both political and ethnic identity.

[3] Latino Institute: *LatStat: Latino Statistics and Data, Latino Origin Groups*, no. 5 (Chicago: Latino Institute, August 1995), 1. In 1970, the census did not report on an Hispanic identification. In this publication the Latino Institute analyzed census data and developed a methodology to determine the estimated number of Mexicans and other Latinos, based on the identified number of Puerto Ricans and Spanish-speaking individuals. The census counted 78,963 Puerto Ricans, and 247,343 Spanish-speaking persons. The determination of

Mexicans and other Latinos is an estimate. The percentages of Latino population may not add up to 100% due to rounding.

[4]Félix M. Padilla, *Latino Ethnic Consciousness: The Case of Mexican Americans and Puerto Ricans in Chicago* (Notre Dame, Indiana: University of Notre Dame Press, 1985), p. 61.

[5]Most of this text summarizes portions of *Latino Institute: A Framework for Influencing Policy*, Latino Institute, 1991. David Luna, Director of Training, largely wrote this document.

[6]Rob Paral, former Research Director of the Latino Institute, is acknowledged for the language of this section and for being the lead staff person in developing the concept of the "Techniques for Policy Analysis and Advocacy Strategies." The concept has been slightly revised by Sylvia Puente.

[7]Latino Institute, *Four Year Progress Report* (March 13, 1979), p 10.

[8]Latino Institute, *Annual Report: 1977* (Chicago: Latino Institute, 1977), p .5.

[9]Latino Institute, *Stepping out into the 90's, Latino Institute, Annual Report: 1989–1990* (Chicago: Latino Institute, 1991.), p.6.

[10]Raymundo Flores, Rufino Osorio, and John Attinasi, *Al Filo/At the Cutting Edge: The Empowerment of Chicago's Latino Electorate* (Chicago: Latino Institute: 1986).

[11]Latino Institute, *Annual Report: 1990-1992,* (Chicago: Latino Institute, 1993).

[12]Illinois Coalition for Immigrant and Refugee Rights, *Federal Budget Deal Abandons Thousands of Illinois' Most Vulnerable Immigrants*, Fact Sheet, May 1997.

[13]Coalition members included the Illinois Coalition for Immigrant and Refugee Rights, the Jewish Federation of Metropolitan Chicago, MALDEF, the American Jewish Committee, the SSI Coalition for a Responsible Safety Net, and the Poverty Law Project. Among the many others that supported this effort were all the Latino and Jewish elected officials in Springfield and countless grassroots community organizations representing various Asian, Jewish, Latino, Polish, Romanian and other immigrant communities.

[14]These States are California, Florida, Illinois, New York, Texas and New Jersey.

[15]*Hopes and Dreams: A Statistical Portrait of Non-Citizens in Metropolitan Chicago,* (Chicago: Latino Institute, 1994); *Indicators for Understanding: A Statistical Portrait of Metropolitan Chicago's Immigrant Community,* (Latino Institute and Northern Illinois University, Office of Social Policy Research, 1995); *A Briefing Book for State and Local Policy Makers* (Chicago: IIPP, 1995); *Estimated Costs of Providing Welfare and Education Services to Immigrants and to the Native Born in Illinois* (Chicago: IIPP, 1996); *Taxes Paid by Illinois Immigrants: A Technical Paper Produced for the Illinois Immigrant*

Policy Project by the Urban Institute (Chicago: IIPP, May 1996); and *Public Aid and Illinois Immigrants: Serving Non-Citizens in the Welfare Reform Era* (Chicago: IIPP, 1996).

[16]Latino Institute, *Annual Report: 1990–1992* (Latino Institute, 1993) p. 7.

[17]Latino Institute, *Latino Institute: A Framework for Influencing Policy* (Latino Institute, 1991).

[18]HACIA website, http://www.hacia.info

[19]UNO website, http://www.uno-online.org

[20]HACE website, http://hace-usa.org

[21]Latinos United fact sheet.

[22]Latino Institute, *Aquí Estamos: Hispanics in Chicago.* Submitted to The Illinois Continental Bank (Reston, Virginia: Latino Institute, 1982), pp. 61–62.

[23]*Working Poor Families in Chicago and the Chicago Metropolitan Area: A Statistical Profile Based on the 1990 Census* (Chicago: Chicago Urban League, Latino Institute, Northern Illinois University, December 1993).

[24]Sylvia Puente, *Race, Ethnicity, and Working Poverty: A Statistical Analysis for Metropolitan Chicago* (Chicago: Chicago Urban League, Latino Institute, Northern Illinois University, February, 1997), p. 6.

[25]These reports were: Latino Institute, *The Condition of Latinas in Illinois and Chicago: A Working Paper* (Latino Institute, 1985); Latino Institute, *Chicago's Working Latinas: Confronting Multiple Roles and Pressures* (Latino Institute, March 1987), and Sylvia Puente, *Latinas in Chicago: A Portrait*, commissioned by Mujeres Latinas in Acción, (Chicago: Latino Institute, October 1996).

[26]Latino Institute, *Chicago's Working Latinas: Confronting Multiple Roles and Pressures* (Latino Institute, March 1987.) p. 2.

[27]Sylvia Puente, *Latinas in Chicago: A Portrait*, commissioned by Mujeres Latinas in Acción, (Chicago: Latino Institute, October 1996), page 40.

[28]1980 data are from Latino Institute, *Chicago's Working Latinas: Confronting Multiple Roles and Pressures,* (Chicago: Latino Institute, March 1987.), page 7–9 and 1990 data are from Sylvia Puente, *Latinas in Chicago: A Portrait*, commissioned by Mujeres Latinas in Acción, (Chicago: Latino Institute, October 1996), pages 23–24.

[29]Most of this section is based on Latino Institute, *Annual Report: 1996* (Latino Institute, 1997), p 6.

[30]These organizations were the Institute for Puerto Rican Policy, based in New York City; the Cuban American National Council, based in Miami, Florida; and the Tomás Rivera Center, based in Claremont, California and Austin, Texas.

[31]Latino Institute, *Toward a Latino Urban Policy Agenda: Selected Demographics*, presented at the Latino Urban Policy Agenda Conference, Washington

D.C., May 29–30, 1996 (Latino Institute, 1996).

[32]Testimony before the office of the Mayor, Legislative Liaison and Intergovernmental Affairs, Regarding Executive Order 83-1, presented by Virginia Martínez, General Counsel, July 13, 1983.

[33]Testimony before the House Labor and Commerce Committee, Subcommittee on Pay Equity, presented by Virginia Martínez, General Counsel, September 13, 2003.

[34]Interview with Virginia Martínez, April 23, 2003, who was General Counsel for the Latino Institute at that time.

[35]Most of this language is drawn from Latino Institute (Chicago: Latino Institute, 1993), p. 13–14.

In Search of Meaningful Voice and Place: The IPO and Latino Community Empowerment in Chicago
María de los Ángeles Torres[1]

I. The Dilemma

The headline "Neither Here Nor There" of the *Chicago Reader's* May 4th, 2001[2] front-page review of Juan Ramírez' *Israel in Exile* may have missed the entire point of the film. The first Latino feature-length film shot and produced in the city, follows Israel, a young Mexican boxer from Zacatecas, as he journeys to Chicago to become a world class boxer, where his dream is cut short as he is disfigured in a fire while saving a young boy. Eventually the boy he rescues grows up and comes back to challenge the older boxer. Mexico is always present as we also watch Israel's mother's life. The manager of the currency exchange in which Israel comes to pick up a weekly check narrates the story. The film has an exquisite linguistic balance between Spanish and English, suggesting not a permanent displacement, but rather a complex existence in multiple cultural, geographic and political locations. Despite the authenticity of this vision, a historical and theoretical understanding of these complexities in the Chicago's region is still lacking.[3]

II. The Historical Setting: Politics, Race and Ethnicity

Four hundred people lived in Chicago when the city was incorporated in 1833. The city's rapid industrialization was accompanied by the relocation of thousands of workers to the area.[4] By 1890, 78% of its population was foreign-born with important concentrations from Ireland, Germany, Scandinavia, Russia (mainly Jews), Italy and Poland. Since then, the metro area has become home to almost eight million residents.

The politics of the Chicago region came to reflect its new communities. New immigrants were relegated to the lowest paying and often most dangerous work. As such, foreign-born labor contributed to radical unionization drives in the 1900s.[5] At the end of the 1800s, labor activism made Chicago the center of support for the eight-hour workday.[6] Indeed, it was confrontations in Chicago that gave the international movement its most renowned martyrs at Haymarket Square. But the union movement in the late 1860s and 70s was deeply divided, and with the absence of a strong central labor voice, ethnic bosses, representing middle-class immigrants, moved into the role of political spokespersons for their communities. For instance, after the Great Chicago Fire of 1871, Anton Hesing led a coalition of Germans and Irish to protest Mayor Joseph Medill's ordinance that allowed only brick homes to be built. Later, he organized the successful movement against temperance laws.[7] Politics became a way to consolidate emerging populations as it gave communities of new immigrants economic and political opportunities.[8]

Nativists, however, argued that immigrants could not be Americanized. Questions of identity became important at the turn of the century as reformers such as Jane Addams advocated for the rights of immigrants and claimed that they could become American. Politicians understood the power of ethnic identification, and in 1919, one of the city's congressional representatives decried that the party that eliminated the hyphen would eliminate itself from politics.[9] Debates about national immigration reform found their way into local politics, as did discussions about the role of the United States in Europe.

Debates about the good citizen were informed with the work of John Dewey and Frances Parker, two theorists who argued that education was the key to sustainable democracies. All individuals, regardless of their background, could become good citizens if they were afforded an education that developed their moral and cognitive skills.

World War I created an unprecedented push on the part of the United States government to "Americanize" ethnics (at the time a derogatory term meaning foreign), particularly those from countries with which the United States was at war. Many states in the Midwest outlawed the use of foreign languages in public spaces, and ethnic newspapers were censored. This trend continued through World War II. In effect, a national policy that demanded patriotic loyalty discouraged ethnic communities, particularly Germans, Italians and Japanese, from maintaining ties with their homeland. Indeed, to preclude such ties, Japanese-Americans were interned throughout the duration of the war.

Ethnicity was relegated to the private realm and in the public realm citizens were rallied around the construction of a *political* American. The impact on local politics was the hyphenated phenomenon; immigrant groups retained a cultural allegiance to their home country, but for political purposes everyone could become an American. It was assumed that by the second generation, immigrants would cut ties with their homeland. Despite a social anti-immigrant backlash, new immigrants became an important part of Anton Cermack's political base that helped him succeed in becoming mayor in 1931, ushering in the era of the Democratic Party local machine.[10]

During this time, Chicago also became a center of organized crime. Gangsters fought out turf wars on city streets, and Chicago gained a reputation as the land of mobsters. And although one of its most infamous, Al Capone, was thrown out of the city and set up his own political machine in the nearby suburb of Cicero, organized crime found important niches in the complex ethnic-political machine of the city. In Cicero it became the basis for the political machine.

Richard Daley would become boss of Chicago's political machine in 1955. By this time, politics was local with occasional forays onto the national scene. Chicago gained the name "The Windy City," not because of its chilling "hawk," (lake winds) but rather because of its politicians.

The demographics of the area changed again during the 1930s and 1940s when five million African-Americans journeyed north in search of jobs and better living conditions.[11] In Chicago their presence created a thriving cultural and commercial district on the south side known as the "Black Metropolis." Politicians vied for their votes and loyal Blacks were included in the political machine. But as the demographics of the city shifted and ethnic whites fled to the suburbs, Daley resisted increasing the number of Black representatives in the changing wards. In addition, racism in every other aspect of life prevented the emergence of an integrated city, and, therefore, the kind of social mobility predicted by the ethnic-assimilation political model did not become a reality for African Americans. By the late 1960s, even African Americans loyal to the machine were finding it hard not to join the civil rights movement.[12]

Daley became a target of civil rights protests that demanded an end to school segregation and poor housing conditions. His response was to declare support for the goals of the civil rights movement while avoiding any substantive changes. But despite official declarations, racism was alive in Chicago. Civil rights workers were met with violence and scorn as they marched through Chicago neighborhoods like Marquette and Gage Parks. Tensions were building. Cicero was a community so racist that even Martin Luther King Jr. refused to march in its streets. The day after the assassination of Martin Luther King, Jr.

riots broke out throughout the city. More than 500 people were injured and nine blacks were killed. The mayor announced that he had given orders to shoot to kill any arsonist or anyone with a Molotov cocktail.

The great social and cultural changes in Chicago's demographics were not reflected in the politics of the city. Daley ran a tight political machine and gained the reputation of being "The Boss." He was unopposed four of his six terms in office. In 1975, two independents ran against him: Bill Singer from the north side and Richard Newhouse, an African-American reformer from the south side. Although the machine had cultivated a Black submachine, independent African-American politicians had started to emerge. The civil rights movement contributed to the beginnings of an independent electoral grassroots movement throughout Chicago. After Daley's death, the ward-based machine unraveled as a struggle ensued for succession. Technically, the president pro tem of the Chicago City Council was supposed to fill the office of mayor until the city council convened and selected one of its own. However, William Frost, the mayor pro tem and an African American, was not permitted to enter the Mayor's office. Instead, Michael Bilalndic, Daley's floor leader, took the office. Special elections were held in 1977 and Bilandic won. Harold Washington, a south side state representative, had opposed him.

In 1979, Jane Byrne defeated Michael Bilandic with a successful grassroots campaign that incorporated Blacks, Latinos and independent white liberals. But early in her term, she turned on her supporters. In the Latino community, Jane Byrne opted for a strategy of privileging business leaders and some community organizations, but she shut the door on grassroots organizations and African American communities that had been critical to her electoral success. For instance, despite the fact that most residents of the Chicago Housing Authority were African-American, Jane Byrne refused to name an African American to its board. In addition, her promises of a more equitable distribution of city resources went unfulfilled. By this time, the numbers of Black elected officials in other cities had increased dramatically. Major cities such as Los Angeles, Detroit, Cleveland and Atlanta had elected Black mayors. This contributed to Black Chicago's search for electoral power. In Chicago, this would be made possible though an alliance with Latinos.

III. Latinos

Latino communities in the Chicago metropolitan area have emerged at the margins of two other demographic phenomena: the immigration of European laborers and migration of southern African Americans. The origins of Latino communities are tied to relations between the United States and the migrants' countries of origins. Mexican workers were the first Latinos to make their presence felt. Agreements between the Mexican and U.S. governments brought thousands of Mexican workers to the steel mills of the Midwest to replace American laborers that were off at war.[13] Despite massive deportations in the 1930s, the emerging communities would continue to grow, fed both by spill-over agricultural migrants and direct immigration from Mexico. In the 1950s, Puerto Ricans also settled in the area[14] and the 1960 federal relocation program of Cuban exiles brought another major wave of Latinos. Latinos from all parts of Latin American continued immigrating to Chicago. The decade of the 1980s saw unprecedented growth of Mexican migration as well as a sharp increase of Central American refugees.

From 1960 to 1980, the Latino population had quadrupled, becoming 14% of the total population of the city. From 1980 to 2000, changes in the economy leading to the creation of an unprecedented number of low-end service jobs became magnets for immigrants looking for work. Surpassing the national average of 58% growth, the Latino population continued to increase by 69% from 1990 to 2000.[15] Most of the increase was represented by Mexican immigrants. In all, more than one million Latinos lived in the metropolitan area, with distinct communities not only in seven geographic localities in Chicago, but also with dramatic increases in suburban areas as well.[16] Today the area's Latino community is the third largest in the United States after Orange (CA) and Dade (FL) counties.

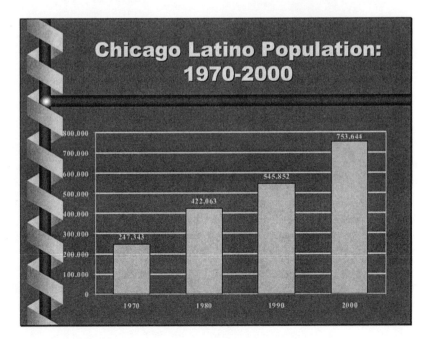

Chicago Latino Population: 1970-2000

1970: 247,343
1980: 422,063
1990: 545,852
2000: 753,644

Although the Latino communities of Chicago and its surrounding area were made up predominately of one or another Latin American or Caribbean origin, *Latinismo* became a way in which to organize politics.[17] The notion itself of "Latinismo" emerged as an ethno-political category in order to leverage numbers of people from communities that have a common linguistic and historical past.[18] The trend seems to be continuing as the percentage of Latinos identifying themselves as such grew from 9% in 1990 to 12.5% in 2000. This creates interesting possibilities for forming political coalitions. (Identity as a merger of Pan-Latin American and U.S. urban experiences raises interesting questions about identity politics in general.[19])

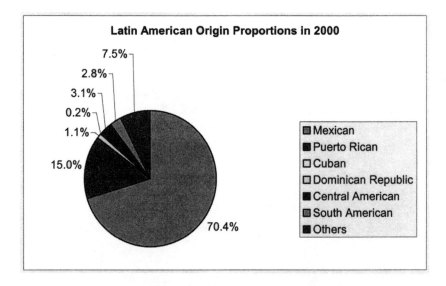

Latin American Origin Proportions in 2000

7.5%
2.8%
3.1%
0.2%
1.1%
15.0%
70.4%

- Mexican
- Puerto Rican
- Cuban
- Dominican Republic
- Central American
- South American
- Others

Demographic and political conditions facilitated the entrance of increasing numbers of Latinos to political offices; however, representation still lags far behind its potential.[20] The vehicle for political involvement in Chicago has been the classic and neo-classic political machine.[21] Latinos incorporated into machine politics often lose their independence and instead of advocating for the needs of their communities, end up being used to detain independent community efforts. Therefore, Latinos' place in politics, with rare exception, has been restricted and their complex realities of having identities and politics informed by both their host and their home country have not fit neatly into the prescribed political practices of the city. The Harold Washington administration in the early 1980s was an exception to this since it set up programs to address issues both in the city and in home countries.[22] Generally, however, Latinos have been forced to choose local machine politics that have not always accommodated the needs or the complexities of the various communities.[23]

Percentage of Latino Elected City Council Members in Chicago
(1980 to Present)

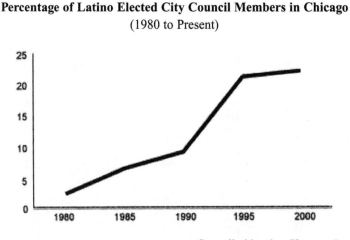

Compiled by the *Chicago Reporter*

Despite barriers posed to independent political action by political machines in the Chicago metropolitan area, Latinos have tried to find an effective voice and place for their politics and identity.

IV. Finding Voice in the Electoral Arena: Independent Political Organization of Little Village

The Independent Political Organization of Little Village (IPO) was first founded in 1981. Its guiding principals were to advocate for services to the community, self-determination in choosing its political representatives, and political unity between the African-American and Latino communities. At first it was named the IPO of the Near West Side, because it also included Pilsen, a predominantly Mexican community directly west of Chicago's downtown, but as the IPO was successful in winning offices in Little Village and not in Pilsen, its members decided to rename it the IPO of Little Village.

The IPO of Little Village is located in the 22nd ward, one of Chicago's fifty aldermanic districts. Until the most recent redistricting, it included Little Village, a southwest community that is predominantly Latino, and North Lawndale and Le Claire Courts, made up of mostly of African-American residents. In total, over 80% of the mainly Mexican residents are Latinos. It is also the ward with the lowest number of eligible voters, a high concentration of legal residents and undocumented workers.

Growth in Latino Concentration for Little Village, Pilsen and New City: 1990–2000

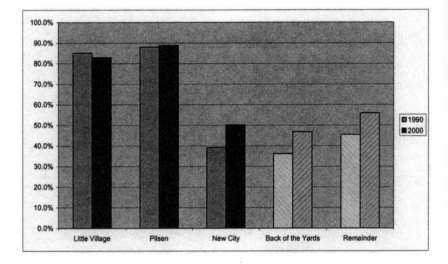

A board of community residents elected annually at a convention governs the IPO. It has an executive committee and a president. While the alderman has usually been the president of the IPO, this is not written into their by-laws. Broad policies are decided upon at their annual convention.

Generally, the work of the IPO is done through its issues committees. Throughout the years these committees have included political action, immigration, citizenship drive, education and health. Special endorsement sessions are held around election time so those members can debate and decide whom they will support as an organization. In addition, the IPO organizes block clubs throughout the ward. To date there are about 250 block clubs covering about half the area of the ward. Anyone living in the ward, regardless of his immigration status, is encouraged to join and work within the IPO. The IPO has about 75 to 200 active members.

The organization has also been active in citizenship drives and in get-out-the-vote campaigns. During election season, the organization becomes active on behalf of the electoral campaigns of candidates which they have endorsed. The organization relies on volunteers and has no paid staff. It does have a close working relationship with alderman's ward office. In general, the IPO sets the agenda and the alderman's office implements it.

History

Today the IPO of Little Village is principally an electoral/political organization, but its roots can be found in an organization established in 1968 by Mexican political refugees. Political repression in Mexico in the late sixties contributed to the exodus of a group of student and community activists. Many of these activists came to the United States, and some founded CASA-HGT (Centro de Acción Social Autónoma, Hermandad General de Trabajadores).

Initially, CASA was an organization of political refugees dedicated to the defense of undocumented workers. As it grew, it recruited young Mexicans, some of whom had been born in Mexico, others who were third generation. For instance, Jesús García was born in 1956 in Los Pinos, a small community in Durango, and came with his mother and three siblings to the United States in February 1965. His father had come to work as a cowboy and had gone back and forth. Finally, the entire family settled in Chicago because of more stable employment opportunities. His longest job was at a cold storage facility on 14th Street. Others, like Linda Coronado, were born in Chicago and raised in the Back of the Yards. Carlos Arango, on the other hand, was one of the student exiles who had sought refuge from Mexican government repression. All of these immigrants became part of the Latino New Left, and their political views reflected a commitment to social justice and socialism. Many had traveled to Cuba and were inspired by the Cuban Revolution.

The members of CASA in Chicago were students, lawyers, community activists and scholars. Unlike other chapters of CASA around the United States that had a significant number of academic members, Chicago's members tended to be rooted in community organizations, although their training ground had been high schools and universities.

Many of the members, like Jesús García, became involved during their high school years. His high school was about 15 to 20 percent Latino, and the political lessons came early. From the beginning, CASA was interested in building ties with the community through high school student organizations. The country was in the midst of the civil rights movement; for Mexican Americans, farm worker rights were at the forefront. Jesús recalls that CASA helped set up a student and community committee in defense of farm workers.

The University of Illinois campus in Chicago turned out to be a center for activism. Linda Coronado had graduated from Northeastern University and was now a counselor at the university. She had become increasingly interested in connecting with struggles throughout the country and in Mexico, and was committed to helping students connect politically, as well. When Jesús García started at the University of Illinois, there was significant activism there. One student organization demanded better services for Latino students and successfully advocated for the establishment of a Latino Cultural Center. In addition, the students wanted to forge links to the community, and thus set up an office in an apartment that they rented in Little Village.

In the summer of 1976, Jesús García met Rudy Lozano. Rudy had dropped out of the university and had begun working with Legal Aid. He was already involved with CASA and was organizing a contingent to attend the bicentennial protest in Washington, DC. On the way to DC, Jesús sat next to Lupe Lozano, Rudy's wife, who told him about their involvement in supporting Mexicans in the United States and about their plans to march in Chicago. Rudy, who had been a pre-med student at University of Illinois at Chicago, had dropped out to become a full-time CASA organizer. At the time, CASA, locally as well as nationally, was focused primarily on organizing undocumented workers into unions and providing them with social services.

Art Vázquez was the director of a Casa Aztlán, a youth-oriented social service organization when Linda Coronado had become the executive director for Mujeres Latinas, an organization that provided services to women, particularly immigrant women in Pilsen. Rudy was working at Legal Aid. Eventually Rudy joined the International Ladies Garment Workers Union, a union that other CASA members were working with in the Southwest. Much of CASA's work involved trying to take away the negative stigma society had placed on immigrants. It also provided undocumented workers with information about their rights and lobbied against anti-immigrant legislation. In one campaign, CASA successfully killed a bill that would have required proof of citizenship to qualify for a driver's license.

The next year, Rudy recruited Jesús to work at the Midwest Coalition in Defense of Immigrants. Part of his job was to travel to Springfield and lobby state legislators on issues concerning immigrant workers. That was García's first experiences in Springfield. These experiences turned out to be crucial in building the first relationships with African American elected officials since some of them were the most responsive to these efforts.

In the early 1980s, Chicago CASA activists began to sense that their focus on community and labor activism was not enough. Some of the Chicago activists had already been involved in running candidates for office. In 1972, Linda Coronado had been involved in an unsuccessful attempt by La Raza Unidad Party to elect a Latino to Congress. As a result, both CASA and LRUP decided that they needed to do more grassroots building.

In Chicago, independent African Americans were getting elected to Congress and were becoming important voices for progressive political visions. CASA activists sought an alliance with African-American activists and other Latinos involved in forming independent political alternatives throughout the city. The Alliance of African American and Latino Independents was then formed to bring together West Town/Humboldt Park activists such as Rev. Jorge Morales and Peter Earle, with Pilsen, Little Village and West Side activists, such as Danny Davis and Richard Barnett. In a sense, there were two coalitions at work here. One was with other Latinos, specifically Puerto Ricans, and the other with African Americans. The issue that united them all was legislative representation; the legal efforts around redistricting for a more equitable map had brought the various communities together.

For many CASA members, linkage to the African American community came naturally. The shared urban experience of being raised in mixed neighborhoods and the height of the civil rights movement made the coalition feasible.

In Pilsen and Little Village, CASA decided to send one of its members to the Illinois state legislature. In 1982, Juan Soliz, an immigration lawyer, was chosen as the candidate, but not without much discussion and some dissension among the members of CASA. Linda Coronado recalls that many felt they did not know him well enough, since he had just moved to the city. Jesús García explains that: "Juan Soliz became an early favorite, because he was a lawyer, and because he was getting a lot of projection in the Spanish-language media, the newspapers at that time, and, he was seen as an emerging champion of immigrants rights in Pilsen, thanks to the CASA base that existed there."[24]

The political machine outmaneuvered him, and his name was kept off the primary ballot. CASA then launched a third-party candidacy and Soliz garnered an impressive 33% of the vote as a write-in candidate, though not enough to win the race. CASA called for a convention at which they formed the Independent Political Organization of the Near West. Juan Soliz was elected president and Rudy Lozano vice-president.

This race laid the groundwork for the precinct organization that would run Harold Washington as an independent mayoral candidate the following year. The mayoral campaign was grounded in local candidates. In the 22nd ward, Rudy Lozano ran against Frank Stemberk, known as the absentee alderman, because he lived out in the suburbs with his girlfriend. In a three-way race, Lozano came up 17 votes short of a run-off.

Independents faced a tougher battle in the infamous 25th ward run by the "Dean of the City Council", Vito Marzullo. The 25th contained Little Italy, Pilsen and the University of Illinois complex. Here, Juan Velázquez, a former brown beret and organizer of farmworkers, received an impressive 42% of the vote running as an independent in the primary election. Consequently, the political machines in these two wards unleashed a campaign of repression against the independents. For instance, Linda Coronado, who was at the time executive director of Mujeres Latinas and had been involved in the campaigns, received visits from city inspectors from every imaginable department trying to find ways to shut down the social service agency.

But while the Latino candidates did not win their primary elections, Harold Washington did. In the primary, the white and Latino votes were split between Richard M. Daley, the son of the late mayor, and Jane Byrne, allowing Harold Washington to win by a slim margin. Washington owed his victory to the overwhelming turnout of African American voters, 15% of white independents and 13% of Latinos. Many of Chicago's machine politicians, including Congressman Lipinsky and Alderman Vito Marzullo, bolted from the Democratic Party and switched to support Bernie Epton, the white Republican candidate. A few, like Michael Madigan, the speaker of the Illinois State House Assembly, gave quiet but important support to Harold Washington. However, white support for Harold Washington remained the same during the general election, as did the Black percentage. The critical change came from Latinos, whose percentage for Harold Washington increased from 13% to 75%. The 50,000 new votes this represented gave him the margin of victory in the general election.

Harold Washington's election was important to establishing an independent ward organization throughout the city, including one in Little Village. It also set the stage for a new governing coalition, which could incorporate both the new immigrant communities and the African-American community. This was possible in part because Harold Washington had a very different governing style than the old machine. He incorporated neighborhood-based agendas and governing structures.[25] He relied on community advisory boards to hold city bureaucrats accountable. Indeed, in the case of Latinos, he gave the community the opportunity to institutionalize an advisory committee within his cabinet that responded not to the mayor, but rather to a board of commissioners. The Mayor's Advisory Commission on Latino Affairs had a broad-based representation of Latinos throughout the city, including the various nationalities and interest groups. Through the Commission, an agenda was set which included community and home-country issues. During Harold Washington's term, Mexico City was chosen as a sister city to Chicago. In addition, the mayor visited Puerto Rico and supported a community-initiated referendum asking the governor not to send the National Guard to Central America. The city also supported cultural organizations involved in exchanges with countries in Latin America. While Washington's politics were grounded locally, he had begun to develop a more national and global perspective in his policies, and Latinos were part of this new vision.

For African American residents of Little Village, the IPO was a place to build coalitions. Ronnel Mustin, who worked with the first electoral campaigns, joined the IPO because he wanted to belong to an organization that showed that African Americans and Latinos could work together.[26]

In the summer of 1983, Rudy Lozano was shot and killed in his home by a young gang member who would eventually be caught and sentenced to twenty years in prison. Weeks earlier, he had provided testimony to the National Labor Relations Board regarding the Del Rey tortilla factory's practices of indenturing immigrant workers. Jesús García, who by this time was the director of Neighborhood Housing Agency, was elected to take his place.

In 1984, Jesús ran for ward committeeman and was elected. The same year, Juan Soliz ran for state representative and won. By this time he had distanced himself from the IPO. After a 1986 court-ordered redistricting of city council wards, the IPO wanted to run candidates in the 22nd and the 25th Wards. Juan Velázquez was the likely candidate for Pilsen, but Juan Soliz insisted on running. He was endorsed by the regular Democratic machine and won the election. However, Jesús García ran for alderman in the 22nd Ward and was elected. Harold Washington died in office in 1987. By 1989, the independents had lost control of city hall. Richard M. Daley was elected mayor and has easily won reelection since then.

The IPO continued its work by expanding its neighborhood organization through block clubs. The clubs functioned not only as neighborhood watch committees, but also as a source of initiatives for the organization and the alderman's office. More than 250 block clubs organized in Little Village. These block organizations became the vehicles for mobilization at the grassroots level. They organized summer festivals, clean-up campaigns, and crime stopping activities. Everyone, regardless of legal status, was encouraged to participate in political discussions to help decide the future of the IPO.

Electoral Growth

In 1992, García ran for the state senate, and the following spring Rick Muñoz became the alderman of the 22nd Ward. Muñoz was twenty-seven years old at the time. Like Jesús, Muñoz was born in Mexico and in 1970 came to the United States when he five years old. His family too first moved to Taylor Street and later to Little Village. Muñoz attended Catholic schools and graduated from Holy Name Cathedral High School. The following year, he moved to DeKalb, Illinois to attend the Northern Illinois University. There he majored in Political Science and minored in Philosophy.

Muñoz's student activism began his junior year and led him into the legisla-

VOTER REGISTRATION BY RACE/ETHNICITY:
Chicago General Elections, 1980-1996

Year/Office	White	African American	Latino	Other	Total
1980 Presidential	82.80%	75%	49.70%	17.80%	75.50%
1982 Governor	78.60%	82.50%	53.70%	21.10%	77.10%
1983 Mayor	83%	84.50%	51.30%	21.40%	79.90%
1984 President	85.20%	81.30%	46.20%	23.10%	78.90%
1986 Governor	77.50%	73.20%	39.50%	23.30%	70.80%
1987 Mayor	83.50%	78%	43.20%	24.20%	75.80%
1988 President	84.40%	75.50%	42.20%	18.50%	74.40%
1989 Mayor	86.10%	73.80%	35.20%	22.10%	73.60%
1990 Governor	86.60%	82.50%	45%	17.90%	78.50%
1991 Mayor	83.20%	88.40%	60.70%	23.40%	81.20%
1992 President	83.30%	93.40%	68%	39%	84.20%
1994 Governor	72.50%	88.50%	41.60%	22.40%	75%
1995 Mayor	77.70%	90.50%	46.90%	20.50%	81.10%
1996 President	80.65%	86.40%	68.50%	35.80%	78.90%

Table from: Metro Chicago Political Atlas - '97-'98

tive process. The tuition hike struggle provided Muñoz an arena in which to coalesce with other minority students.

In the fall of 1987, when Rick Muñoz met Jesús García, he had to come back to his community to volunteer in the alderman's office; his work there was part of the IPO.

The pressure to provide social services caused strains both on the alderman's office and the IPO. For the IPO, the fact that one of their own was the alderman presented a new challenge. Now instead of simply advocating for social services, the IPO became involved in monitoring the delivery of services to the ward. Carl Rosen, one of the early members of the IPO, saw this as an outgrowth of the original purposes of the IPO which was to advocate for better services. Now the IPO was doing it as a way to help a friendly alderman.[27] Having people from the IPO inside city government helped in this process. Some time later, Muñoz got a job at city hall.

In 1989, I went to work in the Department of Health as an administrative assistant in charge of labor relations, basically recording union grievance hearings and fact finding for the hearing, a hearing officer. I was neither management nor labor, I was just the facilitator.

While this job gave Muñoz an insider's view of city hall, in December 1989, Jesús García's chief of staff decided to quit. She had been with him since he had decided to become alderman.

The census numbers had been published and there was considerable discussion about the creation of a majority Latino congressional seat. A city-wide committee came together to explore the possibilities of running Jesús García for U.S. Congress candidacy. But the feeling was that the Daley machine could not be beat in that district, and it had already begun talking to Luis Gutiérrez, a former Washington ally, who had also sought an accommodation with Daley.

In the meantime, a new state senatorial district was drawn to include Little Village, all of Pilsen, some of Back of the Yards, and a little bit of Cicero, Gage Park and Brighton Park.

In March 1992, Jesús García won the nomination for the state senatorial district for the Democratic Party, a factor which practically made him the senator. The question then became who would be alderman. Chicago political protocol calls for the mayor to fill the vacancy with the recommendation of the outgoing alderman. The next step was to convince the mayor to fill the vacancy with Rick Muñoz. Threat of a special election finally convinced his political operatives that Muñoz would be the best bet. Thus, the IPO had succeeded in moving in younger leadership. Muñoz in turn brought in young people to work with him. Mike Rodríguez,[28] leader of a youth organization in Little Village aimed at getting high school students to apply for college, was brought onto his staff.

In 1996, the IPO ran its first female candidate. Women had been critical to the formation of the organization from its inception, working on many of the activities of the IPO, including elections, and holding key staff positions. Evelyn Chinea had begun working in the organization in the early 1980s by organizing block clubs.[29]

Sonia Silva, who had also been an active member of the IPO, was endorsed for the state assembly seat and won her election, making her the first Latina elected to the state assembly. Sonia had gone to high school with Rudy Lozano.[30] Her academic background also focused her on public policy; she had a Master's Degree in Public Policy. During her tenure, Silva was assigned to legislative committees that allowed her to influence education and labor issues as well as day care. This combined nicely with Jesús García's work that had included passing legislation that assisted bilingual students, protected the rights of veterans, and provided tougher sentencing for criminal gun-running.

Having a state senator, state representation and an alderman represented an unprecedented victory for an independent political organization. In 1996, the executive committee was expanded to bring in representatives from all the areas served by these political offices including Back of the Yards, Cicero and Pilsen. In so doing, the IPO succeeded in breaking the ward boundaries imposed by the old political machine.

By the late 1990s, Richard Daley had consolidated his own power within city hall. He initiated a new organization of Latinos called the Hispanic Democratic Organization (HDO), which became Daley's arm in the Latino community. When the alderman of the 25th Ward was sent to jail on federal corruption charges, Daley named Danny Soliz, to fill the vacancy. Soliz, who had headed up a Saul Alinzky community organization, had had a long-running feud with the independents. Along with HDO, he declared war on the independent political movement. In 1998, the IPO decided to try and elect a state representative for the Pilsen portion of Garcia's senatorial district. Guillermo Gómez, a social worker and long-time community activist in Pilsen, ran. But both he and Jesús García were defeated. Two years later, Sonia Silva was also defeated. By 2002, the IPO had one elected official, Rick Muñoz.

> Jesús García admits:
> There was a mistake on my part on concentrating so much time in the campaign in Pilsen, working the issue of displacement, gentrification, and the city's development in Pilsen and UIC. That miscalculation resulted in a tremendous amount of time and energy being expended there, thinking that the 25th Ward was an important entity to win to elect Guillermo Gómez. I spent too many resources in the 25th Ward and on Sonia's campaign and not enough time campaigning in areas where we had done very well in '96, two years prior. So I think those were among the most important lessons. The last one was not sounding the alarm that we could lose.[31]

Underlying the battles between regular Democrats and independents have been two competing visions of development. Symbolic of these two visions were struggles around questions of displacement of the community. One struggle focused on the displacement caused by the University of Illinois's expansion. A city-wide coalition came together to preserve Maxwell Street, an historic area often referred to as Chicago's Ellis Island, from being destroyed. Rick Muñoz was one of the eight aldermen who voted to save the historic district of Maxwell Street. Downstate, Jesús was active in trying to make sure that the community was not displaced; he demanded grassroots input into how to spend revenues generated by Pilsen's designation as a Tax Increment District. At the top of the list was affordable housing and a more open planning process. In contrast, Daley's development plans included the expansion of the University of Illinois and replacement of low and moderate income housing with mainly town homes affordable to a professional middle class. His planning process did not include consultation with community residents.

Dilemmas

Jesús García's loss in 1998 forced a rethinking of the role of an independent political organization in the age of neo-machine politics. The electoral fight had been construed as a Daley versus García battle when in reality the Daley machine had built a complete network of loyal Latino supporters. García admits, "We had not factored in the number of bodies the Hispanic Democratic Organization could pull in on election day. Daley had built an old-style patronage army that was called out on Election Day."

For Muñoz, this vulnerability has meant having to make tough choices at every city council session. Daley demands total loyalty in the city council to the point of absurdity. Criticism is not tolerated and dissenting votes are punished. Therefore, Muñoz has to pick his battles carefully. On the other hand, he is an independent alderman, even if only part of a group of three or four independents in a fifty-member body. This platform allows him to raise issues that may not be surfaced otherwise. For instance, Muñoz along with progressive supporters throughout the city managed to introduce and eventually pass an ordinance demanding that all city contractors pay employees a living wage.

The IPO itself faces another important challenge which relates to the fact that it is really more of a political than electoral organization. While the IPO is clearly interested in electing candidates to public office, it is also a leadership organization through which community residents are encouraged to think about policies that affect their lives. It has met consistently throughout the years on a monthly basis, and held annual or semi-annual conventions in which its executive leadership committee is elected. The organization holds endorsement sessions whenever political seasons are in effect and takes positions on issues, whether it is apartheid in South Africa, U.S. intervention in Central America, or amnesty.

Despite some confusion about the roles of the alderman's office and the IPO, together they have been successful in advocating for building new schools in the ward, infrastructure improvements, increasing the number of Latinos in the police department and in bringing immigrant issues city-wide attention. Questions remain about future elections of independents.

Since Jesús García founded a new development corporation, some of these problems have been solved because of the community development work that was done in the alderman's office is now being done by the Little Village Community Development Corporation.

Strategies/Innovations

The electoral arena is clearly an important part of the Latino civil rights struggle. Even though Chicago has had a unique set of circumstances owing to the legacy of machine politics, nonetheless, some political lessons can be learned from the history and the practice of Little Village's IPO.

1. Transnational grassroots advocacy organizations can be important breeding grounds for increasing civic engagement. The transition of CASA to the IPO clearly shows that for communities marginalized from the political process by either their legal status or the exclusive nature of politics (or both), grassroots community organizations can be a first stage in developing organization and skills necessary to democratize politics and make it more inclusive.

2. The electoral arena is an important place in which to engage struggles for equality. It is through this sector that, in Chicago and many other cities, decisions about the distribution of municipal services are made.

3. Grassroots organizing, particularly in the form of block clubs, can challenge the exclusive nature of elite politics and open the doors for members. In the case of immigrant communities, this is a way for residents, regardless of their legal status, to become involved in the political process.

4. Electoral/political organizations need not be bound by pre-existing political boundaries. The IPO came to include eleven community areas, something that no other independent political organization can claim in the city of Chicago. In addition, it became an important voice on international issues, many of which had direct impact on a community of immigrants.

5. One of the founding principles of the IPO has been to form coalitions among racial/ethnic communities. Again, very few political organizations in Chicago have succeeded in building organizations that facilitated close and equitable relationships among African Americans, whites and Latinos. The relationships built through this principle enrich the lives of all residents and challenge racism.

V. Rethinking Latino Civil Rights Struggles

1. The Geography of Latino politics need not be bound by either national or local political districts.

Latinos' connections to their homelands, as well as the geographic dispersion of populations throughout a wide metropolitan region call into question the effectiveness of politics organized exclusively either by national origin, or ward boundaries, as dictated by machine politics.[32]

Politics in the United States have been conceived along the geographic boundaries of the nation-state. Immigrant communities are affected by policies made in multiple states and as such there is a need to rethink the space in which politics is conducted. Most of the increase in the Latino population is from direct immigration from Latin America; the communities and their needs are informed by this experience.

In addition, within urban areas, particularly those with a strong legacy and or presence of machine style politics, political activity tends to be constrained within wards and city boundaries. In the Chicago metropolitan area, Latinos are spread out though various cities and districts. Organizations that can transgress the local political boundaries stand a better chance of being able to influence the ways people's lives are organized. Pilsen was the port of entry for many; Little Village was the next move up and Cicero, the suburban solution. But families oftentimes move back and forth. Some live in one community area and work in another. The interconnectedness of the three areas is something that should be kept in mind when developing political strategies.

In addition, organizing in a political space not confined exclusively to pre-existing political boundaries makes political organizations less susceptible to concentrated local and neighborhood politics. At times, the activities of the IPO of Little Village have been restricted to one ward and at other times inclusive of other wards and political units. Having a bigger geographic perspective allowed the organization to think beyond just local neighborhood politics.

2. More than one path to incorporation

Historically, new immigrants were quickly incorporated into the electoral arena. But changes in immigration policy have ended up creating a very high percentage of undocumented immigrants within communities. In addition, immigrant communities from Latin America have faced unique discriminatory barriers. Therefore, the path to incorporation may take non-traditional forms.

The IPO did not begin as an electoral organization; instead, it grew from a grassroots effort for protecting the rights of undocumented workers. Activists working with the most vulnerable sectors of the community gained respect from broad sectors, including immigrants who were already legalized. As the organization wanted to make a greater impact on policies that affected immigrants as well as on the delivery of services to the community, it found it necessary to enter into the electoral arena. A unique set of historical circumstances led to the election of a progressive African American mayor in Chicago, which facilitated the entrance of representatives committed to a pro-community agenda. The presence of Latinos within the electoral arena is critical. The difference is the level of impact that can be made.

3. Culture and Politics

Just as identity can be a means of exclusion, it has also become a means to inclusion. Cultural identities are a part of the political process. But there are many ways that immigrant communities reconstruct identities that have either been denied to them or that represent their past and perhaps their future. The most common interpretation of ethnicity and politics in the U.S. experience has been the hyphenated phenomenon, retention of ethnicity in the private sphere and a public political identity called "American". For Latinos in the Chicago metropolitan area, the hyphenated phenomenon has not evolved in quite the same way that it did for other immigrant communities in the past or, for that matter, for other Latinos in other regions of the country.

Many Latin American immigrants hold on to their country-of-origin identity in part because this is one of the identity languages spoken in Chicago. That is, immigrant groups have identified themselves and others by national origin: Mexican, Puerto Rican, and Cuban.

Traditionally, Chicago's political process has been highly segregated along the lines of "Black" and "White", and Latin American immigrants do not fit in either category. As such, another curious phenomenon emerged in this region; that is, the ethnic/political category of "Latino", which provided a political vehicle to increase the numbers of members and it also reflected the racialized environment of politics. Latino become another "racialized" category through which people become involved politically.

This phenomenon has served the political purpose of bringing together disparate groups of different national origins, and it has been particular useful in the political arena. The IPO was founded mainly by Mexican residents, although many Chileans, Puerto Ricans and Cubans contributed to its growth. Therefore, it is a category that helped maximize resources in the political arena. However, the danger is that if it is the only category used, it does obliterate critical cultural, legal and class differences. In addition, if it is the only category used to distribute public goods and services, it can create an unfair mechanism, especially if the proportionality of each national origin group is not taken into consideration. The racialized processing which occurs, simply reproduces inequality in yet another way and does not challenge the exclusive nature of politics in the city.

4. Traditional notions of citizenship need to be reexamined

Both the geography and the identities of Latino politics question the very notion of citizenship as it has been defined in liberal democratic nation/states.[33] Although the IPO's main objective is to engage in the electoral arena, it does not limit its membership to those who can vote or even to those who are legal residents. Everyone is given an opportunity to become a member and participate within the organization. In addition, the IPO has a "sin fronteras" (borderless) view of the reality of their communities. The IPO engages issues that include

Mexico, Puerto Rico, and Cuba and consequently allows it to have an agenda which is more representative of all the members of the community it serves.

5. How to envision a broader social dynamic

Engaging Latinos in civic life is not enough. There is still the question of social and economic inequalities. The leadership of the IPO finally decided that a separate entity was needed that could focus on issues of economic development. To this end, some of the leaders have gone on to found the Little Village Community Development Corporation.

6. Leadership

In recent years, IPO has tried to bring young people onto its staff. In addition, there are interesting lessons to discern about the paths to involvement that shed some light on moments and events that helped each one of them to become involved as adults. The principal actors in the IPO first became involved civically through questions of cultural representation and social justice in high school and at universities. Relationships among community leaders, students and student organizations helped bridge the young people's way back to the community.

It seems that in each of these cases, the leaders themselves were either immigrants or children of immigrants and had lived the experience of not belonging to any particular place. Making both home and host countries more receptive to the needs of immigrants and struggling for a presence and representation within their respective societies became lifelong goals.

The National Context

While the situation of Latinos in the Chicago metropolitan area has unique characteristics, it shares commonalties with other US communities. Increasingly, scholars have pointed out that the Latino reality in the US needs to be understood in the context of *both* host and home country dynamics.[34] Obviously the impact of either locality is dependent on many factors, but to view only the US side of the equation—even in electoral politics—may miss important dynamics at work that have shaped historical and contemporary realities. This broader view does not mean that political borders are not important, but rather that they are also fluid.

Political empowerment of Latino communities has included a variety of strategies from third party movements, such as La Raza Unida to cross border efforts such as the CASA movement of the late 1960s. Labor movements have been central to the quest, particularly in regards to farmworkers. It has also included civil and legal rights organizations, as well as social and public service advocates. Students and women have played a critical role in all of these movements.[35] Home-country issues, such as the independence of Puerto Rico and US policy toward Cuba have been central concerns for these communities.[36] The domestic policy agenda has included education, social services, and language.[37]

The electoral arena has been critical to empowerment movements, as Latinos have tried to incorporate themselves into US political parties. There are group and generation differences in political trajectories thus defying sweeping generalizations.[38] For instance, Cubans in Florida work through the Republican Party, whereas Mexican Americans and Puerto Ricans prefer the Democratic Party. Still, it was grassroots efforts to incorporate all Latinos that finally paid off when in 1975 Congress extended the Voting Rights Act and amended it to protect language-rights minorities.

But the single most important feature of Latino communities is the increased number of recent immigrants. The immediate impact is one of politically disempowering the community overall as the numbers increase as well as their needs, but the overall percentage of real voters decreases.[39] That is why naturalization drives have become part and parcel of electoral movements. Legalization has become an important item on the policy agenda, as well. Despite these obstacles, Latino participation and office holding has increased.[40]

The identities of Latino communities are perhaps one of the most complicated aspects of Latino politics. There are strategic questions about belonging and coalescing, and there are important concerns about the effects of homogenization, and indeed of racialization of Latinos.

Notions about belonging and the composition of political communities have been based on the primacy of the nation/state as its determining organizing principal. Because Latinos have multiple states as political points of reference, the strategic question has been whether or not to include them in their politics. The premium placed on loyalty, particularly in the last half of the twentieth century, led some Latinos to try to focus exclusively on their adopted country for fear of being perceived as un-American. Yet ethnicity is still a means to mobilize and categorize voters. By identifying in part with their Latin American heritage, Latinos could enter the identity game played in politics. The hyphenated phenomenon encouraged the private retention of ethnicity and political parties, and politicians used it as a means to mobilize.

Obviously, these identity struggles differ from region to region, and depend on their timing. For instance, the politics of urban America are structured around the ethnic identities of its various immigrant communities.

The effects of globalization and the formation of free trade alliances have made the interconnectedness among nation/states more visible, thereby making it easier for immigrants to conceive of political identities that are also more inclusive of multiple nations. For Latinos this has meant an expansion of political agendas to include home and host countries. But this has not occurred without debate or differences that have also had an impact on the question of political identities.

Demographic changes, which have resulted in the presence of Latinos from multiple countries in Latin America in U.S. cities have raised the possibility of forming coalitions among Latinos. While this phenomenon first emerged in Chicago, it has also occurred in other areas of the country. It is a way for Latinos to act together; however, it has also become a way to obliterate class, racial and national differences that also exist within and among the communities.

Despite the complexities of Latino immigration and settlements in the Chicago metropolitan area, the prevailing theoretical and historical explanations of identity and politics derive from the European immigrant experience and African American minority mobilization strategies. While Latinos may indeed share commonalties with both groups, including a shared racialized public space, they also have very unique characteristics within each group and among all Latinos.[41] This case study suggests that given these particularities, we also need to rethink the paradigms with which we have tried to understand the incorporation of Latinos into US society.

Latino political empowerment movements aim to make democratic political institutions more inclusive and attentive to diverse populations. In various ways, different organizations and movements have tried to expand notions of citizenship. But expansion is not enough, particularly in a historical context where race and ethnicity have been used as indicators of who belongs. Therefore, the abstract citizen cannot be homogeneous or devoid of culture. Recently, a group of Latino scholars proposed the idea of cultural citizenship.[42] This proposition accepts that politics is tied up with cultural phenomena, particularly in a system in which ethnicity plays such an important role in mobilization and for distribution of goods. Latino claims of equality and justice along ethnic lines are a logical consequence to a distributive system that uses ethnicity.[43] But it is not enough to speak about identity; culture is also political. It is in culture that day to day practice—including how we communicate, how we organize our living arrangements, and how we express ourselves aesthetically—forge a public and consequently, political identity. It is at this multi-layered and complex intersection that Latino communities have battled not only to influence how we are defined but also how to construct communities in which we are included with full rights and privileges.

Notes

[1]Students of DePaul University's Latino Political Empowerment Class[1] August 2002

[2]Cheryl Ross, "Neither Here Nor There," *Chicago Reader*, May 4, 2001, p.1.

[3]There are a few notable exceptions. See Marisa Alicea, "Dual Home Bases," in Félix Padilla, ed. *Hispanic Cultures in the United States: Sociology*, Houston: Arte Público Press, 1994.

[4]See John Allswang, *A House for All Peoples: Ethnic Politics in Chicago, 1890–1936*.

[5]Eric Hirsch, *Urban Revolt: Ethnic Politics in the Nineteenth Century Chicago Labor Movement,* Berkeley: University of California Press, 1990.

[6]Christopher K. Ansell and Arthur L. Burris, "Bosses of the City Unite!Labor Politics and Political Machine Consolidation, 1870–1910," *Studies in American Political Development*, 11 (Spring 1977): 43.

[7]John Jentz, "Class and Politics in an Emerging City: Chicago in the 1860s and 1870s," *Journal of Urban History*, 17/3 (May 1991): 227–263.

[8]Humbert Nelli, *Italians in Chicago, 1880–1930: A Study in Ethnic Mobility*, New York: Oxford University Press, 1970.

[9]John Buenker, "Dynamics of Ethnic Politics 1900–1930," *Journal of the Illinois State Historical Society*, 67/2 (1974): 175–199.

[10]Ira Katznelson, *City Trenches: Urban Politics and the Patterning of Class in the United States*, NY: Pantheon Books, 1981, discusses the decline of class and the rise of ethnic identification in urban areas.

[11]St. Clair Drake and Horace Cayton, *Black Metropolis: A Study of Negro Life in a Northern City*, Chicago: University of Chicago Press, 1993, and James Q. Wilson, *Negro Politicians: The Rise of Negro Politics in Chicago*, Chicago: University of Chicago, 1935.

[12]Paul Kleppner, *Chicago Divided: The Making of a Black Mayor*, DeKalb, IL: Northern Illinois University, 1985.

[13]Louisa Año Nuevo-Kerr, "Mexican Chicago: Assimilation Aborted," in Melvin G. Holli and Peter Jones eds., *Ethnic Chicago*, Grand Rapids, MI: William Eerdman, 1977, 269–299.

[14]Félix Padilla, *Puerto Rican Chicago*, South Bend, IN: Notre Dame University Press, 1990.

[15]Data from the census count, as processed by IUPLR's Census Project, www.iuplr.com.

[16]For the location of the Latino labor force in the city, see John Betancur, Teresa Córdova and María de los Ángeles Torres, "Economic Restructuring and the Process of Incorporation of Latinos into the Chicago Economy," in Frank Bonilla and Rebeca Morales, eds. *Latinos in a Changing U.S. Economy*, CA: Sage Publications, 1993.

[17]Jorge Gracia, *Hispanic/Latino Identity: A Philosophical Perspective*, Malden,

MA: Blackwell Publishers, 2000; Jorge Gracia and Pablo De Greiff, *Hispanics/Latinos in the United States: Ethnicity, Race, and Rights*, NY: Routledge, 2000.

[18]Félix Padilla, *Latino Consciousness: The Case of Mexican Americans and Puerto Ricans in Chicago*. Notre Dame, IN: University of Notre Dame, 1985.

[19]William Flores and Rina Benmayor, *Latino Cultural Citizenship: Claiming Identity, Space and Rights,* Boston: Beacon Press, 1997.

[20]See Latino Institute's *Al Filo/At the Cutting edge: The Empowerment of Chicago's Latino Electorate*, (Chicago: Latino Institute, 1988).

[21]Edward Banfield and James Q. Wilson, *City Politics*, Cambridge: Harvard University Press, 1963; Harold Gosnell, *Machine Politics: Chicago Model,* Chicago: University of Chicago Press, 1977; Milton Rakove, *Don't Make No Waves, Don't Back No Losers: An Insider's Analysis of the Daley Machine*, Bloomington: Indiana University Press, 1975.

[22]Teresa Córdova, "Harold Washington and the Rise of Latino Electoral Politics in Chicago, 1982–1987", in David Montejano, *Chicano Politics and Society in the Late Twentieth Century,* Austin: University of Texas, 1999, 31–57; María de los Ángeles Torres, "The Commission on Latino Affairs: A Case Study of Community Empowerment," in Pierre Clavel and Wim Wiewel, eds. *Harold Washington and the Neighborhoods*, New Brunswick, NJ: Rutgers University Press, 1991; Gary Rivlin, *Fire on the Prairie: Chicago's Harold Washington and the Politics of Race*, NY: Henry Holt, 1992.

[23]On Latino Politics in the Midwest, Richard Santillán, "Latinos in the Midwesersn United States," in Chris García, *Latinos in the Political System*, Notre Dame, IN: University of Notre Dame Press, 1988, 99–118; Luis Fraga, "Prototype from the Midwest: Latinos in Illinois," in Rodolfo de la Garza and Louis DeSipio, *Rhetoric to Reality: Latino Politics in the 1988 Elections.* Boulder: Westview Press, 1992, 111–126; John Valadez, "Latino Politics in Chicago: Pilsen in the 1990 General Election," in Rodolfo de la Garza, Martha Menchaca and Louis DeSipio, *Barrio Ballots: Latino Politics in the 1990 Elections*, Boulder: Westview Press, 1994, 115–136.

[24]Interview with Jesús García, March 2002.

[25]See Pierre Clavel and Wim Wiewel, eds. *Harold Washington and the Neighborhoods*, New Jersey: Rutgers University Press, 1991.

[26]Interview with Ronnelle Mustin, conducted by Alba Santillán and Pamela Mitofsky, March 2002.

[27]Interview with Carl Rosen, conducted by Denise López and Espenosha Williams, March 2002.

[28]Interview of Mike Rodríguez conducted by Paul Kordik and David Méndez, March 6, 2002.

[29]Interview of Evelyn Chinea, conducted by Jose Plascencia and Vannesa Vargas, March 2002.

[30]Jennifer Ducas, interview with Sonia Silva, March 2002.

[31]Interview, March 2002.

[32]See, for instance, Victor Valle and Rodolfo Torres, *Latino Metropolis*, Minneapolis: University of Minnesota Press, 2000.

[33]Rufus Browning, Dale Rogers Marshall and David Tabb, *Protest Is Not Enough: The Struggle of Blacks and Hispanics for Equality in Urban Politics*, Berkeley: University of California Press, 1984.

[34]See Frank Bonilla, Edwin Meléndez, Rebecca Morales and María de los Ángeles Torres, eds., *Borderless Borders: U.S. Latinos, Latin America and the Paradox of Interdependence*, Philadelphia: Temple University Press, 1998.

[35]See Carol Hardy-Fanta, *Latina Politics, Latino Politics: Gender, Culture and Political Participation in Boston*, Philadelphia: Temple University Press, 1993.

[36]See María de los Ángeles Torres, *In the Land of Mirrors: Cuban Exile Politics in the US*. Ann Arbor, MI: University of Michigan Press, 1999.

[37]Pastora San Juan Cafferty and David W. Ergstrom, *Hispanics in the United States: An Agenda for the Twenty-First Century*, New Brunswick, NJ: Transaction Publishers, 2000.

[38]Rodolfo O. de la Garza, Louis DeSipio, F. Chris García, John García, and Angelo Falcón, *Latino Voices: Mexican, Puerto Rican & Cuban Perspectives on American Politics*. Boulder, CO: Westview Press, 1992.

[39]Harry Pachón and Louis DeSipio, *New American By Choice: Political Perspectives of Latino Immigrants*, Boulder: Westview Press, 1994.

[40]Rodney Hero, F.Chris García, John García and Harry Pachón, "Latino Participation, Partisanship, and Office Holding," *Political Science and Politics*, 33/3 (September 2000): 529–534.

[41]Dianne Pinderhughes, *Race and Ethnicity in Chicago Politics: A Reexamination of Pluralist Theory*, Urbana. IL: University of Illinis Press, 1987.

[42]William Flores and Rina Benmayor, *Latino Cultural Citizenship: Claiming Identity, Space, and Rights*.

[43]Iris Marion Young, "Structure, Difference, and Hispanics," *Hispanics/Latino Ethnicity, Race, and Rights*. NY: Routledge, 2000.

Civil Rights and the Latino Community: Education
Judith Murphy

The Civil Rights Acts of the '60s responded to a Civil Rights movement which asserted that people (and peoples) regardless of race, ethnicity, or national origin have the right to be the subjects of their own lives and not merely objects in the lives and plans of others. The commonweal of U.S. society rests on liberty and justice as fundamental rights for all. At the same time, the message that surrounds immigration, amnesty, and employment for undocumented persons who come from Mexico and Central and South America is mixed: the U.S. wants tight borders and cheap labor. Consequently, the civil rights of immigrants, who are both needed and ignored, often get lost in the shuffle. Fundamental among these is the right to education.

Statistics show that since the 1960s the number of Latino children in U.S. public schools has increased 300%, while African-American students have increased 30%, and Whites have decreased 17%. Research in the last 30 years has demonstrated the benefits of respecting the language and culture of immigrant and second-generation students in their education, English acquisition and socialization in this country. Cristo Rey Jesuit High School in Chicago bases its program on research that favors respecting the voice of students by incorporating their culture and language within a Spanish-English college preparatory curriculum. Since its beginnings in 1996, the efficacy of this choice has been affirmed by students' daily attendance, success in the school's innovative work program, graduation rate, and college attendance. These students are empowered as bilingual and bicultural participative citizens and leaders for their community, church, and nation.

What is the promise of the United States? For whom?

In the summer of 1988 I participated in a retreat at the Cuernavaca Center for Intercultural Dialogue on Development (CCIDD) in Cuernavaca, Mexico. CCIDD was founded in 1977 by Don Sergio Mendes Arceo to help North Americans encounter the spirit of social transformation in Latin America. One session was a conversation with Mendes Arceo, by then the retired bishop of Cuernavaca. He challenged the group of American nuns with a question like the one above: "Your Declaration of Independence assures 'liberty and justice'... For whom is there liberty and justice in your country? Does Liberty mean the right to acquire without limit and without regard for the neighbor's need? Is Justice more reflected in a socialist country (he spoke of Cuba) that assures each child a quart of milk every day? How must Liberty and Justice nuance one another?" The questions remain pertinent and challenging.

In the United States, the Latino population in schools is growing rapidly. How is education being developed to empower these young people to be participants in the civic, economic, and political life of this country?

What is the promise of the United States? And who are the beneficiaries of the promise? Martin Luther King and César Chávez led their people to cease colluding in their own diminishment, to see that they had to acknowledge and proclaim their own dignity as human beings, deserving of equity, self-respect and equality as human beings and citizens.

The Civil Rights Movement of the 1960s represented minority peoples' demand to be included in the promise of the U.S. The demand of the movement is for voice, for access, for opportunity, for inclusion, and for equal dignity. The consciousness and self-consciousness of minority peoples was expressed in their demand to have a voice in the conversation and the decision-making that shaped their lives. The Civil Rights Acts of 1964, 1965, and 1968 were a response to the movement and met with varied responses in different regions of the country.

In 1954, the Supreme Court, in *Brown vs. the Board of Education,* had found that segregated schools, "separate but equal," did not satisfy the right of minority children to equal education. Redress was legislated through policies of integration in schools and busing in school systems.

The Immigration Law of 1968 removed the quota system that had kept immigration to the United States dominantly European. By the end of the 1960s, immigrants to the U.S. also included large numbers of Latinos and Asians. A huge migration of Asian peoples occurred as war was waged in Southeast Asia, and Cambodian, Vietnamese, and Hmong refugees sought to build new lives in the United States. Large numbers from other Asian and middle-eastern countries, as well as from Mexico, Central and South America, came as civil unrest and economic turmoil affected their lives and livelihood.

The Civil Rights movement originally was a call for justice between blacks and whites; with the changes in immigration patterns, these issues of justice now are highlighted for all minorities and people of color. Patterns of segregation by race are strongly linked to segregation by poverty, and poverty concentrations are strongly linked to unequal opportunities and outcomes. It is very challenging for minority children to break out of poverty, and education is a most significant core of their being able to envision, prepare for, and obtain such mobility.

There is no greater challenge for the Untied States than race. This was true at the beginning of the last century and remains so at the beginning of the new century. As Professor James Coan of the Union Theological Seminary, paraphrasing W.E.B. Dubois, said at a recent Call to Action conference, "The question of the twentieth century, and it endures, is color." There is no greater challenge for churches than race. There is no greater challenge for the schools than race. Unresolved issues of equal opportunity and access for people of color have an impact on whole segments of U.S. society that remain in poverty. Schools may rightly be expected to be a locus for change, for empowering students to participate actively in their community and world.

This chapter demonstrates how one school was founded to address the role of education in the empowerment of minority Latino students in one area of Chicago. Cristo Rey Jesuit High School was founded for the immigrant community in Pilsen and Little Village in Chicago. The school has as its mission to "advance the human and intellectual capacities, as well as the religious and cultural heritage, of all the families it serves. . . . It intends to maximize the potential of its graduates to assume leadership roles in the civic, religious, business and cultural life of our city and nation." (Mission Statement, Cristo Rey Jesuit High School)

The economies, social and political life of Mexico and the surrounding countries of Central and South America and the Caribbean have been profoundly changed by political and military strife inside and outside their borders, as well as by globalization and the arrival on the scene of multinational corporations. Many people, for economic or political reasons, face the choice of moving to the North when they cannot envision sustaining life for themselves and their family in their home country.

Immigrants from these countries to the south are drawn to the United States in search of work in many cases because the economy at home is not able to sustain them. Workers come; they send money home; eventually, their family comes to be with them where there is work. And even so, they continue to send money home to the extended family. Some travel back and forth across the border, thereby maintaining family ties and traditions.

The influx of non-Europeans since the late 1960s constitutes the largest migration in U.S. history. Nationwide, the number of Hispanic children in public schools nearly equals African American students. Since the 1960s, in the public schools, Hispanics have increased by 300%, African Americans have increased by 30%, and whites have decreased by 17%. For Latinos, the story has been one of steadily rising segregation since the 1960s, with no significant desegregation efforts outside of a few districts.[1] This reality is a consequence of economic status and housing availability; schools are tied to neighborhoods.

The U.S. policy toward people arriving at our southern border is ambiguous and ambivalent. During the last decade of the twentieth century and continuing until now, there has been a beefing up of controls at the border. The INS, "La Migra," builds fences along the southern border, and some states and politicians voice an inhospitable stance toward immigrant families and children, who are portrayed as constituting a burden for local schools, social services and taxpayers.

At the same time, a demand for inexpensive labor has become the foundation for a prosperous economy in various sectors of the United States. The message to immigrants is thus mixed. *"Stay away." "Come."* A large pool of undocumented workers allows corporations to manipulate the work force in some industries, creating or prolonging situations in which working conditions are inhumane and workers are paid less than the minimum wage. Even the minimum wage does not allow people to live above the poverty line, as Barbara Ehrenreich has documented in her recent book.[2]

When children from these families arrive in the classroom, even if they haven't crossed the border themselves, they carry their family's experience within them. They may have difficulty overcoming the negative attitude which society has shown towards them: they may internalize that attitude and carry it within themselves.

Roberto Suro, in *Strangers Among Us: Latino Lives in a Changing America,*[3] chronicles the experience of a number of recent Latino immigrants in cities throughout the United States. The first generation may have come for a dream of "the job" and may be satisfied to have found work; their new situation is better than what they left behind, even though they have given up homeland and the familiar routines of home to come in search of work. The second generation may not experience the dream's fulfillment in the same way. Especially if they are concentrated in central cities with other minority people who experience discrimination routinely, they may pick up an attitude of rebellion as a way to spurn the dream that to them appears unattainable.

The border and its implications are important realities for students, and may influence their attitudes toward the possibility and even the desirability of success in school. Cristo Rey Jesuit High School in Chicago was designed to address the reality of the Latino community of Pilsen and Little Village and the economic, political, and social realities of their lives.

Each September, in neighborhoods all over the country new kindergartners with bright new backpacks and lunchboxes set off for school. Parents hope that their children are beginning a successful and happy journey of twelve or sixteen years of education, that they will be given the tools for the journey of lifelong learning. What happens by the time these children reach high school? How has each child's enthusiasm been supported and affirmed, or dampened?

Depending on where children live and on their place in society, what they are encouraged to hope for may vary. Data indicates that too often the demographics and the socioeconomic profile of a neighborhood continue to predict children's success or failure in the neighborhood schools.

Proponents of school reform identify educational goals to be demanded for *all* in our democracy: academic rigor, equity, personalization, and social and civic growth. These are fundamental bases for education to serve students well, so that they are prepared to participate fully and actively in their own lives, in their communities, and in their world.

This is a story of a school established to do just that.

In 1996, Cristo Rey Jesuit High School opened in the Pilsen-Little Village neighborhood of Chicago. Its mission was to serve this immigrant community by providing college preparatory education in a program that would be culturally sensitive and family centered. Cristo Rey is "the school that works," and this has two meanings: It is a school in which every student goes to work regularly, five days each month, in a corporate office, gaining first-hand knowledge and experience in the business sector of Chicago and earning the major portion of the cost of education. And, it is a school that works for its students, one that has been designed with the students' reality taken into consideration in shaping a curriculum that uses Spanish and English and that values the culture and experience of the students and their families.

Catholic schools are typically tuition-driven and receive little or no support from government funding. For the immigrant community of Pilsen/Little Village, where most families have little discretionary income for tuition, full-cost tuition would constitute an insurmountable barrier. This being the challenge, a creative alternative for funding was developed at Cristo Rey. The financial basis of this private Catholic school is a work program, the Corporate Internship program, in which students earn their tuition. In this program, every student works five days each month in a corporate office and earns 74% of the cost of the year's education. Families are asked to pay the remaining $2200 per year; half of the families receive some financial assistance toward that latter amount.

The school came into existence when the Jesuits of Chicago were drawn to ministry in the Pilsen/Little Village area and conducted a needs assessment, asking community residents what level of educational project would best address the most pressing need. From among all the choices offered—from pre-school up through adult literacy and job skill training—the choice that the people felt was the most needed was a high school. The two local public schools, which Cristo Rey students would have otherwise attended, are very large and over-crowded. In 1992, these two schools had dropout rates of 55% and 73%, respectively.

Often, immigrant or first generation parents find the school system difficult to understand and navigate in large, urban settings. Many of the immigrant parents who first sent their children to Cristo Rey had minimal primary education in rural Mexico. We found anecdotally that the high dropout rate resulted sometimes from parents' choice. When the system is difficult to understand and students feel pressure or intimidation from gangs in the schools, it is not uncommon for parents to choose to have their children leave school before graduating and come to work with them in the factory or at day labor. The reality is that the family needs money to survive, and they know their son will be safe at work with them. (Most often it is a son who would accompany them to work.)

Safety in the neighborhood and within the school is a very significant concern in the light of gang activity that is endemic in this part of the city. Many areas of these neighborhoods are claimed as turf by gangs to control the sale of drugs for profit. Movement across gang "boundaries" is dangerous, especially for young men. Students in schools where gangs have a foothold may be intimidated, shaken down for money, beaten up, or recruited into the gang as it asserts its control at the bus stop or even within the school.

Such gangs may be a natural outgrowth of what was once a block club or a neighborhood group that played sports together. The introduction of guns and the infiltration of these groups sometimes by organized crime involved in the drug trade have raised the stakes monumentally to a deadly situation. It is no wonder that parents choose to have their adolescent sons come to work with them rather than risk the perils of going to school.

Even when the child is at home there is fear. It is common for workers to be paid below minimum wage for their work, especially if they are undocumented and cannot find recourse in the law for unjust hiring and compensation practices. Therefore, one or both parents in a family may need to be working two or more jobs to support the family. If much of the time parents cannot be at home to supervise their children, they mandate restrictive settings and rules that keep young people from going outside to play with other youngsters.

As youth reach adolescence, the lure of gangs may be overwhelming, and they rebel out of frustration, boredom, or fear. Identity, prestige, status, companionship, profit, safety—any one or any combination of these values attract the young person and the reality of the gang may soon be dominant in the young person's life. Parents struggle to maintain influence over their children.

The faculty at Cristo Rey faced the reality that it could not know everything about how to identify gang signs and activity. We determined that we would strive not to be naïve, and we made a strong statement that no gang symbolism, signing or activity would be tolerated within the school. At the same time, we knew that our answer to the gangs was to offer these young people an alternative future that could be achieved. We offered them a high school opportunity that would fill their days and energy and would respect them and their background and family.

The opportunity to *begin* a school is a once-in-a-lifetime opportunity for educators. At Cristo Rey, we had the opportunity to ask questions about the appropriate design of program and curriculum for language-minority, central city adolescents. What should a school look like to engage Latino youth in serious preparation for college? How can parents be empowered to participate in their children's high school education?

The school's founders included religious and lay educators from various backgrounds, Latino and non-Latino. In designing the curriculum, we had assistance from the Illinois Resource Center, a state funded office for teachers of language minority students, where research is gathered both on what does and does not work educationally for language minority and central city students. The IRC helped us to shape pedagogy based in language acquisition theory to engage our students.

From the outset, we determined that this Jesuit Catholic school should be *college preparatory* to help students prepare to take a responsible place in the community and society. It should be *family-centered* and *more culturally sensitive* to serve families in a welcoming and affirming manner, and to affirm and build on the strengths and values that inhere within the families' culture. The school further committed to create a *dual language* curriculum, because language is so significant in the expression and experience of culture. The school would facilitate language acquisition in Spanish and in English. Students who all work to lower the cost of tuition for families would support the school.

We used as a major guide in the formation of the school *Breaking Ranks: Changing an American Institution,* a critique by practitioners of high school in the U.S., commissioned by the National Association of Secondary School Principals. This was published in 1996, the year Cristo Rey began. *Breaking Ranks* strongly asserts that a thorough overhaul of high school education is needed, so that high schools and the professionals that work in them can better serve the needs of adolescents on the brink of adulthood today.

We paid particular attention to the recommendation that time and opportunity for students and teachers to get to know each other as real people is critical, so that the teacher can function as a mentor and coach who can help guide students as they navigate this time of great complexity. We sought ways to integrate the curriculum thematically, so that students would have a coherent educational experience, rather than one that is fractured and seemingly disparate and irrelevant to their lives. This required that the teachers work collaboratively and become a learning community, dynamically and professionally designing college preparatory curriculum and strategies around the students and their reality. The professional conversation, whether in meetings or in individual teacher interactions, consistently dealt with what would lead to more educational success and satisfaction for students.

As part of attending to the reality of the students, respecting their culture and making their parents welcome in the school, we wanted to include both Spanish and English in the curriculum and the school. Bilingual Education is a quite politicized topic in many places. Our research led us to structure the curriculum according to a model that is not so politicized, Dual Language. Our working definition of the two terms is that "Bilingual Education" allows the student to use the home language until he or she is able to learn in content areas in English. "Dual Language" never intends to drop the home language, but rather helps the student maintain the home language and develop language and higher level thinking skills in that home language, while also developing these skills in English.

Research demonstrates that over time a Dual Language approach strengthens the language minority student's acquisition of *English*, in addition to developing skills in the home language, while also valuing the language, history, and culture of the family. Assessment demonstrates that generally, after seven years,

English-learning students in Dual Language programs outperform *in English* their counterparts who have had only total immersion in English. Most of the practice and research has been done in elementary schools, where students from non-English speaking homes can be gradually introduced to instruction in English from the time they start school.

Several such elementary schools in Chicago use a Dual Language Spanish-English program successfully. Typically dual language programs in such schools, when feasible, involve a proportion of the student body that is English-speaking learning another language, and a proportion that is non-English speaking learning English. Students learn to communicate with each other in both languages in the informal settings of the playground and cafeteria, as well as in shared classes, thereby acquiring facility in both languages.

We asked ourselves if we could extrapolate from the experience at the elementary school level and develop a Dual Language program at the high school level. We could not find another high school with such a program. We discovered that some people had considered starting such a high school, but they had backed off because of the difficulty and expense of creating such a program from the ground up. We visited and consulted with several of the elementary schools and the IRC, and then set about to create and shape a Dual Language curriculum for high school.

The anticipated benefits of a Dual Language program for our students were many: to reinvigorate enthusiasm for learning by helping the students see themselves and their background and culture as valuable; to encourage participation by parents in the education of their high-school age children; to capitalize on the benefits of developing academic and professional language skills in two languages; to support self-esteem by respecting the culture and language of the students, and helping their parents feel welcomed and involved into school and in their child's education; to encourage students to consciously embrace the values and heritage of their families, while gaining familiarity and knowledge of the culture of the United States, as well.

The challenges of creating this program were many. Creating the dual language curriculum and selecting materials to support a college preparatory program, as well as the language program, called for teachers who were creative, open to collaboration, skilled in language as well as other content areas, and energetic. It also called for teachers who could share in and support this innovative vision and its new approach to high school education.

The Cristo Rey curriculum is a Dual Language program, with the goal of developing literacy and academic language skills in both Spanish and English by the time of graduation. We found in our research that the more accurate term for this curriculum is "Heritage Language." A Heritage Language program is a language enrichment program for schools with a population that is minority-language dominant. Students study Spanish language and literature each year, and annually each student takes at least one other humanities course (i.e. Religion, Art, or Social Studies) taught in Spanish. Throughout the school, students use both Spanish and English for discussion and for mutual assistance. Students may use either language in journaling assignments, and during the community parts of the school day, at all-school or class level meetings, the two languages receive equal prestige. When parents come to school for meetings about academic progress reports or other issues, these are conducted in whichever language is the more comfortable for parents.

The school schedule includes six 60-minute periods. The extended class periods allow for, and encourage cooperative learning methods, participatory and project learning, use of technology and the Internet within the classroom, as well as relationship building between teachers and students, and student and student—to name some of the pedagogical benefits of the longer class periods.

Since we started the school with sophomores and juniors in 1996, the first class to graduate was that of 1998, with 19 students. Now, with a total of 220 graduates from the first five classes, 172, or 87% of graduates, are in college studies. 100% of the 2002 graduates were accepted and 98% enrolled and went on to college. There is a daily attendance rate at Cristo Rey of 98%, a dropout rate of about 1%, and the work program is meeting with great success in the corporate offices of Chicago.

Most of the students at Cristo Rey are the first in their families to plan to go to college. They may be the first to finish high school. Motivation to tackle and learn college preparatory material and to stay in school is strengthened by the relationship these students develop with their teachers. The teachers are the ones who know what is happening daily on the front lines of student learning. Hence a strong, collegial attitude exists among the teachers to refine and strengthen this student-centered program.

In the school's inaugural year, 102 students enrolled as sophomores and juniors in this new, unknown institution. The next year, 1997-98, there were 200 students in grades 9–12. President John Foley, S.J. and the Board successfully raised funds to build a new 23-classroom building that opened in January 2000. By September 2001, the enrollment was close to 500, the maximum enrollment for the school. Now, there are more applicants than can be accepted, and there is a lengthy admissions process. And a second building, to house a Library, Cafeteria, Gymnasium and Assembly Area, opened in late 2003.

Requirements for admission to Cristo Rey are the following:

1. *"Ganas,"* the desire to participate in this program
2. Familiarity with Spanish, typically oral proficiency
3. Family financial need
4. Motivation and employability to participate in the Corporate Internship Program
5. Openness to religious values
6. Ability to do average college prep work
7. Previous school record that demonstrates motivation to learn
8. Parent and student agreement to participate in the school and work program.

If all these criteria are met, preference is given to families from the identified geographical area the school intends to serve.

Because of its commitment to the Heritage Language program, the school seeks qualified teachers who are bilingual or willing to become so. Teachers are asked to bring a commitment to the continued creation of an integrated, thematic curriculum and the design and construction of learning experiences in student-centered classrooms.

Most students whose home language is Spanish have taken an extra year during the elementary school years to learn or strengthen their English skills and, thus, are already 14 years of age when entering ninth grade, the age required to participate in the work program. These students generally need vocabulary and academic language development in both Spanish and English that continues in high school. But, the fact that they can already navigate their day-to-day lives in two languages encouraged the school to see their bilingual capability as a strength that can be the basis of the enrichment Dual Language program.

The Spanish teachers have developed a curriculum that begins with phonetics and orthography, moves through the reading and writing of literary genres, covers the history of the Americas from before *"el encuentro"* up to the present, and concludes with a study of Hispanic and Latin American literature. In the first four graduating classes, all students have taken (and passed) the Advanced Placement Spanish Language exam, and now most students also take and pass the Advanced Placement Spanish Literature exam, as well.

Graduates of Cristo Rey are expected to go on to college, to have developed academic literacy in both Spanish and English, and to take interest and responsibility for bettering life in their neighborhood, city and world. The Profile of the Cristo Rey Graduate at Graduation calls for them to be "open to growth, religious, intellectually competent, loving, committed to justice, and work experienced."

The results from the first years of the school's existence indicate that the issues of inner-city, language minority education are being successfully addressed by the school's combination of student-centered college prep curriculum and experience in the corporate sector of the city.

The success of the corporate Internship Program as a funding model has led to the establishment of the Cristo Rey Network, an affiliation of groups around the country also seeking to create schools to provide education in poor, educationally underserved areas of minority populations. Three more Cristo Rey model schools now exist in Portland, Austin, and Los Angeles. Others are in the planning stages in Boston, Cleveland, Lawrence, New Bern, New Brunswick, Denver, New York, Tucson, and Waukegan. And more are on the way.

In conclusion, much is known about how to make schools work so that all students can have the opportunity to learn. In a small number of situations, groups of dedicated people demonstrate that schools can apply this knowledge with efficacy so that schools can be places of learning with equity, academic rigor, personalization and growth for all students. Cristo Rey is one such place.

For over twenty years, Dr. Jim Cummins, Professor at the Ontario Institute of Studies in Education of the University of Toronto has researched and written about second language learners and their success in schools. His article, "Empowering Minority Students: a Framework for Intervention," was published in the *Harvard Educational Review*, 56 1 (February 1986). We used this article in establishing our philosophy, as when we set up classrooms and structured pedagogy at Cristo Rey.

The article was reprinted in the *Harvard Educational Review* in 71 4 (Winter 2001). In the reprinted article, no changes were made from the original, but a new introduction was written to accompany it. This introduction includes salient observations that have significant import for schools seeking to serve students and families in the poorest areas of our country. These comments are especially significant in the climate of standardized testing and school reform.

In his new introduction, Cummins says, "I believe that current attempts at reform will fail to boost achievement in any significant way for the same reasons that previous generations of reform were ineffective. These reasons are twofold: (a) empirical data relating to patterns of educational underachievement that challenge the current ideological mindset are systematically ignored or dismissed; (b) there is deep antipathy to acknowledging that schools tend to reflect the power structure of the society and that these power relations are directly relevant to educational outcomes" (650).

Cummins suggests that there are always issues of power in the classroom. "In short, educators define their own identities through their practice and their interactions with students. Students likewise go through a process of defining their identities in interaction with their teachers, peers, and parents. However, this process of negotiating identities can never be fully controlled by forces outside of the teacher-student relationship itself. Thus, educators individually and collectively have the unique potential to work toward the creation of contexts of empowerment. Within these interpersonal spaces where identities are negotiated, students and educators together can generate power that challenges structures of inequity in small but significant ways. . . . Curriculum and instruction focused on empowerment; understood as the collaborative creation of power, start by acknowledging the cultural, linguistic, imaginative, and intellectual resources that children bring to school. These resources reflect the funds of knowledge abundantly present in children's communities" (653).

Cummins' acknowledgement of identity as a rich resource, as opposed to a negative attitude that sees second-language learners as having deficits to overcome, became quite central to our planning of the curriculum. The Dual Language curriculum is built on the students' strength in speaking two languages. That competency was acknowledged as the basis of an enrichment program to develop literacy in the two languages, rather than merely noting underdeveloped English vocabulary and grammar proficiency as a deficit to be overcome.

Teachers very thoughtfully included issues of student and family identity in their curricular planning. For example, teachers developed writing assignments that asked students to interview their parents about the family's experience in coming to this country. Students wrote family biographies and brought parents' and grandparents' experiences into the classroom. Parents commented to us that this was the first time they had had a context in which their children asked these questions. Students composed poems that they wrote interlineally with their parents, alternating theirs and their parent's attitudes or feelings or memories, in some cases also alternating languages. Students wrote about their neighborhoods, describing all the familiar sights and sounds and smells that made it home. Awareness of these issues of identity, self-esteem, and power relationships is important for teachers of all students in our society, but especially so for teachers of minority and language minority students.

Indeed, Cristo Rey's importance as a model lies in its contribution to altering power relationships between students and teachers, school and home, workplace and workers. Students are encouraged to see that their whole selves, with all their experience, are welcomed in the classroom and in their education. Parents are welcomed in the school; conferences about student progress and behavior are conducted in Spanish or English, depending on parent preference, with translators available as needed if the teacher does not speak Spanish, to facilitate their participation in their child's education. Students see themselves as resources for one another when there is a difference in language competency.

Students develop enriched resumes that express the variety of work experiences they have had in the Corporate Internship Program, experiences that include supervision and performance review on a regular basis.

Two examples of students whose lives changed because of attending Cristo Rey are Letty and Manuel (not their actual names). Letty had a diagnosis of learning disabilities for which she had received special help while in elementary school. She had learned to seek out academic assistance in a variety of places, such as the community library and tutoring programs. If she had gone on to one of the large, crowded public high schools in the area, the reality was that the special help would not have been available. She would most likely have gotten lost and possibly dropped out. At Cristo Rey, teachers continued to help her develop competency and assurance. She herself helped to tutor students at the local library and in the local grade school. She became a catechist in her parish. She graduated successfully and is now progressing in her college studies toward becoming a teacher.

Manuel was the kind of student who always seemed to be on the edge of a gang. Not that we could know about this directly in school; with the dress code and admonitions about appropriate haircut and facial hair for the corporate workplace, such signals of gang participation were contained. But his haircut always pushed the limit; his academic performance was average or a bit low; his posture and behavior indicated some holding back from full enthusiasm about the program. And yet, he followed through consistently, received good reviews at work, and graduated.

When he got to college, he helped to start an Honor Society for Hispanic students with high academic requirements, and he is well on his way to graduating with a degree in Business and Marketing. While in high school, he told one teacher that he was surprised to be pretty sure of his high school graduation. He said that only 30% of those he graduated with from grade school were still in school. When asked about the others, he said 50% had dropped out. And the other 20%? They were dead. He had told several teachers that he knew if he could get out of the neighborhood and away from the gang, he could turn things around and move on. Cristo Rey became the opportunity for him to do just that.

In conclusion, the lesson of Cristo Rey is that schools and teachers have the opportunity to further the progress of civil rights for students and their communities by teaching in ways that respect students' talents and reality. This means teaching in a way that expects academic rigor and provides the personal and academic support for students to realistically hope to achieve their goals. This kind of education can empower students so that they may be on their way to having their voices heard, and having something to say. The common good of our democracy is best served when every student grows to be an adult, responsible person who can bring the "funds of knowledge abundantly present in the community" to bear on problem-solving and ethical decision-making.

Notes

[1] Harvard Civil Rights Project website (www.civilrightproject.harvard.edu/research/k-12_ed.ph).

[2] Barbara Ehrenreich, *Nickel and Dimed: On (Not) Getting By in America,* NY: Henry Holt and Company, 2001.

[3] NY: Vintage Books, 1998.

In the Aftermath of September 11, 2001, and the Homeland Security Act of 2002: Implications for Midwest Latinos

Refugio I. Rochín and Alex Santana

Introduction

In response to the terrorist attacks of September 11, 2001, in New York City and Washington D.C., the 107th Congress passed legislation intended to transform twenty-two federal agencies into a large government organization charged with the responsibility to protect Americans at home. The bill that was ultimately passed was called The Homeland Security Act of 2002 (H.R. 5005) and, the new federal agency it created, the Department of Homeland Security, officially began operation on March 1, 2003. There are certain aspects of the Homeland Security Act that will directly and indirectly affect members of the Latino community in the Midwest. Immigrant and non-immigrant Latinos will be profiled and affected on everything from their co-mingling together to their employment of and support for undocumented aliens. Latinos who fit police and security profiles of suspected aliens will be double-checked when they face traffic tickets, loitering, drinking, or are involved in activities that appear to be suspiciously organized as protests or threats to American security. Anyone housing or "harboring" undocumented aliens can face closer surveillance by local police and immigration agents. Some commingling can be as simple as organized protests on issues like the Vieques Island of Puerto Rico or protests against local police or government officials. Local activities for organizing religious fiestas could also be viewed as suspicious, although the risk of being considered terrorists will likely be low. In addition, anyone caught for patronizing undocumented immigrants and providing services such as help with identification cards, drivers licenses, housing and assistance to immigrant families, will face suspicion. Latinos can even be reported by "good citizens," "watchful neighbors," and probably get reported to local authorities, who will have to produce a follow-up report of investigation.

Persons involved in research and data gathering pertaining to public facilities, organizations or Middle Eastern religions or community activities will run the risk of investigation. In fact, telecommunications companies, librarians, news services and other sources of information will have to report suspicious-looking patterns of data gatherers and users to the federal authorities. This is because of the USA Patriot Act of 2003, a federal bill that followed the Homeland Security Act. In fact, the Patriot Act permits unprecedented information sharing between law enforcement and intelligence agencies that make it possible for the federal government to pursue Homeland Security, based upon information produced from a community or place far from Washington. D.C. According to news reports in the popular press at the time of this writing, both the Homeland Security and the Patriot Acts have resulted in numerous criminal investigations by officials of the Department of Justice, local police, immigration authorities, and the FBI. Investigations as of June 6, 2003, have resulted in one significant terrorist-related prosecution, that of Florida professor Sami al-Arian, who is accused of aiding Pakistani suicide bombers.

Efforts underway by Attorney General John D. Ashcroft have also been to use the Patriot Act to a greater degree in pursuing international terrorists within the United States. Concomitantly, congressional leaders are spotting weaknesses in the USA Patriot Act, and some courts, such as the U.S. Court of Appeals for the 9th Circuit, which covers California and other western states, have found the statute vague. Legal authorities are concerned that the Patriot Act goes too far into changing the constitutional protections of American citizens and legal residents at this time.

Despite the serious concerns being raised about the Patriot Act, the Homeland Security Act is in effect and has far reaching implications for Americans and Latinos, in particular. Today, Latinos number 37 million strong within America's population. Latinos constitute the largest minority population. Notwithstanding the fact that Latino growth is primarily due to U.S. born Latinos, the national perception of Latinos is that the population is largely an immigrant population with a relatively high degree of illegal entry. Nationally, according to census figures for 2000, nearly 50% of Latino households are made-up of foreign-born members or children of foreign-born. Latinos of working age are mostly U.S. citizens by birth, but about 40% of today's Latino workers are foreign-born. For the most part, Latinos born in the U.S. or born abroad share many common denominators in terms of Spanish language, concentration in urban areas, and patterns of occupational stratification. It is commonly perceived that Latinos constitute a homogeneous population at the national level, when in fact Latinos are very diverse and complex in terms of socio-economic demographics.

In the aftermath of September 11, 2001 (hereafter referred to as "9/11") and the Homeland Security Act of 2002, Latinos of the Midwest are facing serious challenges to their civil and human rights. The impact has already affected the efforts of immigration reform advocates who have asked for new immigration legislation and policies to ameliorate the adverse conditions and settle hardworking immigrant Latinos. While the Homeland Security agency and its administrators are still in the infant stages of implementing the Homeland Security Act, an analysis and understanding of what is actually written into the law can shed some light on the possible consequences for Latinos of the Midwest. Understanding the structural reforms underway with regard to the handling and processing of immigrants and related U.S. born Latinos can also inform us of the changes in Latino civil and human rights. We can also surmise how defending the homeland through political and administrative reforms will affect all communities in the United States and Midwest Latinos, in particular.

This chapter documents the first six months of the Homeland Security Acts' emergence, its first stages of implementation, and published reports of affects on Latino immigrants and communities. It begins by reviewing the close relationship that prevailed between the Bush administration and advocates for immigration reforms, from passage to before 9/11. The paper then examines the direct effects of the terrorist acts of September 11, 2001, and the immediate reaction of President Bush and his advisors in tightening U.S. borders, strengthening immigration controls, and to implementing new laws and legislation for homeland security. The paper spells out articles of the Homeland Security Act of 2002 and suggests how this act bears directly and indirectly on Latino immigrants and Midwest Latinos and communities. The paper also examines some of the possible secondary and tertiary long-term affects of Homeland Security on Latinos in general. The paper concludes by identifying some of the measures that are important for Latino civil and human rights groups to pursue in the United States today.

II. Midwest Latinos in a Vulnerable Situation

Midwest Latinos face a particular set of circumstances that place them in the center of attention under the laws of Homeland Security.

First, Latinos are a rapidly growing population with concentrations in urban centers of the Midwest. While 75 percent of the Latino population still resides in seven states—California, Texas, New York, Florida, Illinois, Arizona and New

Jersey—by region, the greatest percentage increase of Latinos occurred in the Midwest (81 percent). From 1990 to 2000, the Chicago metro area increased by 73% from 819,676 to 1,416,584. Latinos increased in the central city area of Chicago's PMSA, by 41%, from 535,315 to 753, 644. Although Chicago represents a so-called "established Latino Metro," Latinos increased by 261% in Indianapolis, 189% in Minneapolis-St Paul, 181% in Columbus, 153 % in Grand Rapids, and 106% in Kansas City. It is not so much that the absolute numbers are as dramatic as the fact that Latinos grew at very rapid rates, often generating eye-opening awareness of their influx, especially in new communities that perceived Latinos as "immigrant Latinos."

Second, the communities of Chicago, Illinois and several places in Michigan and Wisconsin have been places for Middle Eastern settlement and growth for many years. Often the concentrations of both Latinos and Middle Easterners exist side by side. In most cases, there is little apparent conflict between Latinos and Middle Easterners, or any notable differences in some of their political or social actions. Both groups share interest in culture, language preservation and justice for fellow immigrants.

Third, with the increase in the numbers of Latinos in the Midwest, there has been a concomitant increase in the number of Latino Muslims. Latino Muslims come from various backgrounds. Some Latino Muslims are immigrants from Latin America, coming from countries that are homes to tens and thousands of Middle Eastern refugees from Palestine, Lebanon, Syria and other parts. Mexico is a country that has long served as refuge and home to Middle Easterners. Today, Latino Muslims are prominent members of Mexican society, for example, and have a unique history and tradition of inter-marriage with others in Mexico. Other Latino Muslims are emanating from domestic Latino populations. They are converts to the Muslim faith, converts who join various religious sects that practice Islam. The movement of Islam is not necessarily of Middle Eastern origin, but an outgrowth of Black Muslim culture and interest groups found in Chicago, Detroit and other parts of the Midwest.

According to an article in the Chicago *Tribune*, July 5, 2002, by James Janega, an Islamic convention was held in the Chicago in July 2002 to develop a cultural unity and a greater network, adding a common voice among Latino Muslims. "The phenomenon [of Latino Muslim growth]is so big, but it's not unified. It's not in one place, they don't know each other."—This is a quote attributed to Sayyid M. Sayeed, secretary general of the Latino Muslim Society of Chicago. The convention at the Holiday Inn O'Hare in Rosemont featured lectures on Islamic literature in Spanish, religious education for Latino Muslims, and profiles on Islam within various Latino cultures.

At this time there is no measure of the influence and growth of Latino Muslim households within the Midwest, but the relationship between Latinos and Muslims is decades old, emanating from a natural outgrowth of Latino diversity and interest in a range of social and religious matters.

II. The Cause of the Homeland Security Act

What compelled the United States government to pass the Homeland Security Act of 2002 was largely the terrorist acts of 9/11. The mandates built into Homeland Security measures were clearly a response to the problems identified in the wake of the terrorism in New York City and Washington DC.

On September 11, 2001, at 8:45 a.m., terrorists crashed a hijacked American Airlines plane into the north tower of the World Trade Center in New York City.Within the next hour and twenty-five minutes, three more hijacked planes were flown into the south tower of the World Trade Center, the Pentagon, and into a field southeast of Pittsburgh, Pennsylvania. Combined, there were more than 2,000 lives lost as a result of these terrorist acts.

On September 27, the Federal Bureau of Investigations released the names of 19 men believed to have been the hijackers of the four planes. The names released were of men who all came from the Middle East. A global investigation soon revealed that they had operated in and out of the United States in organized "cells," connected to Osama bin Ladin, a known Saudi terrorist. The evidence was shocking, calling for immediate action by the FBI, CIA, the Departments of Justice, Defense, Transportation, and Energy. Weak links were identified in the systems of border and immigration controls. The Department of Justice, which administers the INS, admitted that entry and exit data on foreigners could not be relied on for control.

Poll takers chronicled the impact of the terrorist acts on the American public. Besides a growing sense of fear and insecurity, there was a definitive change in the way Americans felt about issues related to immigration and how the United States government should interact with foreigners.

III. Before 9/11, Midwest Latinos Were Expecting More Civil Liberties

Not long before the public's response to 9/11, a Gallup poll showed that 62% of Americans believed immigration was good for the country in general. Also noted by Gallup was that, "Americans are even more positive about immigration when contemplating the past. Seventy-five percent of Americans say immigration has been a good thing for the United States in the past, and less than one in five think it has been a bad thing."

Just a week before 9/11, President George W. Bush and Mexican President Vicente Fox, the first foreign head of state to visit President George W. Bush since taking office, were focused on a more open door between the two nations. In fact, on September 5, 2001, President Bush warm-heartedly addressed President Fox with these words: "I know there are some in this world and our country who want to build walls between Mexico and the United States. I want to remind people, fearful people build walls. Confident people tear them down. And I'm confident . . . that [being] good neighbors [in] a strong relationship is in our nation's best interests."

Clearly evident from President Bush was a positive spirit for a more open border between the United States and Mexico and a more cordial attitude toward Mexican immigrants in particular.

President Bush went on to say in the same speech, "Oh, I know there's a lot of talk about Mexican laborers coming to the United States. But I want to remind my fellow citizens of this fact: Family values do not stop at the Río Bravo. There are mothers and dads in Mexico who love their children just as much as mothers and dads in America do. And if there [is] a mother or dad who can't find work, worried about food on the table, they're going to come and find work in America."

Mexican President Vicente Fox was well in-tune to this dramatic and friendly environment and followed President Bush's comments by saying, "This land of opportunity, the United States, has always kept its door open to countless immigrants from all over the world, remaining true to its founding principles. Let me quote President Bush's remarks, who recently said that 'the United States has traditionally been a welcoming society, where immigration is not a problem to be solved, but a sign of our confident and successful nation. History supports that assertion, because more importantly, we see the proof of that in the innumerable contributions that migrants have made over the last two centuries to the rich and varied American culture.'"

Both Presidents Bush and Fox were further on the road to tying the United States and Mexico into an inter-dependent flow of people, commerce and good will, up to the time of 9/11. There were also advances to promote legislation that would grant amnesty to nearly three million Mexicans living in the United States illegally.

President Bush's embrace of President Fox and Mexico also gained national attention and interest. As noted by an ABC News poll taken in August of 2001, "Overall, 43 percent of Americans say they'd support a plan 'in which illegal immigrants from Mexico would be allowed to live and work legally in the United States,' while 49 percent say they'd oppose it."

On September 6, the President's press secretary commended the Senate for passing legislation allowing immigrants waiting to become residents to remain with their families in the United States. The press secretary went on to say,"The President is heartened by the Senate's action and he looks forward to the House acting quickly to send this legislation to his desk." Another sign of President Bush's commitment to having more open immigration laws in the United States was having National Security Advisor Condoleeza Rice also publicly support the legislation.

On September 7, 2001, *Time Magazine* named Vicente Fox their Person of the Week because of, "The fact that a Mexican president could ask Washington to change its immigration laws—and be applauded for it—signals a new era." In naming Fox, the *Time* piece also added that, ". . . raising the status of the undocumented Mexican underclass could also help Bush grow his share of the increasingly-important Latino vote—an estimated 60 percent of U.S. Latinos are of Mexican origin."

With a President actively pursuing support for the new policies, the Senate's quick work to pass legislation, and the public endorsement of the national security advisor, what could in fact have been a new era for immigration in American was well on its way to becoming reality.

Yet, in a matter of days, the great optimism of both national leaders and legions of interested supporters, would be replaced by a complete reversal in both the government and public views of immigration.

IV. First Affects of 9/11

The terrorist attacks of September 11 changed the relationship between Presidents Bush and Fox by 180 degrees. In the wake of 9/11, President Bush and his advisors moved to secure American borders and to identify the attackers as quickly as possible. Police, Secret Service, FBI, and the military were called in to defend the nation. National Security Advisor Condoleeza Rice focused the presidency on foreign terrorists, to bring them to justice, and to limit foreigners from crossing the border.

The public support that President Bush worked for when pushing his immigration proposals before September 11 was put aside completely. It was not a time for open borders and friendly relations when the nation was clearly attacked by a surprise group of terrorists who took thousands of lives within an hour's time.

By September 25, a poll in Florida on the level of scrutiny that should be put on immigrants reported that, "Eighty-one percent of registered voters responding to the poll said the country should place more restrictions on immigration. Seventy percent said they supported expanding federal police powers to 'indefinitely detain legal immigrants suspected of crimes during a national emergency,' even if that meant suspending civil rights like due process and the right to a speedy trial." The poll also reported that many people supported better policing of the borders by the federal government. This feeling was reported as being widespread despite the fact that none of the September 11 hijackers had entered the United States by crossing a border illegally. Still, the suspicion and fear of foreigners that came from the terrorist attacks translated into a complete fallout of support for legislation meant to ease immigration policies for Latinos living illegally in the United States. There grew in its place an overwhelming support for legislation that would militarize the border region, where high concentrations of Latinos live.

After September 11, the trend in the American public of grouping the controls over the border, immigration and issues of national security was on the rise. Another survey published on September 28 reported that 75% of Americans wanted stricter border control. The article stated, "An overwhelming majority of Americans believe the lack of border control makes it easier for terrorists to enter the country. Those responding think a greater effort in controlling immigration would go a long way in preventing future terrorist assaults on the nation." A majority of those polled believed that weak border control had something to do with the September 11 attacks.

Information released by the FBI later revealed that all 19 hijackers had, ". . . entered the country legally on a temporary visa, mostly B-1 business visas or B-2 tourist visas. One is known to have received an M-1 vocational training visa and two received F-1 student visas." Information revealing that the hijackers did not enter the United States by illegally crossing an American border was widely publicized in the months following the attack. Despite this information, there remained among the American public strong support for increased security at the border. A Texas newspaper reported in February of 2003 that, "Americans view immigration with regard to safety rather than social and economic stances." With the emphasis on immigration and the border remaining on security rather than the social and economic issues that the President used to sell the plan prior to September 11th, it is unlikely that the legislation that was once so close to passing will ever recover from the shock left by the terrorist attacks.

V. Secondary Effects

The idea for a Department of Homeland Security quickly surfaced, and the White House called for securing the border and checking foreigners that enter the country. As information mounted that the Immigration and Naturalization Service had granted visas to all nineteen hijackers, questions began to be asked about the effectiveness of the agency in preventing terrorists from entering the country and making decisions as to whom should be allowed to enter. Government inquiries discovered that three of the hijackers had lost their legal status in the United States, yet the Immigration and Naturalization Service had done nothing to find them and deport them.

More revealing was information showing that exactly six months after the September 11 terrorist acts, two of the hijackers who flew planes into the World Trade Center had approval forms for student visas sent to the flight school they had attended in Florida.

An INS spokesman said, "It does serve to illustrate what we have been saying since 1995—that the current system for collecting information and tracking foreign students is antiquated, outdated, inaccurate and untimely." The President, after hearing of the report, was quoted as saying to Tom Ridge and John Ashcroft, "Get to the bottom of this immediately." A Justice Department official was also quoted as saying, "The attorney general is extremely concerned and furious about the situation." With controversy surrounding the agency over its failures in relation to the September 11 attacks, the INS did not appear to have a future in the Department of Justice.

The Immigration and Naturalization Service had many critics long before 9/11. For several years, representatives from the Latino community and advocacy groups, such as the National Council of La Raza and the Mexican American Legal Defense and Education Fund, had charged the Immigration and Naturalization Service with poor and inadequate service in handling legal immigrants. NCLR and other organizations proposed changes to the INS, such as separating services and enforcement functions and providing adequate funding for immigrant services so as to eliminate the huge INS backlog of visa, residency, and citizenship applications.

VII. Homeland Security Measures

Within weeks of 9/11, the Office of the President moved swiftly to advance security on the home front. Former Governor Tom Ridge, once a candidate for Vice-President, was chosen for the task. Time was of the essence in re-structuring the agencies responsible for immigration, defense, and national security. The White House internal decision paved the way for the Homeland Security Act. Legislators ultimately eliminated the Immigration and Naturalization Service with Section 471 of The Homeland Security Act, which reads:

SEC. 471. ABOLISHMENT OF INS.
(a) IN GENERAL. -Upon completion of all transfers from the Immigration

and Naturalization Service as provided for by this Act, the Immigration and Naturalization Service of the Department of Justice is abolished.

On March 1, 2003, the Immigration and Naturalization Service officially ceased to exist.

VIII. Bureau of Citizenship and Immigration Services

Washington essentially heeded the call from advocacy groups in the Latino community to separate the enforcement and services functions of the INS. Lawmakers created the Bureau of Citizenship and Immigrant Services (BCIS) to handle the immigrant services formerly provided by the INS. Section 451 of the Homeland Security Act sets out the responsibilities of the BCIS, which reads:

SEC. 451. ESTABLISHMENT OF BUREAU OF CITIZENSHIP AND IMMIGRATION SERVICES.
(a) ESTABLISHMENT OF BUREAU.-
(1) IN GENERAL.-There shall be in the Department a bureau to be known as the "Bureau of citizenship and Immigration Services".
(b) TRANSFER OF FUNCTIONS FROM COMMISSIONER.-In accordance with title XV (relating to transition provisions), there are transferred from the Commissioner of Immigration and Naturalization to the Director of the Bureau of Citizenship and Immigration Services the following functions, and all personnel, infrastructure, and funding provided to the Commissioner in support of such functions immediately before the effective date specified in section 455:
(1) Adjudications of immigrant visa petitions.
(2) Adjudications of naturalization petitions.
(3) Adjudications of asylum and refugee applications.
(4) Adjudications performed at service centers.
(5) All other adjudications performed by the Immigration and Naturalization Service immediately before the effective date specified in section 455.

The Bureau of Citizenship and Immigration Services assumed control over all property, funding, personnel and responsibilities that belonged to the former Services Division of the INS. A spokeswoman for the Chicago office of the Bureau of Citizenship and Immigration Services said, "It's a new name, but it will be the same office, the same officers, the same forms, the same fees."

Soon, thereafter, proponents for greater immigration services noted that: "If the Bureau of Citizenship and Immigration Services simply keeps the status quo, it would not be a good thing for the millions of Latinos trying to obtain services necessary to establish legal residence in the United States."

The huge INS backlogs that existed before September 11 turned into even greater backlogs as the agency changed its focus to security and enforcement. The number of entries into the United States that needed to be processed rose by over one million in the first months of Homeland Security.

The Immigration Services and Infrastructure Act of 2000 mandated that the INS backlog be eliminated within one year of the Act's enactment but the mandate was not accomplished. When writing the Homeland Security Act, lawmakers simply gave the same mandate but extended the starting point of the one year time frame to the date of the enactment of the Homeland Security Act. Section 458 states the following:

SEC. 458. BACKLOG ELIMINATION.

Section 204(a)(1) of the Immigration Services and Infrastructure Improvements Act of 2000 (8 U.S.C. 1573(a)(1)) is amended by striking "not later than one year after the date of enactment of this Act;" and inserting "1 year after the date of the enactment of the Homeland Security Act of 2002;".

Legislators also included Section 451(a)(5) which states:

(5) PILOT INITIATIVES FOR BACKLOG ELIMINATION.-The Director of the Bureau of Citizenship and Immigration Services is authorized to implement innovative pilot initiatives to eliminate any remaining backlog in the processing of immigration benefit applications, and to prevent any backlog in processing of such applications from recurring, in accordance with section 204(a) of the Immigration Services and infrastructure Improvements Act of 2000 (8 U.S.C. 1573(a)). Such initiatives may include measures such as increasing personnel, transferring personnel to focus on areas with the largest potential for backlog, and streamlining paperwork.

This section gives the BCIS Director, Eduardo Aguirre, the power to try different programs with the budget that has been allocated to the agency. The Bush Administration wanted an elimination of the backlog and a six-month processing time for all applications. The President also mandated that this be done with a $100 million per year initiative that will not give the BCIS a chance to change its funding until 2006. With an existing backlog of more than five million applications, it will be difficult for the BCIS to meet the standards put forth by the President.

Many immigration watch dogs fear that services will be brushed aside and forgotten in the large agency whose main mission is to prevent terrorism. Marshall Fitz of the American Immigration Lawyers Association said, "Our concerns are broader. They are not directed toward what is going to happen in the next week or the next month, but the more long term of what is going to happen to immigration services now that they are being folded really under the umbrella of what is more a security apparatus than a welcome mat."

IX. Directorate of Border and Transportation Security

The enforcement end of the Department of Homeland Security is the Directorate of Border and Transportation Security. This Directorate goes well beyond the obligations of the Immigration and Naturalization Service, which is just one part of this Directorate. Sec. 401 sets out the responsibilities of this division of the Department and reads as follows:

Sec. 401. UNDER SECRETARY FOR BORDER AND TRANSPORTATION SECURITY.

There shall be in the Department a Directorate of Border and Transportation Security headed by an Under Secretary for Border and Transportation Security.

SEC. 402. RESPONSIBILITIES

The Secretary, acting through the Under Secretary for Border and Transportation Security, shall be responsible for the following:

(1) Preventing the entry of terrorists and the instruments of terrorism into the United States.

(2) Securing the borders, territorial waters, ports, terminals, waterways, and air, land and sea transportation systems of the United States, including managing and coordinating those functions transferred to the Department of ports of entry.

(3) Carrying out immigration enforcement functions vested by statue in, or performed by, the Commissioner of Immigration and Naturalization (or any officer, employee, or component of the Immigration and Naturalization Service) immediately before the date on which the transfer of functions specified under 441 takes effect.

(4) Establishing and administering rules, in accordance with section 428, governing the granting of visas or other forms of permission, including parole, to enter the United States to individuals who are not a citizen or an alien lawfully admitted for permanent residence in the United States.

(5) Establishing national immigration enforcement policies and priorities.

(6) Except as provided in subtitle C, administering the customs laws of the Unites States.

(7) Conducting the inspection and related administrative functions of the Department of Agriculture transferred to the Secretary of Homeland Security under section 421.

(8) In carrying out the foregoing responsibilities, ensuring the speedy, orderly, and efficient flow of lawful traffic and commerce.

This Directorate is the broad enforcement arm and security arm of the Department. The Department of Homeland Security budget for the fiscal year of 2004 is $36.2 billion. Of this amount, $18.1 billion is going to the Directorate of Border and Transportation Security. This directorate will oversee the enforcement functions that were previously handled by the INS.

The Immigration and Naturalization Service enforcement functions will be split up into two divisions within the Directorate of Border and Transportation Security. The Bureau of Customs and Border Protection is in charge of security matters at all borders, airports and seaports. The other division is the Bureau of Immigration and Customs Enforcement, which is in charge of finding and deporting illegal aliens, plus the securing all federal buildings. Section 474 states that both the enforcement and services segments of the Department of Homeland Security are important and will be funded sufficiently. The Section reads as follows:

SEC. 474. SENSE OF CONGRESS.

It is the sense of Congress that-

(1) the missions of the Bureau of Border Security and the Bureau of Citizenship and Immigration Services are equally important and, accordingly, they each should be adequately funded; and

(2) the functions transferred under this subtitle should not, after such transfers take effect, operate at levels below those in effect prior to the enactment of this Act.

While the Act may state this, a comparison of the monetary resources available to the enforcement segment of the Department of Homeland Security as compared to those of the services division shows how small a role the services division has in the Department as a whole.

The mission of the Bureau of Citizenship and Immigration Services does not fit in with the rest of the agency. This situation presents a dangerous scenario for the Latino community because the immigrant services sector of the federal government is at risk of being pushed aside, over-shadowed and under-funded. The ability of Latinos and other immigrant groups to draw attention to the needs and problems of the immigrant services will be harder than it has ever been before. This is because it is the piece that does not fit in the gigantic puzzle that is the Department of Homeland Security.

There is also the problem of the public maintaining a lingering negative sentiment toward foreigners stemming from the attacks of September 11. While the terrorist attacks alone may not have institutionalized this sentiment toward foreigners in the minds of Americans, the hastily assembled Department of Homeland Security may very well do just that. This can have tremendously negative effects on the experiences that future generations of immigrants will have interacting with the federal government.

X. Tertiary and Long Term Implications for Latinos

There is a slight ray of hope that the new Department of Homeland Security, of 170,000 employees, will be more efficient and better run than the INS. At the same time, the backlog of immigration papers and news accounts of arrests and detentions of Latinos along the Mexican border is raising concern that Latinos will not achieve support from the Bush administration, at least on a level afforded President Fox before 9/11. These fears are being justified by newspaper articles chronicling how the Department of Homeland Security has used anti-terrorism resources to pursue immigrants from Latin America.

New interpretations of immigration laws that the Department of Homeland Security has brought about, with the help of the Department of Justice, will severely challenge the rights of many Latin American immigrants who enter the United States illegally. Attorney General John Ashcroft has ruled that, "Broad categories of foreigners who arrive in this country illegally can be detained indefinitely without consideration of their individual circumstances if immigration officials say their release would endanger national security." The decision gives the Department of Homeland Security much more discretion in deeming an individual a threat to national security. The ruling has been applied to Latin Americans who have been deemed threats to national security, despite not having any connections to terrorist organizations or any intentions of committing terrorist acts upon arrival in the United States.

In the case of 18-year-old David Joseph, a Haitian who was apprehended after entering the country illegally, the Department of Homeland Security decided to hold him indefinitely and will decide his fate without affording him the right to a trial before an immigration judge. David Joseph was deemed a national security threat because Pakistani terrorists have used Haiti to enter the United States illegally and Joseph's entry takes Homeland Security resources away from finding those terrorists.

Eleanor Acer from the Committee for Human Rights has said, "The ruling affects not only asylum seekers, but also those others who might be picked up in this as undocumented aliens, on a workplace raid, for example." Under these new provisions, the Department of Homeland Security could deem any illegal individual that crossed the border between the United States and Mexico a threat to national security if it is believed that terrorists also use the US-Mexico border to gain entry into the United States. Once an individual is deemed a threat to national security, his rights would be much more limited. The fate of such an individual would no longer be decided by immigration judges or boards but rather by the Department of Homeland Security.

The Department of Homeland Security has also asked for the help of state and local law enforcement agencies in apprehending illegal immigrants. Attorney General John Ashcroft again re-interpreted former affirmations from the Department of Justice in 1996 and 2001 that local police departments should not track and arrest illegal immigrants. This has resulted in state and local law enforcement agencies, ". . . arresting people accused of civil violations of immigration law like overstaying visas."

The rulings by the Attorney General and the Department of Homeland Security will have considerable bearing on "illegal" Latin Americans living in the United States, as well as on the large Latino communities that they live in. The new levels of enforcement also affect the ways in which police departments operate and interact with illegal immigrants. It will change the system from one of cooperation and protection for human rights to one of fear.

There is also concern that undocumented Latinos will face even greater risk of assault and robbery as a result of a fear of reporting crimes to police. This would also undermine cooperation between illegal immigrants and police departments in solving crimes committed in the Latino communities. Along with a deterioration of cooperation between Latino communities and police departments, the level of service provided by police may deteriorate as resources are shifted to performing immigration functions. This will have the largest effect on the large Latino communities that are made up of legal and illegal immigrants, residents and citizens.

XI. Summary and Conclusions

September 11, 2001 has already changed a number of the ways that Latinos behave and feel in the Midwest. It has certainly transformed a period of positive relationships between Midwest Latinos with relatives in Mexico, Central America and the Caribbean who have immigrated to the region. The complete change from a sense of relief from *la migra* (before 9/11) to the fear that now prevails is startling, to say the least. The end is not in sight for a period of peace and security within the United States. At the forefront of challenges to civil and human rights are U.S. and immigrant Latinos, especially of the Midwest.

It would be a year and a half later that most of America would know some of the consequences of President Bush's defensive actions taken in response to 9/11. What we know today is being released gradually in the public record. According to a 198-page report issued by the Federal Office of the Inspector

General in June 2003, the Justice Department instituted a "no bond" policy for all detainees connected to the terrorism probe of the attacks. The Immigration and Naturalization Service was employed to quickly respond with lists of possible immigrant suspects and possible terrorists for detention and/or capture by the FBI. The call for duty resulted in the detention of more than 1,200 immigrants deemed "of interest," brought in for questioning and/or were arrested.

According to the report, federal and state authorities violated the civil rights of many who were detained. There was a pattern of physical and verbal abuse against some detainees. According to the June 9, 2003 Section B5 edition of *The Washington Post*, from October 1, 2002, to March 31, 2003, U.S. authorities deported 898 citizens from the two dozen countries under special scrutiny, triple the number that was deported the year before. Of the 67,000 people deported in the six months after October 1, 2002, nearly three quarters were Mexicans.

The report of the Office of the Inspector General cited some of the forms of round-up and abuse that faced detainees. In one example reported by Steve Fainaru in *The Washington Post* (June, 3, 2003, A-1), ". . . three Middle Eastern men were detained after a traffic stop on September 15, 2001, in New York because police found the building plans for a school in their car. Even though the men were construction workers at the school, a fact verified by their boss the next day, 'they remained detained' as part of the Sept. 11 probe."

Overall, the full effect of 9/11 and the follow-up measures of Homeland Security are being worked out. The record of impact is also being divulged, piece by piece, as government records become available to the news media and researchers.

In sum:

1. Latinos have been negatively affected by the turn-around in public opinion resulting from the terrorist attacks of 9/11.
2. Latinos have been negatively affected by the changes in legislation that came as a result of the terrorist attacks of 9/11.
3. Civil and human rights must be defended and upheld at every stage of the war on terror and in the writing of legislation in order to ensure true American values.

Clearly, September 11, 2001 changed Latino behavior and their sense of security and freedom in the Midwest. They now share a common belief that Latinos are primary targets of anti-immigration measures of Homeland Security, despite the fact that no Latino has been court-judged a terrorist agent in this nation. Under these circumstances, Midwest Latinos have lost ground in their struggle for social justice.

Latinos Struggle for Equality: A Case Study of Nebraska's Latino Communities
Miguel A. Carranza

INTRODUCTION

Background

In January 2000, *Legislative Bill 1363* was introduced into the Nebraska legislature by a group of seventeen state senators led by Senator Matt Connealy. The purpose of *LB 1363* was to create the Task Force on the Productive Integration of the Immigrant Workforce Population. The bill was passed by the Nebraska legislature and signed by Governor Johanns in April 2000. One of the primary directives for the newly established task force was to "investigate current statutes and practices of the state and local government regarding the access and use of human services provided to the immigrant workforce in Nebraska, but not limited to: education, housing, transportation, justice system, and health services." As part of its initiative, the Task Force held a series of public hearings which gave individual citizens across the state an opportunity to express their views and ideas about the opportunities and challenges "old timers" and new arrivals in Nebraska face as a result of an increasing immigrant workforce population in the state and their respective communities. The second component of the research initiative was to sponsor a study on this same topic. We were subsequently selected by the State of Nebraska Mexican American Commission to conduct such a study, the results of which will be discussed below.

Purpose and Methodology

The main purpose of the study was to explore the degree to which Latino newcomers are being effectively and positively integrated into the economic, social, and political lives and institutions of the state and local communities. The project consisted of three phases. The first was based on the analysis of recent releases of U.S. Census 2000 figures as well as other government documents, media archives, and published research. We utilized this information primarily to construct a general, albeit partial, demographic and socio-economic profile of Nebraska's Latino immigrant and native-born population and workforce. The second phase was the development of a survey questionnaire mailed to a wide array of agencies and organizations directly or indirectly charged with the process of integrating newcomer populations. In the third phase, we conducted focus groups with newcomers and key organizations in three Nebraska communities. These last two phases are described in more detail later in the study. This research project represents an important step on the part of state institutions to address the serious dearth of research on the state's Latino population. Our findings, however, must be interpreted with some caution because the data are still insufficient. Additionally, it is too early in the process to arrive at definitive conclusions or accurately predict the direction that integration for Latino newcomers and their children will take and the speed at which it will occur.

Theoretical Assumptions and Guiding Research

The research process was informed by a vast body of national and regional research on immigrant incorporation processes conducted by nationally recognized scholars. Among some of the most important insights we gleaned from this body of research were:

- The productive incorporation of new immigrants and their children has never been as simple, linear, and predictable as popular and nostalgic tales, based largely on earlier European immigrants' assimilation trajectories, seem to suggest.
- It is largely true that, in time, all immigrants assimilate into American society. In fact, research continues to show that even newly arrived children of immigrants prefer to speak English within a year of attending school in the United States, and it is the native language and culture that are soon lost. However, to which social and economic segment of American society, and with what level of difficulty or success, immigrants will assimilate will vary greatly depending on a combination of factors. Critical among such factors are the reservoir of human and social capital[1] contained in newcomer communities and, perhaps more importantly, the social and economic barriers newcomers confront on their road to successful integration.

- Large national studies have convincingly demonstrated that one of the most important components of a positive "context of reception" has to do with the receiving governments' laws and policies.[2] To the extent that these policies promote inclusion rather than passive acceptance or outright exclusion, immigrant workers and their children are most likely to commit to, as well as experience, a positive, productive, and long-term process of incorporation into their host communities and societies.

- Other factors shaping the incorporation process include the degree to which host communities welcome diversity and provide economic and social opportunities for newcomers and the political and economic strength of the more established ethnic community.

- Research on the so-called "second generation" (children of immigrants born in the United States) provides strong evidence for the thesis that, when these children and their parents experience a hostile context of reception, framed in large part by low wages and adverse policy and cultural environments, time actually diminishes the original immigrant drive and has a negative impact on children's adaptation process.

- Assimilation is thus a segmented process and, lacking access to the key institutions of society and mechanisms that reinforce a strong sense of identity, children of immigrants will assimilate into the lower and most socially troubled segments of our societies. In this manner their contributions to the future of these societies, whether at the national, state or local level, are effectively undermined.

- In sum, positive integration is always a two-way process and its effectiveness is not simply determined by what immigrants bring with them in the way of human capital. On the contrary, it is the extent to which newcomers encounter a welcoming economic, social and political environment that is most determining of successful integration and assimilation.

THE LATINO POPULATION AND WORKFORCE

Demographic Transformations

Much of the focus on immigrant populations in the United States is fueled by the demographic changes that have occurred during the past two decades. One need only review the dramatic growth of the Hispanic/Latino population in the United States to recognize these changes and their tremendous social, economic and political impacts. Whereas the overall population in the United State increased by slightly more than 13% in the decade between 1990 and 2000, the Hispanic/Latino population increased 58% during that same period, reaching a population totaling approximately 35 million people. This unprecedented growth did not just occur in those regions where Hispanics/Latinos have traditionally been found, e.g. California, Florida and Texas. To the surprise of many demographers, major surges in growth were found in what are being called "new destinations" in regions such as the South where states such as Georgia, Tennessee, Alabama, Arkansas and others experienced record growths in their Latino population. North Carolina, a new destination state, had the greatest growth proportionately, with its Hispanic/Latino population increasing by nearly 400 percent in the past decade.

Table 1 provides a glimpse of how Great Plains states were also beneficiaries of these immigration patterns. The overall population increases in each of these states was well below the national average of 12.4 % ranging from .5% to 8.9 %. However, the Hispanic/Latino percentage change far exceeded the overall population change in all of the states. In all cases, states would have had little or no growth had it not been for the increase of their Latino populations in the past decade. Kansas and Missouri experienced nearly 100 percent growth in their Latino population, and Nebraska and Iowa ranked even higher among the ten states experiencing the largest Latino population growth between the last two decennial census counts (U.S. Census 2000). A common denominator underpinning these demographic changes and migration toward new destinations has been their relationship to the restructuring and revitalization of industries, such as meat and poultry processing.[3] This has been a particularly important factor in Nebraska, a state whose Latino population growth exceeded all others listed in Table 1. We discuss these trends below in more detail.

TABLE 1. Growth and Percentage Change for Total Population and Hispanic/ Latino Population for Selected Northern Plains States, 1990 and 2000

	1990		2000		% Change 1990–2000	
State	**Total Population**	**Hispanic/ Latino Population**	**Total Population**	**Hispanic/ Latino Population**	**Total Population**	**Hispanic/ Latino Population**
Iowa	2,776,755	32,647	2,926,324	82,473	5.4	152.6
Kansas	2,477,574	93,670	2,688,418	188,252	8.5	101.0
Missouri	5,117,073	61,702	5,595,211	118,592	9.3	92.2
Nebraska	1,578,385	36,969	1,711,263	94,425	8.4	155.4
North Dakota	638,800	4,472	642,200	7,786	.5	74.1
South Dakota	696,004	5,568	754,844	10,903	8.5	95.8

Source: U.S. Census Bureau, Census 2000 Redistricting Data (Public Law 94-171) Summary File, Matrices PL1 and PL2

From 1990 to 2000 Nebraska experienced dramatic changes in its Hispanic/Latino population. According to U.S. Census Bureau figures, the Hispanic/Latino population increased more than 155%, going from 36,969 to 94,425. Tables 2 and 3 provide a glimpse at the changes that have occurred in Nebraska counties and cities in the past decade, according to U.S. Census figures. Table 2 lists the 15 counties that recorded the largest Hispanic/Latino populations in 2002. Most of these counties had small to moderate growths in population. However, one-third of the counties had increases of 17% or greater, with Dawson and Dakota counties reflecting the largest percentage increase in total population. When viewing the percentage change in the Hispanic/Latino population, it is clear this population had significant increases in all of the counties and helped contribute to the overall positive population growth that occurred in these counties. This remains true even in such counties as Box Butte, which had a slight decrease in total population, yet still had almost a 29% increase in its Hispanic/Latino population. In looking at Table 3, the comparison of percentage

TABLE 2. Growth and Percentage Change for Total Population and Hispanic/
Latino Population for Selected Nebraska Counties, 1990 and 2000

	1990		2000		% Change 1990–2000	
State	Total Population	Hispanic/ Latino Population	Total Population	Hispanic/ Latino Population	Total Population	Hispanic/ Latino Population
Douglas	416,444	11,368	463,585	30,928	11.3	172.1
Lancaster	213,641	3,938	250,291	8,437	17.2	114.2
Hall*	48,925	2,116	53,534	7,497	9.4	254.3
Scotts Bluff*	36,025	5,237	36,951	6,352	2.6	21.3
Dawson*	19,940	663	24,365	6,178	22.2	831.8
Sarpy	102,583	3,383	122,595	5,538	19.5	58.4
Dakota	16,742	1,016	20,253	4,581	21.0	350.9
Madison*	32,655	569	35,226	3,042	7.9	434.6
Colfax*	9,139	224	10,441	2,732	14.2	1119.6
Platte*	29,820	255	31,662	2,072	6.2	712.5
Buffalo*	37,447	1,023	42,259	1,970	12.8	92.6
Lincoln*	32,508	1,623	34,632	1,880	6.5	15.8
Adams*	29,625	303	31,151	1,428	5.2	371.3
Dodge*	34,500	223	36,160	1,421	4.8	537.2
Box Butte*	13,130	722	12,158	930	–7.4	28.8

*Indicates non-metropolitan counties
Source: U.S. Census Bureau, Census 2000 Redistricting Data (Public Law 94-171) Summary File, Matrices PL1 and PL2.

TABLE 3. Growth and Percentage Change for Total Population and Hispanic/
Latino Population for Selected Nebraska Cities, 1990 and 2000

	1990		2000		% Change 1990–2000	
Cities	Total Population	Hispanic/ Latino Population	Total Population	Hispanic/ Latino Population	Total Population	Hispanic/ Latino Population
Omaha	335,719	10,288	390,007	29,397	16.2	185.7
Lincoln	191,972	3,764	225,581	8,154	17.5	116.6
Grand Island*	39,386	1,887	42,940	6,845	9.0	262.7
Lexington*	6,601	329	10,011	5,121	51.6	1456.5
Scottsbluff*	13,711	2,720	14,732	3,476	7.4	27.8
S Sioux City	9,677	545	11,925	2,958	23.2	442.8
Bellevue	30,928	1,213	44,382	2,609	43.5	115.1
Schuyler*	4,052	164	5,371	2,423	32.6	1377.4
Norfolk*	21,476	299	23,516	1,790	9.5	498.7
North Platte*	22,605	1,355	23,878	1,596	5.6	17.8
Columbus*	19,480	167	20,971	1,395	7.7	735.3
Hastings*	22,837	268	24,064	1,343	5.4	401.1
Kearney*	24,396	667	27,431	1,118	12.4	67.6
Fremont*	23,680	165	25,174	1,085	6.3	557.6
Gering*	7,946	944	7,751	1,039	-2.5	10.1

*Indicates cities located in non-metropolitan counties

Source: U.S. Census Bureau, Census 2000 Redistricting Data (Public Law 94-171) Summary File, Matrices PL1 and PL2.

change from 1990 to 2000 between the total population and the Hispanic/Latino population is even more dramatic. Overall, for these cities the Hispanic/Latino population growth has significantly contributed to the changes occurring within the total population. Again, this occurrence holds true even in a community such as Gering, which had a 2.5% *decrease* in overall population, yet still had an increase of more than 10% in their Hispanic/Latino population. It should be noted these figures do not take into account persistent problems of undercounting groups, such as Hispanics/Latinos, particularly undocumented immigrants and their families.

There are no adequate means to calculate the precise number of undocumented workers and their families living in the United States or Nebraska. Omaha's district office for the Immigration and Naturalization Service (INS) initially estimated that about 25% of the meatpacking labor force in Nebraska was undocumented. Its subsequent review of the entire industry's employment records did not confirm such a high estimate, albeit it did not totally disprove it either (INS Task Force 2000). Nationally, estimates are similar to the local INS estimates. They range from a low of 5.9 million to a high of 9.9 million, with a midrange of nearly 8 million, or about 25% of the estimated foreign-born population.[4] Our own field experiences suggest numbers can vary depending on periods of low or aggressive labor recruitment by employers (who may or may not be specifically targeting undocumented workers) and time of arrival of particular migration streams. Such estimates may range from a low of 10% or 15% to a high of 25 or 30% in different communities and at different times.

Age and Fertility: Contributions to Growth

While the majority of the Latino population growth between 1990 and 2000 was due to immigration, additional factors contributing to these demographic trends were age and fertility. Nationally, the Hispanic/Latino population has a median age of 25.9 years, as compared to the total population's 35.3 years–about a nine-year difference. The difference between whites and Latinos is more dramatic in the new destination states, such as Nebraska. Here, the Latino median age is 13 years below that of non-Latino white median age. Similarly, the state's crude birth rate was 14.4 live births per 1,000 population in 2000, while the Hispanic population's birth rate was more than twice that (about 30 live births per 1,000, which is the same as the national rate). The city of Lexington, where Latinos are now a majority, recorded the highest birth rate among communities with a population of at least 2,500 (25.9 total birth rate).[5]

Latinos' higher birth rate has particularly broad implications for schools, where there will be a higher proportion of these children in our Pre K-12 classrooms. In fact, recent figures from the Nebraska Department of Education show that the number of Hispanic children enrolled in Pre K to 12 grades in Nebraska schools increased from 7,147 in 1990-1991 to 20,659 in 2000-2001—a nearly 300% increase. For example, in the communities of Lexington and Schuyler, Latino children constitute 64% and 65% respectively in these school districts.[6] If we narrow the focus only to the elementary-level (grades K-6),then the numbers and percentages are even more pronounced. Lexington again is illustrative. According to School Superintendent Dick Eisenhauer, 80% of the children enrolled in Kindergarten in 2002 were Hispanic.[7] It is this second generation that will shape the future character of these communities.

Diversity within the Latino Population

An additional dimension to the growing Hispanic/Latino population in Nebraska is the group's increasing diversity based on country of origin. Table 4

illustrates the diverse number of countries from which the Latino population orig-
inates. Historically, immigrants of Mexican origin have constituted the largest
part of the Latino population, and clearly they remain the majority of Nebraska's
Hispanic/Latino population (75.2%). Nonetheless, the figures from the 2000
Census indicate a sizeable increase in the "Other Hispanic or Latino" category,

TABLE 4. Hispanic or Latino Origin for Nebraska, 2000

	Number	Percent
TOTAL POPULATION	1,711,263	100.0
Not Hispanic or Latino	1,616,838	94.5
Hispanic or Latino (of any race)	94,425	5.5
HISPANIC OR LATINO BY TYPE	94,425	100.0
Mexican	71,030	75.2
Puerto Rican	1,993	2.1
Cuban	859	0.9
Other Hispanic or Latino	20,543	21.8
Dominican (Dominican Republic)	129	0.1
Central American (excludes Mexican)	5,270	5.6
Costa Rican	67	0.1
Guatemalan	2,508	2.7
Honduran	476	0.5
Nicaraguan	116	0.1
Panamanian	232	0.2
Salvadoran	1,626	1.7
Other Central American	245	0.3
South American	1,197	1.3
Argentinean	79	0.1
Bolivian	47	—
Chilean	130	0.1
Colombian	397	0.4
Ecuadorian	77	0.1
Paraguayan	9	—
Peruvian	241	0.3
Uruguayan	7	—
Venezuelan	157	0.2
Other South American	53	0.1
Spaniard	180	0.2
All Other Hispanic or Latino	13,767	14.6

Source: U.S. Census Bureau, Census 2000, Summary File 1 and unpublished data. Internet Release Date: October 22, 2001.

which now comprises almost 22% of the state's Hispanic/Latino population. In Nebraska, foreign-born immigrants from Central and South America, together with their U.S. children, the so-called "immigrant-stock" population, make up the bulk of the new Latino population. According to the 2000 Census, there are 39,991 Nebraska foreign-born from Latin America, or about 42% of the total Hispanic population. Census 2000 data on the number of Nebraska children born to Latino immigrant parents are not yet available. However, it is safe to say that they will elevate the percentage of immigrant-stock Latinos considerably above those who consider themselves third- or fourth-generation Latinos or, for that matter, pioneer Hispanic (primarily Mexican) settlers of the United States. This contrasts sharply with 1990 when only about 16% percent of the Latino population was foreign-born. Mirroring national trends, in 1990, the majority of Nebraska's foreign-born came from Europe (about 38%) and only 22% came from Latin America; today nearly 54% come from Latin America and only 14.5% come from Europe. Asians are the second-largest foreign-born population, with 25.7%. Positive international migration actually offset the state's negative domestic in-migration in recent years. The majority of these new immigrants are also young and thus important replenishments to the state's dwindling workforce.[8]

Re-Populating Rural Communities

A final point about the demographic shift that has occurred in the last ten years has to do with the large number of Latinos who have settled in Nebraska's rural counties and small towns between 1990 and today. Nearly half of the total Hispanic/Latino population as enumerated by the 2000 Census today lives in communities of less than 25,000 people, and new Latino immigrants have settled primarily in non-metropolitan counties. As Tables 1 and 2 indicate, Hispanic population growth in these counties far outpaced that of metropolitan counties. Latinos have settled, not in the smallest, but in the mid-size communities of these non-metropolitan counties (those with cities of at least 8,000 population), where meatpacking plants and other immigrant labor-dependent industries have also relocated or expanded.[9] Not surprisingly, as we will discuss later, it is from these cities that we obtained the largest number of survey responses, attesting perhaps to their heightened awareness about the presence of immigrants and the need to positively integrate this newcomer population.

Socio-Economic Indicators of Integration

Unfortunately, much of the data necessary to construct a complete and accurate socio-economic profile of Latino newcomers are not readily available. We have made an effort to define or infer additional characteristics of the Latino old timer and newcomer populations from published research and other data sources. Nor is it always possible to differentiate clearly between older generations and more recent arrivals. Subsequent Census 2000 releases and analyses will make significant contributions to filling this data void. We will be producing additional publications based on such releases and additional research.

Despite these difficulties, we are confident that the following trends accurately reflect key socio-economic characteristics of the Latino population. Interpreted against the backdrop of the national research findings outlined earlier, these trends contain ample warning signs of the barriers newcomers may confront as they proceed in their journey to successful adaptation. They also reveal potential sources of knowledge and skills, which, through enlightened policies, can be deployed in the service of this integration process and the citizens of Nebraska as a whole.

- *Old timers' Socio-economic Status and Social Capital.* Census data suggest that, not unlike today and despite high rates of labor force participation, Latino old timers in Nebraska have tended to concentrate in "blue collar" jobs, have higher poverty rates, lower rates of home ownership, and lower median incomes than non-Latino whites. In 1990, half as many Latinos as non-Latino whites had completed college degrees.[10] Nevertheless, there is a visible, though relatively small, middle class of Latino old timers made up of professionals who have completed some college (about an equal number of Latinos and non-Latino whites had completed associates degrees in 1990). Latinos in Nebraska also slightly surpassed the national average for Latinos with a college degree. Finally, this population has maintained strong ties to its historic, primarily Mexican, roots and a strong sense of collective responsibility and community solidarity.[11] This speaks well for the social capital contained in the larger Latino community and thus for newcomers' chances for positive integration.
- *Employment and Newcomers.* Nebraska in general suffers from a deficit of middle and higher-wage jobs. Wages and benefits in industries such as meatpacking or construction, where Latino newcomers are heavily represented, are insufficient springboards toward meaningful economic advancement. Our research, for example, as well as periodic industry reports, has consistently shown that these newcomers typically make up between 50 and 80 percent of a meatpacking plant's labor force (Gouveia and Saenz 2000). While working conditions and wage scales may vary from locality to local-

ity, industry to industry, and even from plant to plant, there is little doubt that Latinos in Nebraska, particularly newcomers, are heavily represented in the bottommost jobs. Not unlike what research at the national level shows, many of these workers view self-employment as their best chance to achieve some semblance of the American Dream. Newcomers have revitalized downtowns in communities where they are settling. However, institutional efforts to support this entrepreneurial drive appear to be rather minimal.[12]

• *Education and the Children of Immigrants.* Latino high-school students' dropout rates far exceed the state's average. From 1993 to 1999, an average of 7.9 Latino students enrolled in grades 7 to 12 quit each year, compared to an average of 2.8 in the overall student body. There are initial signs of a downward trend in Latino dropout rates. Latino enrollment in Nebraska universities continues to lag far behind the state's average. We need to learn more about the factors that propel or impede these positive changes (theIndependent.com 2000).

• *Immigration and Social Policies.* In today's political climate, policies often promote exclusion and isolation rather than inclusion and integration. Particularly problematic are the multiplication of barriers to legalization of newcomers and policies blocking access of undocumented children to higher education.[13] Also counterproductive are policies denying newcomers access to minimum types of governmental assistance required to complement low wages and improve newcomers' opportunities for economic advancement. Among other issues, Latino newcomers lack sufficient access to unemployment and medical benefits, health, mental health and child care (Fix and Zimmermann 2000, Blankenau et al. 2000, Saint Francis Medical Center 2000).[14]

• *Newcomers' social capital.* There is evidence of abundant social capital and family solidarity within the new immigrant community. This ranges from informal credit mechanisms to establish businesses and purchase homes, to the provision of services such as child-care, translation, transportation, tax preparations, instilling strong cultural values in community children, healing the sick or burying the dead (Gouveia and Sanchez 2000). However, communities with large numbers of politically-vulnerable and below-poverty individuals often lack sufficient social capital to cancel out the negative effects of exclusionary immigration policies, segregation, racism, and institutional barriers to academic achievement (Portes and Rumbaut 2001).

• *Citizenship.* Nationally, The INS naturalized nearly 840,000 individuals in fiscal year 1999; this represents an increase of 81 percent over naturalization rates in 1998, which the INS attributes to improvements in application processes. In Nebraska, naturalization rates vary widely from year to year, with the highest rates reported during 1993, 1994, and 1995, when more than 11,500 individuals became naturalized. For 1999, the latest year for which data is available, 407 individuals became naturalized, most of them from the Philippines. Media reports and field research observations suggest Latinos' naturalization rates have climbed significantly during the last three years, as some of these immigrant streams reach maturity and services at the local INS office also improve.[15] We will be tracking this information in future publications.

- *English Language Proficiency and Bilingualism.* As expected, new immigrant adults have a lower level of English language proficiency than their children. However, many adult immigrants acquire at least a functional knowledge of English after a few years of being in the United States.[16] Census 2000 figures show that the share of individuals who speak English less than very well has increased from 1.5% to 4%. In communities such as Schuyler, where Latino population growth reached beyond 1,000%, nearly 20% of the population speaks English less than very well. Tearing down barriers to English language acquisition, while fostering true bilingualism, is critical to positive integration trajectories.

- *Housing Tenure and Neighborhood Segregation.* Census 2000 shows that 46% of Latinos in Nebraska own their own home, when compared to 67% of the total Nebraska population. Rates vary from community to community, with the highest rates found among historic Latino settlers in a county such as Scottsbluff (57%, or about 8% below the county's rate), and even Dawson (52%), to those where large numbers of newcomers can be found, such as Douglas or Colfax counties where home ownership rates are much lower (42% and 44% respectively). Latinos are highly concentrated in low-income neighborhoods in cities such as Omaha.[17] However, initial reviews of census data suggest that Latinos' residential patterns in the same city are beginning to resemble those of older European immigrants, slowly expanding from the southeastern to the southwestern part of Omaha.

- *Latino-Owned Businesses.* Mirroring national trends, Latin-owned businesses in Nebraska have increased dramatically in the last years. According to the 1997 Economic Census, the latest data available for minority-owned businesses, the number of Hispanic-owned businesses in the state was slightly below Black-owned businesses (1437 and 1565 respectively). Latino businesses also generated a higher number of "Sales and Receipts" and employed a larger number of workers than Black-owned businesses (US Census 1997).

• *Racism and Discrimination.* Reports of community tensions and cultural conflicts vary from community to community, although some common trends are also evident. Communities with no recent history of multi-cultural immigration, or where such history reveals patterns of past discrimination, are likely to be poorer contexts of reception than those deviating from these patterns (Gouveia and Sánchez 2002). For example, a recent survey conducted among newcomers by Saint Francis Hospital in Grand Island revealed that more than 60% of respondents felt racism was an obstacle to obtaining adequate health Care.[18]

Summary

Nebraska's Latino population growth outpaced that of neighboring states. Their presence in urban as well as non-metropolitan counties has contributed to a reversal in population decline evident in the 1990 census. A significant number of these Latino newcomers have settled in rural communities, largely as a result of meat-packing recruitment efforts. While the majority of Latinos still trace their roots to Mexico, an increasing number now come from Central and South America.

One of the most urgent questions various experts and community leaders are now asking is whether those communities benefiting from the arrival of Latino newcomers will be able to retain this population in years to come.[19] This is especially the case for rural communities where young people as a whole often find few opportunities for economic advancement.[20] For Latinos and other minorities, the challenge may be even more serious and dependent not only on economic opportunities, but also on the local community's reception to cultural and ethnic/racial diversity. Despite their tendency to put down roots in their local communities and stay close to home, Latino youth are not impervious to the same forces affecting non-Latino youths. Comparisons from the 1980 and 1990 censuses, for example, reveal that in the aftermath of the farm crisis of the early 1980s, young and educated Hispanics left small towns like Lexington at similar or even higher rates than non-Hispanics. Their permanence in these non-metropolitan counties in the future is not to be taken for granted. Their exodus could totally devastate rural communities that have recently prospered.[21]

The benefits of this demographic shift to urban areas are just as contingent. Here, the issue may not be so much whether the next generation of Latinos will stay, but whether the local socio-economic, educational, and cultural context in which they assimilate will foster a positive process of incorporation or downward mobility and integration into the lower tiers of society. Powerful research findings, as well as common sense, compel us to understand that whether or not this demographic shift becomes an asset is highly dependent on the capacity of our institutions and leaders to creatively harness the skills, cultural richness, and energy contained within these new communities of labor. Failure to do so will constitute an enormous loss of opportunity by the state and a predictably stormy future. The indicators outlined in this section provide initial warning, as well as hopeful signs with regard to newcomers' chances for successful integration.

This brief and necessarily incomplete review of Latino old timers and newcomers socio-economic conditions reveals a mixed picture with regard to Latinos' past successes in, and future chances for, overcoming negative contexts of reception and achieving successful integration. Latino old timers in Nebraska lag behind on a series of socio-economic measures when compared to the state's averages. However, they often do better than Latinos in other parts of the country. The challenge for us will be to achieve an even greater understanding of those unique characteristics of Nebraska's context of reception that both impede and facilitate successful integration. The challenge for policy makers and community leaders will be to enhance these reservoirs of old timer and newcomer social and human capital. The state's future hinges largely on our capacity to construct a welcoming environment for newcomers and spaces for mutual understanding and communication among old timers and newcomers. Our survey and focus groups, which we analyze in the next two sections, disclose a growing recognition across all segments of Nebraska society and its institutions, that newcomers are indeed a major economic asset, as well as important contributors to the enrichment of cultural and family values that are held dear by older and newer residents of the state alike.

MAIL QUESTIONNAIRE SURVEY

Methods

We selected communities where Hispanic/Latino settlements have existed for a long time, as well as those communities whose Latino population has been a more recent phenomenon. First, we utilized 1990 and 2000 Census figures to discover those cities that had the largest absolute numbers of Hispanics/Latinos according to the 2000 figures, and, second, those cities that had experienced the largest percentage growth between 1990 and 2000. In the case of some communities, their overall population might have been quite smaller, but proportionately their Hispanic/Latino population growth was greater than many of the larger cities. As a result, we came up with a list of 54 communities that met one or both of these criteria for inclusion.

We constructed a survey instrument that would not take so great an amount of time to fill out so that agency/organization representatives would not participate, but, at the same time, the survey would provide us with enough useful information for a meaningful investigation of the integration of the immigrant workforce. The survey was sent to 1173 agencies/organizations in 54 communities, and we had 81 returned for inadequate addresses or the organizations were no longer in existence. We sent follow-up reminder postcards as well as made follow-up telephone calls. Finally, we ended up receiving 237 responses. After adjusting for duplicates and agencies no longer in existence, the response rate was approximately 25 percent. This is within the margins of acceptable response rates for mailed questionnaires, although lower than we had hoped.

Community Size and Types of Agencies/Organizations

We wanted to ensure adequate representation from agencies in a wide variety of communities and, therefore, we established the following categories according to population size: less than 2,500; 2,500–9,999; 10,000–24,999; 25,000–49,9991; and 50,000 or larger. Figure 1 (see below) shows the agencies/organizations that completed our survey, according to the size of their community. Of the 237 responses, agencies in cities in the 2,500–9,999 range represented almost 28% of the total respondents, followed by 22% of the responses coming from cities 10,000–24,999. Overall, 72% of the responses came from agencies/organizations with populations of less than 25,000.

We grouped our agencies/organizations into the following eight categories: schools/education, city/state government, justice/law enforcement, economic/business, churches/civic organizations, human/social services, media and a resid-

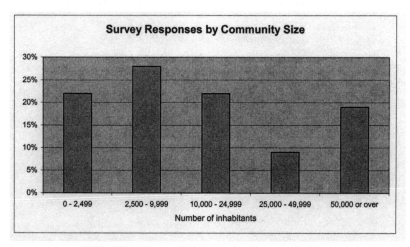

FIGURE 1. Survey Responses by Community Size

ual "other" category. Figure 2 indicates the breakdown from those who responded. Clearly, school/education agencies were the largest group of respondents, comprising 30% of the respondents, followed by churches/civic organizations (18%), human/social service agencies (14%) and city/state government (13%).

Latino-serving agencies and employers of Latinos

As part of our study we were interested in looking at what agencies/organizations were primary service providers for Latinos and what proportion of these same agencies were employers of Latinos in their workplace. Of the 237 respondents, 110 of the agencies (approximately 46%) served Latinos in some capacity. Also, 73% (174) of the total number of agencies employed Latinos either as full-time or part-time employees. When looking at the issue of whether or not those who provide services for Latinos also employed them, we constructed the following table:

The results indicate that 75% of these service providers have workforces of which Latinos comprise less than 10% of their employees. Only 8 of these agencies (7%) indicated that Latinos make up more than 50% of their workforce populations. Unfortunately we did not have available the total number of people served by these service providers so as to be able to calculate the percentage of Latinos served and compare it with the percentage of Latinos employed. Nevertheless, it is important to continue to assess the connection between service providers and employers. If real integration is to take place, then employment of

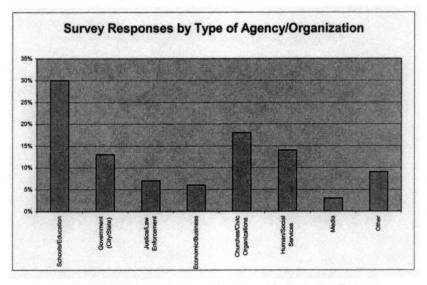

FIGURE 2. Survey Responses by Agency/Organization Type

TABLE 5. Percentage of Latino Employees by Latino-Serving Agencies

Latinos Served Monthly	Percentage of Latino Employees					
	>10%	11–25%	26–50%	51–75%	<75%	Total
1–10	23	1				24
11–25	14	1	1			16
26–50	9	1			1	11
51–100	9			1		10
More than 100	28	11	4		6	49
Total	83	14	5	1	7	110

Latinos should increase, particularly in those businesses that provide services to the Latino population.

Hispanic/Latino Immigrants as Community Assets

We felt it was important to see whether or not agencies/organizations view Hispanic/Latino immigrants as contributors or potential contributors to their respective communities. In order to address this issue we asked the following question—"What are the three greatest assets Hispanic/Latino immigrants bring to your community?" When looking at the greatest strengths Latino immigrants bring to their communities, we found the following trends as reflected below in Figure 3:

- Responses related to labor/work ethic contributions, cultural enrichment of the community, and the strength of family and religious values were the most frequently mentioned assets.
- Labor/work ethic contributions and cultural diversity/enrichment were consistently the top two answers, thereby highlighting the real and potential economic contributions these immigrants make, while at the same time recognizing the cultural richness the newcomers bring to the community.
- Another dimension of culture was also a part of the third most frequently mentioned set of assets—strong religious and family values.

When analyzed by organizational type, differences were found between types of agencies (see Figure 4). For example, forty-six percent of the school/education organizations answering this question mentioned as the major asset various factors which we grouped under a category called **"Rich Culture/Diversity."** Thirty four percent referred to **"Labor/Work Ethic"** as the second most important asset. Twenty percent (20%) mentioned as an additional asset, those related to **"Religiosity/Family Values."** Law enforcement agencies also exhibited a similar

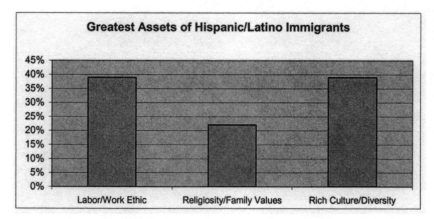

Figure 3. Greatest Assets of Hispanic/Latino Immigrants

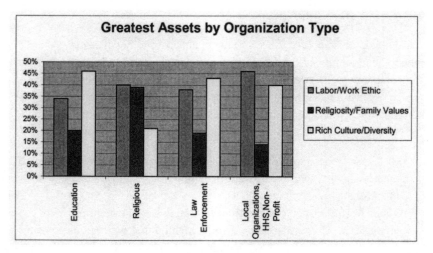

FIGURE 4. Greatest Assets by Organization Type

ranking order. However, local organizations, including health and human services and non-profit organizations, demonstrated a slightly different ranking pattern with labor/work ethic listed first followed by rich culture/diversity and then religiosity/family values. We found that religious organizations ranked religiosity/family values and labor/work ethic equally, followed by rich culture/ diversity.

Respondents often elaborated on what they meant by these various answers. For example, the contributions of newcomers to the workforce were not perceived by respondents as being simply a numerical contribution. Instead, they stressed newcomers' strong work ethic and used adjectives such as "industrious," and "reliable." Moreover, these workers' economic contribution was not viewed as one that was confined to providing a much needed workforce, but also as consumers and energetic entrepreneurs and professionals who revitalized downtowns and brought new enthusiasm to their organizations.

Challenges and Barriers to Integration

As part of our interview we asked, "What are the three greatest challenges Hispanic/Latino immigrants pose to your community?" This particular question assesses more directly the issue of barriers to integration. The responses revealed the following trends:

• Across all agencies, the most commonly mentioned barriers to integration had to do with language, cultural conflicts/racism, and lack of assimilation and understanding the law (See Figure 5). There are, however, differences between these various groups of organizations, which are discussed below in more detail in Table 6.

As would be expected, when categorized according to organizational types (see Table 6), there were some important differences which seem to derive from differences in the types of problems, barriers, issues with which each of these

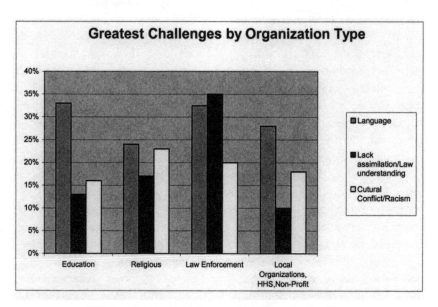

FIGURE 5. Greatest Challenges by Organization Type

TABLE 6. Greatest Challenges by Organization Type

| Organization

Challenges | Education | Religious | Law
Enforcement | Local
Organizations,
HHS, Non-Profit |
|---|---|---|---|---|
| Language | 33% | 24% | 32.5% | 28% |
| Lack assimilation/
Law understanding | 13% | 17% | 35% | 10% |
| Cultural Conflict/Racism | 16% | 23% | 20% | 18% |
| Poor jobs/Low wages | 12% | 9% | 2.5% | 9% |
| Education/Training needs | 13% | 8% | 2.5% | 11% |
| Basic Needs | 11% | 11% | 5% | 14% |
| Lack of access to legal
status and advice | 2% | 8% | 2.5% | 10% |

organizations is most likely to encounter in their daily work. The ability to view a combination of answers across all organizational types allows us to capture the multi-dimensional and reinforcing nature of these barriers. Language was by far the most common response across educational organizations (33%), religious organizations (24%) and local organizations, HHS and non-profit agencies (28%). Each of these organizations also ranked cultural conflicts/racism as the second major challenge to integrating Latino immigrants into the community. In the case of law enforcement agencies, they saw lack of assimilation/under-standing of the law as the greatest barrier, followed closely by language issues and then cultural conflicts/racism as a distant third. However, while lack of assimilation and knowledge of laws and community norms were the next most important responses for law enforcement agencies (35%), only 17% of religious organizations and only 13% and 10% of education and local government and non-profit organizations respectively thought these were a serious barrier to integration. Finally, in varying degrees of importance, all of the organizations also highlighted poor jobs/low wages, the need for education and training, basic needs for housing, health and transportation, and lack of access to legal status and advice as potential barriers for the integration of Latino immigrants.

Here a word about language barriers is in order. Language is a much more complex variable than it appears on the surface, although not in surprising ways. Language provides an important entry point for communication with and inte-gration of Latino newcomers. When analyzing the various ways in which respondents mentioned this barrier, a split of sorts becomes obvious between those who place the burden of responsibility for this barrier squarely on the shoulders of Latinos who "refuse to learn English" and those who view it as a two-way communication issue where the burden is shared by the newcomers themselves and community members and agencies/organizations alike. Those who viewed language as a two-way process tended to stress barriers, such as excessive work hours or lack of transportation and easy access to ESL classes, as the true barriers to English language proficiency. Additionally, respondents in social agencies as well as private organizations stressed the serious lack of bilingual and bicultural staff and leaders as very serious barriers to integration. Bilingualism was valued by many as a much needed skill, not a luxury, to be possessed by all and, as one respondent noted, "We should all learn Spanish."

Community Success at Integration of Latino Immigrants

In a separate question we asked respondents to "circle the response that over-all best reflects, in your opinion, *the success your community has had in inte-grating Hispanic/Latino immigrants into your community*: 'Very successful,' 'Successful,' 'Unsuccessful,' or 'Very Unsuccessful.'"

Although 26% feel their communities have been unsuccessful in their inte-gration efforts, an overwhelming 65% of the respondents feel their communities have been "successful" in integrating Latino immigrants. Very few respondents felt that their efforts had been either very successful (3%) or very unsuccessful (3%). The combination of very successful and successful (68%) establishes a strong base of support for future integration efforts.

When looking at this answer by type of organization (see Table 7), sixty-four percent (64%) of the education/school organization respondents that answered this question, for example, agreed that their communities had been successful and, in a few of those cases (3%), very successful in facilitating the integration of newcomers. Local organizations, health and human service agencies, and non-profits also reflected a similar pattern of responses, although indicating slightly higher percentage for the unsuccessful category. While religious orga-nizations had the highest percentage for unsuccessful (33%), they also had the strongest indication for very successful at 17%. In the case of law enforcement, the responses were either strongly in support of successful (73%) or unsuccess-ful (27%). Law enforcement agencies did not feel that community efforts at integration had been either very successful or very unsuccessful.

Optimism for Agency Contributions to Latino Integration

We wanted to see how respondents felt about the future role their own agen-cies will play in the integration of Latino newcomers. As a result, we asked respondents: "Overall, are you optimistic or pessimistic about your agency's

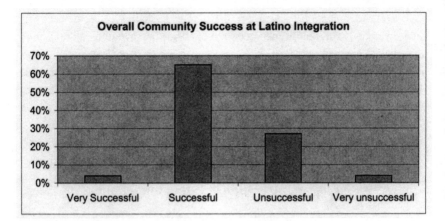

FIGURE 6. Community Success at Latino Integration

TABLE 7. Community Success at Integration by Organization Type

Organization Challenges	Education	Religious	Law Enforcement	Local Organizations, HHS, Non-Profit
Very Successful	3%	17%		3%
Successful	64%	44%	73%	64%
Unsuccessful	19%	33%	27%	32%
Very unsuccessful	3%	6%		1%

*Education does not equal 100% because several respondents indicated answers that were between two of the four categories listed.

contribution to the positive integration of Hispanic/Latino immigrants in your community?"

As shown in Figure 7, when respondents were taking into consideration their own agency's role in the integration of this workforce, they demonstrated a strong inclination for being either optimistic (59%) or very optimistic (27%). Only fourteen percent of the respondents were pessimistic (11%) or very pessimistic (3%) about the role their agency will provide in integration efforts. Ninety-one percent of the schools that answered this question said they were "optimistic" or "very optimistic."

Optimism and City Size

This overall strong feeling of being optimistic and/or very optimistic was also evident when looking at city size and overall optimism. Table 8 illustrates the distribution of overall optimism by city size.

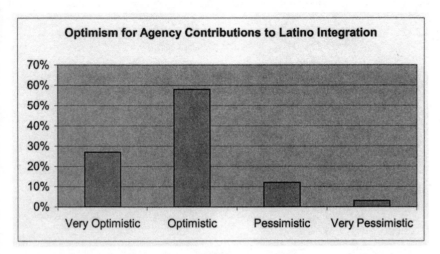

FIGURE 7. Optimism for Agency Contributions to Latino Integration

It is clear that for many communities, especially those ranging from 1,000–10,000 in size, a cautious optimism remains. These agencies recognize the kinds of changes taking place in their communities and are optimistic, but also recognize the resistance from some community members to achieve the constructive outcomes that can result from the positive integration of the immigrant workforce population.

A small rural county agency representative expressed this gained wisdom as her reason for being optimistic in this way: "I have been in this community for 15 years. Looking back where we started, I've seen tremendous gains; they just didn't happen overnight. There is still a lot of work to be done."

Summary

A preliminary conclusion can be drawn from an analysis of the mail questionnaire responses. To some extent, organizations closer to the plight of newcomers as workers and families trying to improve their lives, are more likely to focus on institutional and social-context barriers to integration, while agencies such as local, state and federal law enforcement groups are somewhat more likely to locate the barriers to integration within the immigrant community itself. Lack of information provided in culturally appropriate and accessible formats, less than welcoming attitudes by some of their social agency co-workers, and problematic immigration laws, are the types of answers that resonated among the former rather than the latter organizational types.

However, this was not a perfect relationship. It is interesting to note, for

TABLE 8. Overall Optimism By City Size

City Size	Overall Optimism				
	Very Pessimistic	Pessimistic	Optimistic	Very Optimistic	Total
0–999		1	4	1	6
1,000–2,499	2	7	11	7	27
2,500–9,999	3	7	29	6	45
10,000–24,999		3	28	15	46
25,000–49,999		2	9	8	19
50,000–99,999			1		1
100,000 or more	1	1	24	11	37
Total	6	21	106	48	181

example, that intolerant, racist, and prejudicial attitudes found among older residents were a source of concern across organizational types, including law enforcement agencies. As one law enforcement respondent put it, "the racist actions of others" in the community preclude a smooth incorporation of newcomers. Answers given by some religious organizations were equally revealing. While at times adopting a paternalistic tone toward newcomers and focusing primarily on what they viewed as cultural deficiencies of this population (e.g., their "disregard for the laws and community norms"), a significant number of respondents also spoke of their frustration with their older congregations' lack of acceptance, and respect for the Hispanic/Latino population. As one respondent put it, "Many/most of the members with power in the church don't want them in our congregation."

Moreover, as we try to make sense of the combined answers about assets and challenges, some seemingly paradoxical trends are revealed and require further analysis. As suggested earlier, an overwhelming number of respondents presented a very positive picture of the Latino workers and families and of their contributions to their communities. "These are good people" was a typical characterization. Yet, the question on challenges at times seemed to emphasize a contradictory set of less positive traits found among this same Latino or newcomer population. We believe, based not only on survey by focus group responses discussed later, that there is a logical way to reconcile these seemingly schizophrenic views about newcomers. Respondents seem to be making a distinction between what they see are two very different segments of the newcomer population—not unlike the kinds of distinctions many of us make about the population as a whole. The first and largest segment by far is being conceived as the core of the newcomer population, characterized by its strong work ethic and family values. The second, and much smaller segment, is characterized as those in the periphery of this larger segment and is composed by the minority who violate norms, participate in some criminal activity, or exhibit behavioral problems at school.

Moreover, as mentioned earlier, many respondents argue that this segmented process of integration is at least partly driven by the institutional barriers to communication, learning, access to legal documents, poverty and isolation. It is in the focus group discussions where these more nuanced community analyses of the barriers to integration and their multiple and confounding impacts become clearer.

FOCUS GROUPS

Methods

We conducted a total of six focus groups in three different metropolitan and non-metropolitan communities. The selection was guided by our advanced knowledge of these communities and issues we wished to explore in each of them. The groups were composed of either Latino newcomers to the state, agency representatives or a combination of both. A list of open-ended questions was distributed to participants at the start of the meeting. The questions required that participants think about the major economic, social and political issues confronting the Latino newcomer and immigrant population and the community.

Results

The following is a brief overview of some of the major barriers to integration highlighted during focus group sessions. We illustrate these themes with selective testimonies offered by various participants.

Poverty, Working Conditions, and Safety Nets

The mutually reinforcing barriers of poor work conditions, poverty, precarious employment and legal status were underscored in all of our focus groups. The quote below is representative of their comments:

This [the immigrant community] is a very unstable community. The main reason is their economic situation. Maybe their jobs are new and they cannot pay the deposit, or the husband lost his job. They don't have a safety net that can help them get back on their feet. Or they are stuck in a low-wage job because they are not able to adjust their legal status or don't speak English. The families are young and are having children, the husband gets injured in a job and they have no health insurance, usually because they don't think they can afford it or even be eligible for it. . . . They often don't qualify for benefits from the county or state help or this is simply not sufficient. . . . All these health issues we see everyday are related to poverty. . . . I think they just need an opportunity to start, get a job, have some money, and they will prosper from there.

Participants often connected these concerns directly with the negative impact these socio-economic conditions will have on their children, the second generation. An issue that received significant attention was the link between these conditions and the loss of parental supervision and involvement in their children's lives, as well as the erosion of parental authority. This situation can in turn lead to "dissonant" or negative modes of incorporation:

All this vacuum is caused by their parents needing to work, because salaries are low, parents cannot sit together with their children, they do not have time, they are working two jobs, sometimes they are ill . . . their parents cannot be there for them.

Latino newcomers reiterated old complaints about working conditions, line speeds, and treatment by supervisors in meatpacking plants and other places of employment, such as local restaurants. During a focus group conducted with thirty Latino workers, the view that the Governor's Meatpacking Workers' Bill of Rights is routinely ignored by employers was widely held:

What happens is that what it says out there [on the Bill posted outside the working area] *is not followed inside. They don't even let us go to the bathroom. One asks for permission to go and they don't let us, and it is difficult because sometimes comes a point when you almost want to go right there, standing up.*

In a prominent meatpacking town, a group of Latino and non-Latino professionals agreed that, while these jobs can be a good start for many newcomers, some of the problematic practices connected with this industry die hard, especially when it comes to the way management tends to deal with injuries and other worker grievances:

I could say that at this table there is no one who does not know someone personally who has been injured [at the meatpacking plant] *and who has not gotten a fair treatment.*

Education and Training

Focus group participants across the state overwhelmingly agreed that one of the most critical needs the state and federal governments must address is that of facilitating college entry and adjustment of legal status for a large number of students who are undocumented and yet comprise a critical component of Nebraska's dwindling and future labor force.

A teacher illustrated this issue well:

One of my students right now, he's going to graduate this coming May . . . Since Kindergarten he has had straight A's. He's too much brain for the school he's in and the teachers recognize that. He wants to go to school, [college] but he's not legal.

One mother expressed her dilemma this way:

My children are eight and six years old. The oldest has no papers and the youngest was born in the U.S. We are very thankful about the fact that our children have access to free public education until the twelfth grade. But at the same time that one pushes our kids to get an education and aspire to a professional career, we know that at the end of the road everything stops because they have no papers and no social security. We work from sun up to sun down hoping that our children will have a better life. But we have no way to get legal papers so they can do so. Today I got the reports from my eight year old. He got the honors band and he was so excited about having earned the honor to have lunch with the principal. It breaks my heart when I think that some day soon I will have to tell him, "No more education." We contribute a lot to the economy of this state. This is not fair.

An INS representative in the focus group shared the following legal opinion:

The Supreme Court has ruled that any child can go to school and then, in terms of college, a lot of times you hear colleges saying they don't want to take the responsibility. Well, that's baloney. If they want to give the kid a full ride, then they can give him a full ride.

Community agency representatives also expressed concerns about adult newcomers' limited access to language classes, vocational training and opportunities to pursue or complete their higher education. They spoke at length about the absence of mechanisms to accept or validate professional degrees earned in native countries in areas such as teaching, medical fields, and business.

A school administrator provided one among numerous examples:

We need teachers to be role models. We need to grow our own bilingual staff members, we know two or three women who have quite a bit of education, who could be wonderful teachers . . . we need to support them . . . these people are not in the position to drop everything and go to school. We have to find some flexible way to bring the programs to them and to be able to utilize the education they bring with them.

A worker expresses the same issue from the vantage point of a newcomer:

I was a teacher in Mexico, but here I am nothing.

Finally, every focus group yielded concerns about the economic and social barriers inhibiting parents' involvement in their children's schools and educational progress:

[Women think] *"I have to work, I have to clean the house, I have to take care of my kids . . ." They do all that and they don't feel they have time to go to their child's school; and, again, it is always the mothers the ones that have to go to school and get involved, and she is the one also that takes care of the family.*

A local pastor pondered the long-term impacts of these barriers to parental involvement:

The most affected are the children, you know. They reflect the family problems. Some of them have very low levels of self-esteem. Parents don't have time because they are working two, sometimes three, jobs a day. . . .

Leadership and Community Involvement

The theme of the need for Latino role models was commonly expressed as a call, by Latino and non-Latino participants alike, for a more equitable inclusion of newcomer and old timer Latino residents in positions of leadership as well as in leadership training programs. Work schedules, language, lack of transportation, limited efforts or creativity on the part of local institutions or policies were some of the perceived barriers that community participants identified.

Language Barriers

Language barriers, figured prominently among all of our focus group responses. Participants expressed their view of language barriers not solely as the absence of English language skills among newcomers but, more generally, as a communication problem. This problem, most of them believed, was also exacerbated by a serious shortage of bilingual translators, reluctance among some old timers to even consider gaining some functional knowledge of a second language, or make any real effort to communicate with newcomers.

The sound of a foreign language seems to elicit irrational fears among some community members. A U.S.-born Latina was told by a neighbor, while shopping in a supermarket where Spanish-speaking shoppers could be overheard:

I hate Hispanics. "So you hate me?" [asked the Latina neighbor] *Oh no, you are different, you speak English.*

Lack of transportation and child care, as well as excessive work hours and double shifts, were mentioned as barriers to community integration in their own right and to newcomers' participation in English as a Second Language (ESL) classes. Women appear particularly disadvantaged by these structural barriers. In addition, ESL teachers often reported that husbands are sometimes reluctant to let their wives attend classes because they feel that they interfere with their home and child care responsibilities.

A former ESL teacher expressed widely known problems among Latino community members and agency representatives:

One of the things I saw were the barriers for people that came to the room, even though it [class] *was free, is that classes were at times when people were working, and the other problem was for a lot of the women—it was mostly women who took these classes—their husbands did not approve of them leaving the house. And, second of all, it was a child care issue—because we didn't provide child care and they were not allowed to bring their children.*

On the other hand, local community representatives report that ESL classes are constantly full and there are waiting lists in some cases. However, ESL teachers also told us that newcomers tend to get discouraged after realizing these classes are not accelerated language programs. "They just stop coming; time is extremely costly and valuable to them," said one teacher. Community representatives concur in their views that, more often than not, ESL classes lack standardization, consistent curriculum, qualified staff, and are not equipped to provide students with English-language skills beyond relatively elementary levels.[22] Latino workers in the focus groups expressed their frustration in this manner:

Let's accept the fact that there may be people who don't want to learn English; but there are many more who do because they want to improve their lives. Because, after all, that's why we came, to improve our lives. . . . English is not an easy language; experts say it takes about ten years to learn English. Precisely because we don't speak English, we have to take the hardest jobs, then many times it becomes physically impossible to study after such hard work all day. That is one of the most difficult things.

A proposed solution, echoed by Latino and non-Latino focus group participants, was that employers who recruit and rely heavily on large number of immigrant workers, be encouraged or required to offer English classes during working hours as an expected component of employee training.

Health

Lack of health, particularly mental health, services was a major concern of social service agency participants. The problem is particularly serious in nonmetropolitan or smaller communities. Participants explained this as a consequence of the same combination of mutually reinforcing barriers alluded to previously, and a problem that ranged from sheer absence of services to a lack of bilingual and culturally-sensitive staff.

Housing

The lack of adequate housing was particularly salient in the metropolitan area focus groups, although it is a theme that emerged in non-metropolitan community focus groups as well.

A church Pastor expressed what is now common knowledge in his metropolitan community:

There is too much exploitation. There are not lots of housing facilities. Others live in very bad conditions. Some have difficulty maintaining the apartment in good condition and the landlords do not help them. If the heating breaks down, well their solution is that they should buy a small, personal [space] heater. So they are paying for these expensive apartments that are in very bad conditions.

Assimilation and Successful Integration

Very few focus group participants wondered out loud about the "assimilation-ability" of newcomers. In fact, most seemed to take for granted that these workers and their families came to try to make a better life and the rest would come in time. However, their comments suggested the same concerns, captured in literature about assimilation, about the dangers of segmented assimilation and the fact that fast-paced assimilation and the simultaneous loss of their historical culture does not necessarily equal successful integration.

A social agency director's quote best captured this concern:

I think that we will have two layers. One are the kids that become successful, that get their high school and college degrees and become medium-size business owners. And the other will be those kids who get into the system [become assimilated] but are not able to make it because of social and economic situations.

A second agency director continues this thought process thus:

However, those who get into the system are losing their cultural connection, their cultural values. Their parents want them to become Americanized, to speak English without an accent . . . so these kids become "American," but that does not necessarily make them successful. They end up assimilating into all these material values and want new and expensive shoes and other things their parents cannot afford. They become frustrated and have no system in place or their own cultural values they have now rejected to protect them.

The loss of cultural values and their native language was mentioned, as it is in the research literature, as leading to the loss of parental authority and family cohesion which can in turn direct children toward the destructive route of segmented or dissonant assimilation. It is this process that scholars refer to as "downward" as opposed to "upward" assimilation.

Racism and Cultural Separateness

Problems of community prejudice and cultural tensions were mentioned in each of our focus groups. In some cases, they ranked at the top of participants' barriers to integration, while in others racism was second to other issues such as language or education. Often, it was mentioned by social agency representatives who wished to highlight the problem of poorly trained, culturally insensitive, and biased staff in health and human service agencies:

There are some very good people out there, but there are more of the [ones that practice] *discrimination and have nasty attitudes.*

A Latino newcomer expressed it this way:

For example, if one goes to request some kind of service from a person, then they treat people with a bad attitude or they judge us people . . . sometimes I imagine that they look at Latinos as if we are worse than animals, that we don't think, that we have no intelligence; they have no idea if we received an education in our country; they don't really know who we are, but they immediately catalogue us.

Immigration and Social Policies

Particular laws and policies were considered especially problematic in the effort to integrate newcomer communities. Among them were those denying undocumented children a college education, and legal or mixed-status immigrant families access to insurance, public benefits and Nebraska driver's licenses.

The following quote captured the spirit of these exchanges:

Sometimes they require a bank account number [to secure housing, for example] *and you can't open a bank account if you don't have a social security number. What I feel is that they are here, they have been here, for generations; they will be here after you and me are gone. And the United States is losing a lot economically because if they pay for their drivers' license, it is better security for all of us, for all of society to identify them. When there is an accident, we need to know where to go to make that person responsible. But as long as we deny all these things to them, and society gets angry.* . . . *I guess where I am coming from is* [from the point of view of] *a teacher. If I want them to come here and live in my town, I need to help them and guide them because I want a nice town to live in.*

The INS representative disagreed:

This is a nation of immigrants, but it is also a nation of laws. . . . *We would be opening the doors* . . . *not too many people have the standard of living of the United States. I think that the bigger picture is to help Mexico with their infrastructure as opposed to anything else.*

Another participant responded:

But when in the world are we going to help Mexico and see that happen? The United States might have a better standard of living, but we still want these people over here anyway . . . *so the best thing is to try to do the right thing. Don't try to tell me about crime; my only crime is that my kids are hungry.*

Summary

Many of the same topics and themes found in our survey questionnaires also emerged in our focus groups. However, the open-ended nature of the focus group discussions often yielded richer responses and allowed for a more in-depth exploration of these themes. In general, focus group participants concentrated on barriers to integration associated with poor jobs and lack of access to key community institutions and benefits. These discussions provided us with findings easily supported in the literature, as well as more subjective impressions that confirmed the presence of a complex picture when it comes to Latino newcomer integration. These immigrant communities work extremely hard but face uphill battles in their road to successful socio-economic adaptation. Some of those challenges are due to deficient education, absence of legal status, and the mere fact of having migrated—regardless of education—via labor as opposed to more socio-economically privileged networks.

Communities in Nebraska, and the many agencies and organizations they house, have also worked hard–albeit some more than others–to integrate Latinos into their midst. Participants spoke about how, early on, their communities were in denial, thinking Latinos and their jobs would soon leave. Today, they are beginning to recognize how critical the contributions of these newcomers are for the future of their communities. Many listed a growing number of programs and "good practices" their communities can now showcase as creative actions to facilitate Latino newcomer integration. These initiatives range from Headstart and new Early Start programs to inter-agency committees, bilingual classes for newcomers and old timers alike, youth leadership and information technology programs for kids, and even constructive relationships with local INS offices.

Prejudice and cultural separateness are still prominent, yet we also encountered a significant number of people who have done everything possible to create a welcoming context of reception. Latino newcomers have also worked very hard to get involved in their new home. Focus group discussions richly captured the same optimism revealed by our surveys, even if most participants admitted that they are not yet "very" successful in their Latino integration efforts.

CONCLUSION

Our research findings support previously documented assumptions that view integration as a two-way process whereby its trajectory and outcomes are largely shaped by the extent to which immigrants and newcomers experience a welcoming or hostile environment and accompanying attitudes. Historically, immigrant groups have availed themselves of a number of resources and institutional support from the larger community—albeit these experiences have varied widely from group to group. They have also tapped into their abundant energy and unsurpassed motivation to better themselves, their children, and the community in which they hope to live for a long time.

The combination of data sources utilized in this report reveals a daunting number of mutually reinforcing barriers and challenges to integration. It is important to note, however, that while many of these barriers are unique to newcomers, many apply equally to all low-income and politically vulnerable populations in the state. We also identify critical reservoirs of human potential and social capital, as well as good practices and innovative policies, which can be mobilized to tear down barriers to successful socio-economic adaptation. In fact, we have reason to think that Nebraska may very well turn out to be a much more welcoming destination, and produce more positive measures of incorporation than states where elected officials have adopted more punitive and shortsighted nativist attitudes toward newcomers. However, all of this is contingent on how proactive we, as a state, become in steering these socio-demographic transformations toward constructive actions and policies. Already, numerous communities, schools, human and social service agencies, advocacy organizations, policy-makers and churches put into action a growing number of good practices, the evaluation of which could teach us a great deal.

These best practices include:

- School programs promoting true bilingualism among all Nebraska children, regardless of national origin
- The passage of the Meatpacking Workers Bill of Rights
- Significant improvements in Nebraska's Primary Care for the newborn
- Efforts by state and federal legislators to introduce bills addressing educational barriers forced by undocumented children
- The establishment of a Mexican consulate in Omaha
- Multicultural celebrations that strive to include old timers and newcomers
- Use of Latino and non-Latino media to educate and inform the community about issues that promote integration
- Parents Training Parents programs devoted to involve Latino parents in the school and educational lives of their children
- Chambers of Commerce diversity committees to support emerging Latino businesses and consumers
- Bilingual programs for children such as Headstart, Latino Book Club and "My World"
- Computer and language classes for Latino and Latina adults
- Growth of unions and other forms of worker organizations
- Proliferation of advocacy organizations tracking and defending newcomers' civil and human rights
- Proliferation of Latino community social and health services agencies
- Establishment of legal clinics to service the newcomer population

Research summarized at the beginning of this report alluded to the dangers of adopting a *laissez faire* attitude toward the barriers that stand in the way of the successful integration of newcomers. Particularly costly to the state's future is the high risk of downward assimilation facing the children of newcomers, most of whom are U.S. citizens. Research shows that most newcomers arrive as adults; their education and other expensive facets of their earlier years are paid by their native countries. Savings to the U.S. are estimated to be at least $69,000 per immigrant. Conversely, our failure to educate undocumented children can amount to income losses in the thousands of dollars, not only for the immigrant child and his or her family, but also for universities, potential employers, and state coffers.

The voices captured in our research generally reflected an understanding of the link between strong ties to one's own cultural and linguistic roots and the secure footing from which journeys toward successful adaptation can be launched. The very core of U.S. identity and supporting lore are reaffirmed periodically by immigrant stories of successful integration. Whether we realize it or not, U.S. identity is not something fixed or its definition owned by a particular cultural, linguistic, or racial group. Instead it is continuously being re-constructed, re-negotiated and re-validated through, not despite of, our endless exchanges with the multiple groups that make up our diverse society. Today this re-examination of identity is again at one of its more salient moments, but it should not be cause for concern. The true essence of "American" identity is ultimately anchored on such universal values as freedom, democracy, justice and equality, rather than on a presumption of monolithic language and cultural traditions. Thus, American identity has and will continue to withstand the test of time—but only for as long as such core values continue to be reaffirmed through our actions and policies.

Policy Recommendations

1. Immigration policy. Erase barriers to undocumented children's education, immigrant family cohesiveness and reunification, acquisition of driver's license, immigrant's access to benefits and work support services given to other low-income families, as well as access to legal status and the full range of labor rights and benefits afforded to all Nebraska workers.

2. Eliminate economic barriers via support for living wages, workers' organizing efforts, inclusion of English language acquisition as an allowable work activity, and effective monitoring of the Meatpacking Workers Bill of Rights.

3. Allocate additional resources for communities and agencies shouldering the task of facilitating the integration of newcomers.

4. Encourage employers, local communities and educational institutions to create training and education programs to truly capitalize on the assets brought by newcomers and fulfill our mission to create a productive and economically healthy labor force.

5. Invest in children's educational opportunities, including the encouragement of cultural identity and bilingualism to prevent a process of segmented assimilation.

6. Support parents in their efforts to preserve their children's ties to their native culture and language and to participate in their children's education and school activities.

7. Expand programs designed specifically to support the integration of immigrant women who often face additional barriers and, conversely, perform most of the unpaid work contributing to their family's socio-economic adaptation.

8. Declare Latinos and newcomers' lack of access to health insurance a health and socio-economic crisis and implement programs to address this serious problem.

9. Increase bilingual language training opportunities and the hiring and promotion of bilingual staff.

10. Invest in neighborhoods, housing, libraries, recreational facilities and multicultural programs which, together, can create a welcoming environment in areas where newcomers tend to settle.

11. Introduce new mechanisms for monitoring local and non-local law enforcement agencies dealing with newcomer populations to prevent practices that may violate civil rights and ultimately undermine the state's efforts to retain newcomers.

12. Support the development of innovative programs that promote integration and educational excellence among Latino students in higher education.

13. Promote programs that capitalize on newcomers' entrepreneurial spirit and help rebuild or expand small business sectors in our communities.

14. Support programs and policies aimed at including Latinos in the political process and enhancing their political, education and leadership capacities.

Notes

[1]Social capital is defined as "the ability to gain access to needed resources by virtue of membership in social networks" as well as in societal institutions of various kinds. (Portes and Rumbaut, *Legacies: The Story of the Immigrant Second Generation* (Berkeley: University of California Press, 2001) 313.

[2]See, for example, Portes and Rumbaut,; Also, Michael Fix and Wendy Zimmermann. "The Integration of Immigrant Families," Washington DC: The Urban Institute (2000).

[3]For a more detailed discussion on the combination of global and regional forces shaping the formation of recent migratory streams toward the Midwest and the Great Plains, see Lourdes Gouveia and Rogelio Saenz, "Global and Latino Population Growth in the Midwest: A Regional and Subregional Analysis," *Great Plains Research* 10/2 (2000): 305–28.

[4]B. Lindsay Lowell and Robert Suro, "How Many Undocumented: the Num-

bers behind the U.S.-Mexico Migration Talks" (Washington, DV: The Pew Center, 2002).

[5]Nebraska Department of Health and Human Services, *2000 Births by Sex, Race and Hispanic Origin by Place of Residence* (2001). www.hhs.state.ne.us/cedtabl5.htm.

[6]Nebraska Department of Education, *2001–2002 Membership by Grade, Race & Gender, by School with County and State Totals* (Lincoln, NE: Nebraska Department of Education Data Center, 2001.)

[7]Joan Knapple Olson, "Lexington has a stake in school quality," *Lexington Clipper Herald.* (January 26, 2002): 1–2.

[8]Nebraska Department of Economic Development, "Midwest States Remain Static, but Nebraska's Population Is 'On-the-Go.'" *Nebraska Development News* (Lincoln, NE: Nebraska Department of Economic Development, 2000.)

[9]Jerome Deichert, "Components of Population Change, Nebraska Counties, 1990-2000. Focus," Center for Public Affairs Research, Nebraska State Data Center (June 2001):1–10; Sara Tiennessen, "Hispanic Population Growing with Industry," *Sunday Journal Star* (August 26, 2001):1–2.

[10]Bureau of Business Research, *The Educational Status of Hispanics/Latinos in Nebraska: A Statistical Profile,* Vol. 2 (Lincoln, NE: University of Nebraska-Lincoln, 1997.)

[11]David Lopez, "Latinos in Omaha: a Socio-economic Comparison of Non-Latino Whites and Latinos in the City of Omaha," *JSRI Statistical Brief Number 12* (East Lansing, MI: Julian Samora Research Institute, Michigan State University, 2000.)

[12]Lourdes Gouveia and Thomas Sánchez, "Incorporation of Latinos/Immigrants in Rural Nebraska Communities: Grand Island and Schuyler," *A Report to Texas A&M Research Foundation* (College Station, TX: Texas A&M University, 2000); David Lopez, *Latinos in Omaha: A Visual Essay* (Lewiston, ME: Mellen Press, 2001.)

[13]Cindy Gonzalez, "For Latino Students, a Wall," *Sunday World Herald* (February 11, 2001): 6B; Ray Parker, "No Green Card Turns Them Blue," *Lincoln Journal Star* (July 29, 2000):1A–2A.

[14]For discussions and updates on policies hindering or facilitating the integration of newcomers to U.S societies and regional states see, for example, immigrantsrightsnetwork@yahoogroups.com student_adjustment@yahoogroups.com and web sites for the National Immigration Forum, The National Council of La Raza, the Immigration Law Center and the International Migration News web bulletin maintained by the University of California-Davis. Also see Michael Fix and Wendy Zimmerman, "The Integration of Immigrant Families" (Washington,

DC: The Urban Institute, 2000.)

[15]Joan Knapple Olson, "U.S. Adds 209 Citizens Friday," *Lexington Clipper Herald*. (July 7, 2001): 1, 8.

[16]Cindy Gonzalez and Paul Goodsell, "More Nebraskans Lack English Fluency," *Omaha World Herald* (June 2, 2002): 1–2.

[17]Blanca Ramírez-Salazar, "Omaha, Nebraska Block Maps: Geographic Distribution of Racial/Ethnic Minorities—Census 2000," (Lincoln, NE: Nebraska Equal Employment Opportunity Commission, 2002.)

[18]St. Francis Medical Center, "Hispanic Health Needs Survey," (Grand Island, NE: St. Francis Medical Center, 2001.)

[19]Communities in Transition Project, *Report to the University of Nebraska Public Policy Center Advisory Board* (Lincoln, NE: University of Nebraska Public Policy Center, 2002.)

[20]See, for example, Center for Applied Rural Innovation, *Nebraska Rural Poll* (Lincoln, NE: University of Nebraska-Lincoln, 2002.) <www.cari.unl.edu/ruralpoll.htm>

[21]Lourdes Gouveia and Donald D. Stull, "Latino Immigrants, Meatpacking and Rural Communities: A Case Study of Lexington, Nebraska" *JSRI Research Report No. 26* (East Lansing: Michigan State University, 1997.)

[22]The seriousness of this problem is underscored by the recent organization of an ad hoc coalition of representatives from various Omaha agencies and individuals concerned with this issue. They have recently mailed a questionnaire to governmental and non-governmental agencies teaching ESL as a first step to find more adequate solutions.

Mujeres Latinas en Acción: A Case Study of Latina Civil Rights

Martha Zurita

Civil rights *is used to imply that the state has a positive role in ensuring all citizens equal protection under law and equal opportunity to exercise the privileges of citizenship and otherwise to participate fully in national life, regardless of race, religion, sex, or other characteristics unrelated to the worth of the individual.*[1]

Domestic violence (DV) *is a pattern of physical and psychological abuse, threats, intimidation, isolation, or economic coercion used by one person to exert power and control over another person in the context of a dating, family or household relationship. Domestic violence is maintained by societal and cultural attitudes, institutes and laws that are not consistent in naming this violence as a wrong.*[2]

Domestic violence and a person's civil rights cannot be any more opposite than night and day. Civil rights deal with equality, protection, and participation, whereas domestic violence denotes abuse, coercion, and unequal power and control. Yet, the one commonality is that the state perpetuates both domestic violence through its inconsistency and civil rights by its laws.

This contradiction cannot be truer than for Latina victims of domestic violence. Latinas and other immigrant groups may experience additional forms of domestic violence through legal coercion in that the abuser may threaten deportation or the withholding of residency papers, as well as distortion of the legal system and criminal laws because the immigrant women may not understand the U.S. systems (as indicated in interview conducted for this chapter). As such, their lack of knowledge of their own civil rights places them in more risk of continued violence. For this reason, a domestic violence program focusing on Latinas and other immigrants may have additional obstacles to overcome in attempting to end the cycle of abuse.

This chapter discusses the impact of domestic violence from different perspectives: the victim, the children, and society at large. It also introduces a nonprofit agency in Chicago, Mujeres Latinas en Acción, which focuses on Latinas and is well-known for its work on domestic violence, particularly on its work to ensure Latinas' knowledge of and access to their civil rights. Finally, this chapter puts a face to domestic violence by focusing on a Mujeres client who shared her ordeal with the author and how the agency provided her with the support, knowledge, and services necessary to help her rise out of her abusive situation.

Going Full Circle: Impacts of Domestic Violence

Many people do not fully understand how large and severe a social problem domestic violence truly is. Some feel that it is a private, family issue, whereas others simply do not comprehend how many people are victims of domestic violence. Nationally, domestic violence is a very common crime, and yet it is the least reported. One statistic reveals that nearly one-third of American women (31 percent) report being physically or sexually abused by a husband or boyfriend at some point in their lives.[3] And the effects of this abuse do not just have an impact on the victim and the abuser; there is significant impact of domestic violence on children and other individuals present in the home, and on society at large.

Clearly, being abused by someone you trust and are close to, such as your partner, has negative effect on a person's psyche, self-esteem, and physical well-being. Many people, however, do not take the effects of domestic violence to their logical conclusions, which for some victims may be hospitals and cemeteries. In 1994, 37% of women who sought treatment in emergency rooms for violence-related injuries were injured by a spouse or partner.[4] In 1996, among all of the female murder victims in the U.S., 30% were slain by their husbands or boyfriends.[5] Although some may disagree, domestic violence is a social issue, particularly when it means harm and death to members of society.

There is significant impact on the children in a home where domestic violence is taking place. Children of battered women are 15 times more likely to be battered than children whose mothers are not abused, which then repeats the vicious cycle through generations.[6] There are detrimental psychological effects to children who have witnessed abuse. They often suffer low self-esteem, depression, stress disorders, poor impulse control and feelings of powerlessness.

They are also at high risk for alcohol and drug abuse, sexual acting out, running away, isolation, fear and suicide.[7] Considering these children will become the future generation, by not providing societal systems to end the cycle of domestic violence, the country as a whole will undoubtedly suffer along with children raised in abusive homes.

It is obvious that domestic violence has serious effects on the human fabric of society in that it tears down individuals and families. Domestic violence also poses society with significant medical and financial issues. It is the leading cause of injury to women between the ages of 15 to 44 and ranks as one of the nation's most expensive health problems.[8] Abused women experience a 50% to 70% increase in gynecological, neurological, and stress-related problems either as aftereffects of the abuse or the result of the increased stress levels caused by the abuse.[9] Furthermore, family violence costs the nation from $5 to $10 billion annually in medical expenses, police and court costs, shelters and foster care, sick leave, absenteeism, and non-productivity. As a society, can we continue to *afford* financially and in terms of human capital to leave this ill untreated and ignored?

Individuals, organizations, and public systems attempting to eradicate or diminish acts and effects of domestic violence have a very large charge. Not only must these entities take into account the negative implications of abuse on the individual, the future generations, and social well-being, but they must also educate and ensure that the victims' civil rights are intact. This feat has been made a bit easier with the passage of the Violence against Women Act (VAWA) of 1994, which reflects a growing national recognition that domestic violence is not merely a private family matter, but an issue of crime prevention, public safety, and prevention of gender-based discrimination. In essence, the VAWA recognizes that domestic violence is an issue of civil rights for women. However, the protection of immigrant women under law is narrower than that of non-immigrant women, which makes them a more vulnerable population. For example, an application of legal permanent status may be denied if the applicant is likely to become a "public charge."[10]

Mujeres Latinas en Acción: Opening the Door

Many groups are working to stop the cycle of domestic violence and rebuild individuals, families, and communities. One organization in particular, focuses solely on Latinas: Mujeres Latinas en Acción.[11] Mujeres, a non-profit agency in Chicago, is a bilingual/bicultural agency seeking to empower Latina women and their families to become self-reliant, take full advantage of available opportunities, and create new opportunities to improve the quality of their lives. In order to carry out their mission, Mujeres provides comprehensive services that help women explore choices, make informed decisions, develop self-esteem, and enhance daily living and problem-solving skills. Through its work, Mujeres also undertakes policy analysis and advocacy with and on behalf of Latinas. Mujeres strives to maintain a balance between clinical work and consciousness-raising, and is committed to bringing about systemic changes and long-term solutions to the problems of personal safety and development facing Latinas.

Started in 1973 by a group of women, Mujeres Latinas en Acción is one of the oldest agencies that focuses specifically on Latinas in the country and is currently the only organization in the state that is primarily administered by and working on behalf of Latinas and their families. The impetus for the organization was a statewide Latina women's conference, "La Mujer Despierta" (The Awakening Women), held in June 1973. It became clear through dialogue at the conference that few services existed to meet the needs of women, especially Latinas.

After the conference, a group of women from two predominantly Latino communities in Chicago, Pilsen and Little Village continued to meet with the goal of developing services for women. The initial group of women served as volunteers to provide limited services and sponsor educational events for two years without funds. They borrowed space from other community organizations to hold meetings and events.

One event that may have stopped the existence of the organization was a fire in September of 1974. The organization had leased a rectory, which subsequently was burned to the ground. The fire was the last event in a series of threats that the women had experienced. Just a few days before the fire, a founder of the organization was physically assaulted by gang members at a local bar. Other Mujeres members had received suspicious phone calls in the preceding weeks. Although they did not know for certain, the women of Mujeres felt that the fire had been set intentionally because the men in the community had perceived the organization as a potential threat.

In 1975, this group of women began a grassroots fundraising effort to secure a storefront from which to offer services. Soon, they had held enough dances, bake sales, and raffles to pay the rent and utilities on a storefront. Through securing this location and through their efforts, they increased their visibility in the community, which increased the number of volunteers. The core group of women, which was made up of teachers, businesswomen, students, housewives, social workers, and teens, kept the storefront open, ran summer youth programs, held education workshops, and provided referrals to women.

The organization has grown substantially over the last thirty years. Although the organization has continually changed leadership over the three decades, it has managed to survive shifting economic and political tides. Currently, Mujeres has 32 full-time staff members, a core group of 50 volunteers, and an annual budget of $1.3 million. It has gained recognition at all levels: local, state, national, and international. There are 11 different programs running today. The programs include the following: Domestic Violence, Parent Support, Latina Leadership, Peace Program, Child Care Services, Women in Transition, Youth Counseling (SASS), Sex Assault, Mother and Daughter Leadership, Project Sanctuary, Teen Reach. Each year, Mujeres provides support, guidance, and counseling to 7,000 Latinas and their families.

Mujeres is well known nationally and internationally for its Domestic Violence (DV) program. In fact, Mujeres is the only bilingual, bicultural agency with DV programs focusing specifically on Latinas. Through its services to youth, it became clear that a strong link existed between violence within homes and children's delinquency, such as truancy, running away, drug abuse, and gang affiliation. In response to this link, Mujeres created its Domestic Violence program in 1981. One of the major challenges of the program was breaking the taboo of raising the issue of DV in the community.

The Domestic Violence program provides clients with crisis assessment and intervention. The program has a 24-hour hotline staffed by 30 volunteers. Clients are also provided individual and group counseling, court advocacy, and referrals. The program also has a community education component reaching a larger group of people with its anti-violence message. The Domestic Violence program currently has eight full-time staff members: a coordinator who also supervises the Sexual Assault program, three court advocates (two for criminal cases and one for civil cases), one community educator, one volunteer supervisor for the hotline, and one assistant.

As a tireless advocate on behalf of DV victims and their families, Mujeres has made significant policy changes in Illinois over the years. Much of this work was done despite the fact that the organization did not have a full-time policy advocate on staff. Many of the policy changes were realized through grassroots efforts, such as letter-writing campaigns, organizing marches, and hosting busloads of women to travel to the state's capital to push for certain legislation. Mujeres also worked in collaboration with other organizations that focus on domestic violence to bring about change.

Mujeres was instrumental in creating a safer environment for victims by advocating and securing a separate courthouse for domestic violence cases, as opposed to sharing space with criminal court, as was previously the case. Mujeres also advocated for and secured multiple entrances into the courthouse, whereas previously there was only one entrance, and the victims would be frightened to go to court because chances were high that they would encounter their abusers. As such, victims of domestic violence could not have access to equal protection under the law because they were fearful of appearing at the courthouse. In addition, Mujeres was instrumental in ensuring that translators were available in court at all times, whereas previously court translators were only available during certain hours, which, in essence, denied those who did not have full command of the English language full representation. The DV staff at Mujeres is currently focused on establishing different waiting rooms at the courthouse because today victims and their alleged abusers must wait in the same waiting room, which is very intimidating for the victims of abuse.

Marisa: Walking through the Door to Civil Rights

Él dijo que la policía no me iba a ayudar porque era inmigrante. Y yo le creí. [He told me that the police would not help me because I was an immigrant. And I believed him.]

The customers at McDonald's do not know that this hard worker is a single mother of three who starts work at 6:00 am and ends at 2pm and is paid minimum wage.

Nor do they know that this worker came into this country illegally with her youngest child seven years ago, leaving behind her two eldest until she could save enough money to bring them across the border with coyotes.[12]

Nor do they know that this worker who stands near five feet tall is a powerful survivor who has lived through immeasurable terrors at the hands of her former husband in order to improve her children's opportunities.

Marisa[13] is typical of the domestic violence clients served at Mujeres Latinas en Acción. She was an undocumented Mexican immigrant who had arrived in Chicago in 1994. She was the mother of three children and spoke no English. Marisa had been abused for many years at the hands of her husband and his family before being directed to Mujeres. Her husband, Adolfo, was an alcoholic at first and then a drug addict, which only increased the intensity and frequency of the abuse upon her and her children. In essence, Marisa was a perfect victim because she was extremely isolated. She had no family support in Chicago, no social network, and no understanding of the U.S. legal system or protections offered to her. Marisa and her children were on the verge of finalizing their paperwork for legal residency when she went to Mujeres for help.

Marisa began her life in a Mexican pueblo almost 40 years ago. She came to Chicago after her husband of 11 years, Adolfo, brought her and their youngest child across the border. Technically, as Marisa points out, it was her father who had brought them because her father had lent them the money for *coyotes* to provide them illegal means to enter the country. And after she could raise enough money for another *coyote*, it was she who brought their two eldest children to live with them in Chicago.

Although they both came from the same pueblo, Marisa and Adolfo could not have been more different. She came from a close-knit, religious family, whereas he came from a dysfunctional, broken home. Marisa was cherished by her family, particularly her parents, and was often teased by her siblings for being her parents' favorite child. To this day, Marisa cannot understand how she went from a home where she was so treasured to a marriage where she was so hated, hurt, and mistreated. Adolfo, on the other hand, had lived in the U.S. independently since the age of 12. Marisa had an eighth grade education and Adolfo had less. They met through a cousin, who was also working in the U.S. and began writing letters to each other. After two years, they wed.

In Marisa's mind, she has never had a marriage. During the first 11 years of their marriage, Adolfo came home to Mexico erratically, staying the maximum of two months in that country. As Marisa puts it, "He came home to impregnate me and that's it." He rarely sent money home and when he did, his family demanded a portion of the money from Marisa. Although she was married and remained true to a husband she rarely saw, Marisa was a single parent. She worked to provide for her children. At times, her father, who was also working in the U.S., would send her additional money and gifts. With help from her parents, she purchased a house in Mexico, where she and the children lived and her husband visited when in the country.

Although her husband was not present most of the time during the first decade of their marriage, Marisa and her children were still being physically abused—at the hands of *his* family. And when Adolfo came home, she reported the abuse to him. It did nothing to improve the situation and simply made it worse. That is the reason Marisa agreed to come to Chicago: to escape the abuse at the hands of his family. Unknowingly, she put herself and her children in a much more hazardous zone by living with her husband.

Once in Chicago, Marisa's life did not change much. She was still in essence a single mother, but to a higher degree because she did not have any of her family in Chicago. Marisa quickly became painfully aware that her husband was a severe alcoholic. She knew that he drank but did not realize the extent of his addiction due to the fact that they lived in separate countries for so long. Always placing his friends and his vice ahead of his wife and children, he never had enough money to support his family and, as with any addict, his paycheck went to feed his addictions. As a way to survive, Marisa and her eldest son worked in a factory and they worked very long and very hard. She secretly saved their over-time checks and, by 1999, had enough money for a down payment on a home. Not being a legal resident, her name was not included on the mortgage contract, although she and her son had made the down payment, as well as all of the mort-gage payments for two years. The names on the deed were that of her husband and his friend, who co-signed the $115,000 loan.

Marisa recounted a time her husband severely beat her. Her eldest son, then 16, came home and saw what Adolfo had done to his mother. When her son was little, Marisa's father had secretly taken him aside and informed him that when he was older, he was to protect his mother, should his father ever physically abuse her. Upon seeing his battered mother, he confronted his father. He told Adolfo that he had no right to hit his mother and if he did not love her, he should just leave the family. He informed Adolfo that he would assist his mother finan-cially, so in essence, there was no need for Adolfo to stay. An infuriated Adolfo lunged at his son's neck and began choking him. A frantic Marisa attempted to come to her son's rescue, screaming at her husband that he was going to kill him—which was his goal. She unsuccessfully tried time and time again to phys-ically remove her husband from on top of their son. The youngest son, who was the only one with command of the English language, called the police to help his brother. The police arrived to find Adolfo still choking the eldest son. According to Marisa, it took three officers to get the father off of his son.

Marisa did not leave or pursue charges against her husband after this inci-dent, for several reasons. The first reason was her children. Like many victims of domestic violence with children, after the incident, her children pleaded with Marisa not to leave their father because they did not want to come from a home with divorced parents. The second reason was her lack of knowledge of the court system. Marisa indicated that she knew absolutely nothing about the court system in the United States. She did not know where the courts were located or how to get there. Finally, common to other victims of domestic violence, her husband threatened that if she put him in jail, he'd kill her upon his release.

Eventually, Marisa realized that her husband was addicted to more than just alcohol. She would see traces of white powder (cocaine) around his nostrils after he would come home. Syringes from heroine were found lying around the house. Her clothes and her children's jewelry disappeared. He completely dis-tanced himself from Marisa, sleeping on the couch during the last two years of their marriage. And all the while, he grew increasingly violent, erratic, and para-noid, all of which meant more incidences of abuse for the family, particularly when she confronted him about her suspicions and concerns.

The last straw was when Adolfo tried to kill the entire family. One year after he had tried to choke their eldest son, he came home obviously on drugs—Marisa remembers his eyes bulging out of their sockets. As she tells the story, the kids were doing their homework and eating at the kitchen table. They were holding a conversation with their mother and enjoying themselves. From out of nowhere, Adolfo appeared and began beating his chest shouting, "¡Soy el Diablo!" (I am the Devil!) And he looked the part; he was manic and crazed. He disconnected the gas pipes leading to the stove. He was waving them around the room screaming that they were all going to die and go to hell. All the while, he was searching for a lighter by which to blow the house up. The fact that he did not have a lighter on hand, being that he was a chain smoker and always had a lighter in his pockets, is something that Marisa cannot understand to this day. She attributes it to divine intervention.

In realizing that he was looking for a lighter by which to kill everyone, Marisa attempted to wrestle the pipe out of his hand or, at the very least, distract him from locating a lighter. With chaos erupting, the youngest son called the police for help, yet again. Upon arriving at the house, the police arrested Adolfo and transported Marisa and the children to the hospital, because they had become ill from the gas fumes.

At this point, Marisa knew nothing about Mujeres Latinas en Acción, not even that an agency focusing on domestic violence existed, particularly one that was dedicated to Latinas. Because Chicago is a large city with very rigid neighborhood boundaries, most community-based organizations provide services largely within their neighborhood boundaries. As such, it was not uncommon that Marisa, who lived on the north side of the city, had never heard of Mujeres, an agency in the south side of the city, although they were only six miles apart. Fortunately for Marisa, when she went to her children's school to inform teachers why her children had missed school, the principal and the social worker took her to Mujeres, a move for which she is eternally grateful.

Mujeres immediately assisted Marisa in obtaining an order of protection against her husband. Adolfo, however, did not let it stop him from harassing his family. He continued to threaten his family by constantly going to the house and screaming out obscenities and letting them know that they could not do anything to him. He would also scream out lies about his wife, so that he could humiliate her in front of their children and neighbors. Adolfo would often break the windows of the family home. After almost every incident, the youngest son, who was the only one to speak English (one of the reasons his father came to despise him), would call the police to notify them that his father was there to harm the family. In total, he technically violated the order of protection 12 times, in that the police found him, took him to the station and recorded 12 violations. After the twelfth violation, a frustrated Marisa confronted the police. "How many times is it going to take for you to understand that he's not going to stop?" she asked. "Will it be when I'm finally dead?"

And it was that time that the police took her whole family down to the station to interview each one individually. The police officers admitted to Marisa that the system had failed her and her children. They then told her that it was a miracle that she and her children were still alive. It was their professional opinion that she had been living with a psychopath. And in a move not to intimidate her or sway her into a decision either way, they informed her that if she was to return to her husband, they would have no choice but to remove her children from the home for safety reasons. Marisa posed them with the question, "Being that I am undocumented, why would I risk deportation if I was going to reconcile with my husband? Clearly, I want help and do not want to reconcile with him." As a result of his numerous violations against the orders of protection, Adolfo was deported back to Mexico. However, being an abuser with a mission, Adolfo re-entered the country through *coyotes* and continues to seek out and harass Marisa and their children.

During this stressful process of hospitals, constant threats, violations of orders of protection, and police interviews, Marisa missed work. As a result, she missed two mortgage payments. A few months later, the bank foreclosed on Marisa's house. Until our interview, Marisa was under the impression that Adolfo had forged her signature and sold the house. Although the story was not very clear to either of us, Marisa asked me to read papers proving his guilt—they were foreclosure papers. No one had explained this to Marisa and, not being able to read or speak English, she assumed that her husband had taken the house illegally. This was a clear example of how little understanding of legal procedures Marisa had.

Marisa attributes much of her present status and success to Mujeres Latinas en Acción. She expresses sincere gratitude for all that the agency has done for her, as well as for illustrating just how much she can accomplish. The following are examples of Mujeres Latinas en Acción's critical involvement in Marisa's life:

- Assisted her in enrolling for public assistance.
- Aided Marisa with the surmounting hospital bills for her and her children as a result of her husband's attempted homicide.
- Helped Marisa in obtaining orders of protection against her abuser.
- Drove to Marisa's home to give her a ride to the courthouse, provided support while in the waiting area, and stayed with her throughout the proceedings. On occasion, her Mujeres court advocate even had verbal exchanges with Marisa's husband when he felt the need to "unleash."

• Assisted Marisa's daughter in also filing charges against her father, after she had seen his arrogance and lack of remorse in the courtroom.

• Referred Marisa to a divorce lawyer, which resulted in Marisa having full custody of the children.

• Assisted her in regaining her house in Mexico from her ex-husband through a collaboration with the Mexican Consulate in Chicago.

• Facilitated her and her children receiving their residency status as a result of being victims of domestic violence. [14] They were on the verge of becoming residents before the final incident with her husband.

A person does not know what she is capable of overcoming until she is placed in a situation where she must make the ultimate choice. As an individual, Marisa had the will and strength to prevail over her abuser and her situation. She did not, however, have the knowledge and understanding of her rights and protections provided by the state. And without this knowledge, there is a strong possibility that Marisa and her children may not have been triumphant in their ordeal. In fact, without the knowledge of their rights and protections, they may have all been dead at the hands of their abuser. And it is the bilingual, bicultural staff of Mujeres Latinas en Acción who assisted her in understanding these rights afforded to her by law. In addition, being that Marisa was virtually alone in Chicago, Mujeres staff provided her with the support and reassurance to make it through this ordeal.

Currently, Marisa and her children are attempting to rebuild their lives. They have many psychological and physical scars as a result of Adolfo's years of abuse. Marisa and her two youngest children are in therapy. The youngest two, who are still enrolled in school, do well academically, which she sees as a good sign of their progress and a fact of which she is very proud. Her oldest son continues to work full-time to assist his mother. The family has recently been relocated to a high rent, gentrified area of the city by the police because her ex-husband found out where they had been living. She lives in constant fear and continues to be isolated because she cannot relocate to be with her family, since his family lives in the same town as her family. She does not want her family to suffer at the hands of her husband or his family. Marisa is positive, however, that she did the right thing for herself and her children. She is committed to working very hard to increase the quality of her children's lives. Finally, Marisa is amazed at how powerful she feels for having lived through and having overcome her ordeal.

Civil Rights and DV: Completing the Circle

Marisa's experience clearly illustrates that domestic violence diminishes a victim's civil rights. As stated earlier, given that nearly one-third of American women (31 percent) report being physically or sexually abused by a husband or boyfriend at some point in their lives, clearly the civil rights of many Americans are not protected. The key components of civil rights include the following for all citizens: (1) equal protection under law; (2) equal opportunity to exercise the privileges of citizenship; and (3) the ability to participate fully in national life, regardless of race, religion, sex, or other characteristics unrelated to the worth of the individual.[15]

Like other victims of domestic violence, Marisa did not have equal protection under the law. Being an undocumented immigrant, she believed her ex-husband when he told her that the police would not protect her because she was an immigrant. As a result, Marisa did not have equal access and protection under the law, whether it was real or perceived. Even with an order of protection, her ex-husband continued to threaten and psychologically torment her and her children. It took 12 violations of the order before action was taken and he was finally deported. This is yet another example of Marisa not having equal protection under the law.

Although Marisa was not a citizen or a permanent resident at the time, one could argue that she should not have access to privileges of citizenship or be allowed to participate fully in national life. Being that this chapter is not the forum by which to discuss this issue, examining victims of domestic violence as a group reveals that they would not have access to privileges of citizenship as a result of the violence. As stated earlier, domestic violence is fundamentally about an exertion of power and control over another person in an intimate relationship. This exertion of power is carried out through physical and psychological abuse, threats, intimidation, isolation, or economic coercion. As such, this abuse, intimidation, and coercion drastically reduce the victim's movements, actions, and overall well-being. In Marisa's case, for example, her movements are very restricted. She still cannot relocate to live with her family in another state because her ex-husband's family lives in the same town. She is afraid to be seen because he still comes back into the country illegally and attempts to locate her and her children. In addition, Mujeres Latinas en Acción has made several requests of Marisa to appear on television programs focusing on domestic violence. Marisa has continually declined because she fears that her husband will find her and continue to terrorize her and her children. And although she tells her story to help other victims, Marisa insists that no identifying traits be used, in the event that her ex-husband read or hear the story. In essence, Marisa, like many other victims of domestic abuse, lives in fear and hides from her abuser. As such, she does not have access to the privileges of citizenship or full participation in national life.

Using Marisa's ordeal as a case study clearly illustrates that the civil rights of victims of domestic violence are not protected. Hopefully, through the telling of Marisa's story, the reader can come to a clearer understanding of how the civil rights of DV victims are being violated, how the issue is more severe for Latinas and immigrants, and why the work of organizations like Mujeres Latinas en Acción is critically needed.

Notes

[1]"Civil Rights and Civil Liberties," Microsoft Encarta Online Encyclopedia 2002.

[2]Chicago-Area Domestic Violence Services website, 2003.

[3]The Commonwealth Fund Survey, "Health Concerns across a Woman's Lifespan." 1998 Survey of Women's Health (www.cmwf.org.)

[4]Bureau of Justice Statistics, "Special Report: Intimate Partner Violence and Age of Victim, 1993–94," 2001.

[5]Federal Bureau of Investigation, "Uniform Crime Reports of the U.S.," 1996.

[6]US Senate Judiciary Hearing, August/December 1990, "Women and Violence," as cited on "A Friends Place" website.

[7]Jaffe, Wolfe & Wilson, 1990, pp. 28–29, as cited in "A Friends Place" website.

[8]American Medical Association, *American Medical News,* 1992, as cited in "A Friends Place" website.

[9]Elliott, V.S., "Doctors Make a Difference in Treating Abuse." *American Medical News,* July 22, 2002. (www.amednews.com).

[10]Mo Matthews, "Addressing the Effects of Domestic Violence on Children," National CASA Association website (www.casanet.org).

[11]"Mujeres Latinas en Acción" is also referred to as "Mujeres" throughout this chapter, as is done in practice.

[12]A *coyote* is a "smuggler" who, for a considerable fee, assists people in illegally entering the United States.

[13]Names have been changed for the protection and privacy of the individuals.

[14]The passage of the Violence Against Women Act (VAWA) of 1994 allows for those who are battered, or whose children are abused, by a citizen or legal permanent resident spouse to "self-petition" for their own legal permanent resident status.

[15]"Civil Rights and Civil Liberties," Microsoft Encarta Online Encyclopedia, 2002.

Bibliograpy

Acuña, Rodolfo. *Occupied America: A History of Chicanos.* Harper Collins, 1988.

Alicea, Marisa. "Dual Home Bases." Ed. Félix Padilla. *Handbook of Hispanic Culture the United States.* Houston: Arte Público Press, 1988.

Alinsky, Saul D. *Rules for Radicals, A Pragmatic Primer for Realistic Radicals.* New York: Random House, 1971.

Allsup, Carl. "Concerned Latins Organization." *Forging A Community: The Latino* Experience in Northern Indiana 1919–1975. Eds. James B. Lane and Edward J. Escobar. Volume 2. Chicago: Cattails Press, 1987.

Allswang, John. *A House for All Peoples: Ethnic Politics in Chicago.* Lexington: University of Kentucky Press, 1971.

Ansell, Christopher K. and Arthur L. Burris. "Bosses of the City Unite! Labor Politics and Political Machine Consolidation, 1870–1910." *Studies in American Political Development* 11 (Spring 1977): 1–43.

Austin, John and Members of the Nebraska Business Forecast Council. "Nebraska Reacts to the National Recession." *Business in Nebraska.* 57 (2001): 662.

"Chicanos in the Midwest." *Aztlán* (Thematic Issue) 7/2 (Summer 1978).

Banfield, Edward and James Q. Wilson. *City Politics.* Cambridge: Harvard University Press, 1963.

Barger, W.K. and Ernesto Reza. The Farm Labor Movements in the Midwest: Social Change and Adaptations among Migrant Farmworkers. Austin: The University of Texas Press, 1994.

Betancur, John, Teresa Córdova, and María de los Angeles Torres. "Latinos in

Chicago." Eds. Frank Bonilla and Rebecca Morales. *Latinos in a Changing U.S. Economy.* Newbury Park, CA: Sage Publications, 1993.

Blankenau, Joe, Joni Boye-Beaman, and Keith Mueller. "Health-Care Utilization and the Status of Latinos in Rural Meat-Processing Communities." *Great Plains Research.* 10/2 (2000): 275–94.

Bonilla, Frank. *Borderless Borders: U.S. Latinos, Latin America and the Paradox of Interdependence.* Eds. Frank Bonilla, Edwin Meléndez, Rebecca Morales and María de los Angeles Torres. Philadelphia: Temple University Press, 1998.

Breaking Ranks: Changing an American Institution. Reston, Va: National Association of Secondary School Principals, 1996.

Browning, Rufus, Dale Rogers Marshall, and David Tabb. *Protest Is Not Enough: The Struggle of Blacks and Hispanics for Equality in Urban Politics.* Berkeley: University of California Press, 1984.

Buenker, John. "Dynamics of Ethnic Politics 1900–1930." *Journal of the Illinois State Historical Society.* 67/2 (1974): 175–199.

Bureau of Business Research. *The Educational Status of Hispanics/Latinos in Nebraska: A Statistical Profile.* Vol. 2. Lincoln, NE: University of Nebraska-Lincoln, 1997.

Bureau of the Census, U.S. Dept. of Commerce. *Statistical Abstract of the United States: 1981.* 25–26, 499.

Bureau of Justice Statistics. Special Report: Intimate Partner Violence and Age of Victim 1993-99. 2001.

Campuzano v. Ilinois State Board of Elections, No. 01 C 50376 (U.S. Dist. Ct., N.D. Ill.).

Cárdenas, Gilbert. "Los Desarraigados: Chicanos in the Midwestern Region of the United States." *Aztlán,* 7/2 (1978).

Carlo, Gustavo, Miguel A. Carranza, and Byron L. Zamboanga. "Culture, Ecology, and Latinos on the Great Plains: An Introduction." *Great Plains Research.* 12/1 (2002): 3–12.

Carranza, Miguel A., Gustavo Carlo, and María Rosario T. de Guzmán. "The Role of Research and Scholarship in Enhancing the Quality of Life for Latinos on the Great Plains." *Great Plains Research.* 10/2 (2000): 409–21.

Chicago Urban League. *Working Poor Families in Chicago and the Chicago Metropolitan Area: A Statistical Profile Based on the 1990 Census.* (Prepared for the Working Poor Policy Forum.) Chicago: Chicago Urban League, Latino Institute, Northern Illinois University (December 1993).

Clavel, Pierre, and Wim Wiewel. *Harold Washington and the Neighborhoods.* New Brunswick: Rutgers University Press, 1991.

Communities in Transition Project (COMIT). *Report to the University of Nebraska Public Policy Center Advisory Board.* Lincoln, NE: University of Nebraska Public Policy Center, 2002.

Córdova, Teresa, and Harold Washington. "The Rise of Latino Electoral Politics in Chicago, 1982-1987." Ed. David Montejano. *Chicano Politics and Society in the Late Twentieth Century.* Austin: University of Texas, 1999. 31–57.

de la Garza, Rodolfo O., Louis DeSipio, F. Chris García, John García, and Angelo Falcón. *Latino Voices: Mexican, Puerto Rican & Cuban Perspectives on American Politics.* Boulder: Westview Press, 1992.

de los Ángeles Torres, María. "The Commission on Latino Affairs: A Case Study of Community Empowerment." Eds. Pierre Clavel and Wim Wiewel. *Harold Washington and the Neighborhoods.* New Brunswick: Rutgers University Press, 1991.

_____. *In the Land of Mirrors: Cuban Exile Politics in the US.* Ann Arbor: University of Michigan Press, 1999.

Estimated Costs of Providing Welfare and Education Services to Immigrants and to the Native Born in Illinois. Chicago: IIPP, 1996.

Estrada, Daniel and Richard Santillán. "Chicanos in the Northwest and Midwest United States: A History of Cultural and Political Commonalty." *Perspectives in Mexican American Studies.* Tucson: University of Arizona Mexican American Studies and Research Center, 1997.

Fix, Michael, and Wendy Zimmerman. "The Integration of Immigrant Families." Washington, DC: The Urban Institute, 2000.

Flores, Raymundo, Rufino Osorio, and John Attinasi. *Al Filo/At the Cutting Edge: The Empowerment of Chicago's Latino Electorate.* Chicago: Latino Institute, 1986.

Flores, William, and Rina Benmayor. *Latino Cultural Citizenship: Claiming Identity, Space and Rights.* Boston: Beacon Press, 1997.

Fraga, Luis. "Prototype from the Midwest: Latinos in Illinois." Eds. Rodolfo de la Garza and Louis DeSipio. *Rhetoric to Reality: Latino Politics in the 1988 Elections.* Boulder: Westview Press, 1992. 111–126.

García, F. Chris. *La Causa Política: A Chicano Politics Reader.* Notre Dame, Indiana: University of Notre Dame Press, 1974.

_____. *Pursuing Power: Latinos and the Political System.* Notre Dame: University of Notre Dame Press, 1997 and 1988.

Gomez-Quiñonez, Juan. *Reality & Promise 1940–1960.* Albuquerque: University of New Mexico Press, 1990.

Gosnell, Harold. *Machine Politics: Chicago Model.* Chicago: University of Chicago Press, 1977.

Gouveia, Lourdes, and Rogelio Saenz. "Global Forces and Latino Population Growth in the Midwest: A Regional and Subregional Analysis." *Great Plains Research.* 10/2 (2000): 305–28.

_____ and Thomas Sánchez. "Incorporation of Latinos/Immigrants in Rural Nebraska Communities: Grand Island and Schuyler." A report to Texas A&M, 2000.

_____ and Donald D. Stull. "Latino Immigrants, Meatpacking and Rural Communities: A Case Study of Lexington, Nebraska." *JSRI Research Report No. 26.* East Lansing: Michigan State University, 1997.

Gracia, Jorge. *Hispanic/Latino Identity: A Philosophical Perspective.* Malden Massachusetts: Blackwell Publishers, 2000.

— and Pablo De Greiff. *Hispanics/Latinos in the United States: Ethnicity, Race, and Rights.* New York: Routledge, 2000.

Guthrie, Charles, Dan Briere, and Mary Moore. *The Indianapolis Hispanic Community.* Indianapolis: University of Indianapolis Press, 1995.

Hardy-Fanta, Carol. *Latina Politics, Latino Politics: Gender, Culture and Political Participation in Boston.* Philadelphia: Temple University Press, 1993.

Hernández Gómez, Carlos. "Latino Leadership: Population Soars, but Political Power Lags." *Chicago Reporter.* September/October 2001.

Hernández-Leon, Rubén, and Víctor Zúñiga. "Mexican Immigrant Communities in the South and Social Capital: The Case of Dalton, Georgia." *Southern Rural Sociology.* Forthcoming.

Hero, Rodney, F. Chris García, John García, and Harry Pachón. "Latino Participation, Partisanship, and Office Holding." *Political Science and Politics.* 33/3 (September 2000): 529–534.

Hirsch, Eric. *Urban Revolt: Ethnic Politics in the Nineteenth-Century Chicago Labor Movement.* Berkeley: University of California Press, 1990.

Illinois and Immigrant Policy: A Briefing Book for State and Local Policy Makers. Chicago: IIPP, November 1995.

INS Task Force. "INS Task Force: Recommendations on the Impact of Immigration and Naturalization Service Enforcement in Nebraska." *Report to Governor Mike Johanns.* Facilitated by Lt. Governor David Maurstad. Lincoln, NE: State of Nebraska, 2000.

Jentz, John. "Class and Politics in an Emerging City: Chicago in the 1860s and 1870s." *Journal of Urban History.* 17/3 (May 1991): 227–263.

Jurasek, Rita Arias, and Carlos Tortolero. "Images of America." *Mexican Chicago.* Chicago: Arcadia Publishing, 2001.

Katznelson, Ira. *City Trenches: Urban Politics and the Patterning of Class in the United States.* New York: Pantheon Books, 1981.

Kleppner, Paul. *Chicago Divided: The Making of a Black Mayor.* DeKalb, Illinois: Northern Illinois University, 1985.

Lane, James B., and Edward J. Escobar. *Forging a Community: The Latino Experience in Northern Indiana 1919–1975.* Vol. 2. Chicago: Cattails Press, 1987.

Latino Institute. *Annual Report: 1990–1992.* Chicago: Latino Institute, 1993.

_____. *Annual Report 1996.* Chicago: Latino Institute, 1997, p. 6.

_____. *Aquí Estamos: Hispanics in Chicago.* Reston,Virginia: Latino Institute, 1982.

_____. *Chicago's Working Latinas: Confronting Multiple Roles and Pressures.*

Chicago: Latino Institute, March 1987, p. 2.

_____. *Four Year Progress Report. Chicago: Latino Institute,* 1979.

_____. *Hopes and Dreams: A Statistical Portrait of Non-Citizens in Metropolitan Chicago.* Chicago: Latino Institute, 1994.

_____. Indicators for Understanding: A Statistical Portrait of Metropolitan Chicago's Immigrant Community. Chicago: Latino Institute, 1995.

_____. LatStat: Latino Statistics and Data, Latino Origin Groups. Chicago: Latino Institute, August 1995, p. 1.

_____.*1977 Annual Report.* Chicago: Latino Institute, 1977.

_____. *Stepping out into the 90s: Latino Institute, Annual Report 1989-1990.* Chicago: Latino Institute, 1991.

_____. *The Condition of Latinas in Illinois and Chicago: A Working Paper.* Chicago: Latino Institute, 1985.

_____. *Toward a Latino Urban Policy Agenda: Selected Demographics.* Chicago: Latino Institute, 1996.

Lemann, Nicholas. *The Promised Land: The Great Black Migration and How It Changed America.* New York: A.A. Knopf, 1991.

López, David. *Latinos in Omaha: A Visual Essay.* Lewiston, ME: Mellen Press, 2001.

_____. "Latinos in Omaha: a socio-economic comparison of non-Latino whites and Latinos in the city of Omaha." *JSRI Statistical Brief Number 12.* East Lansing, MI: Julián Samora Research Institute, Michigan State University, 2000.

Lowell, B. Lindsay, and Roberto Suro. *How Many Undocumented: The Numbers Behind the U.S.-Mexico Migration Talks.* Washington, DC: The Pew Center, 2002.

Luna, David. *Latino Institute: A Framework for Influencing Policy.* Chicago: Latino Institute, 1991.

Maldonado, Edwin. "Contract Labor and the Origins of Puerto Rican Communities in the United States." *International Migration Review.* 13 (1979): 103–121.

Meléndez, Edwin and Edgar Meléndez. *Colonial Dilemma: Critical Perspectives on Contemporary Puerto Rico.* Boston: South End Press, 1993.

Montejano, David. *Chicano Politics and Society in the Late Twentieth Century.* Austin: University of Texas Press, 1999.

Morín, Raúl. *Among the Valiant: Mexican Americans in World War II and Korea.* Alhambra, California: Border Publishing Company, 1966.

National Council of La Raza. *The Mainstreaming of Hate: A Report on Latinos and Harassment, Hate Violence, and Law Enforcement Abuse in the '90s.* Washington, D.C.: National Council of La Raza, 1999.

Nuevo-Kerr, Louisa Año. "Mexican Chicago: Assimilation Aborted." *Ethnic Chicago.* Eds. Melvin G. Holli and Peter Jones eds. Grand Rapids, MI:

William Erdman, 1977. 269–299.

Pachón, Harry, and Louis DeSipio. New American by Choice: Political Perspectives of Latino Immigrants. Boulder: Westview Press, 1994.

Padilla, Félix M. Latino Ethnic Consciousness: The Case of Mexican-Americans and Puerto Ricans in Chicago. Notre Dame, IN: University of Notre Dame Press, 1985.

_____. Puerto Rican Chicago. Notre Dame, IN: Notre Dame University Press, 1990.

Parra, Ricardo, Victor Ríos, and Armando Gutiérrez. "Chicano Organizations in the Midwest: Past, Present and Possibilities." Aztlán. 7/2 (1978).

Pew Hispanic Center. 2002 National Survey of Latinos. Washington, D.C.: Pew Hispanic Center and the Kaiser Family Foundation, December 2002.

Pinderhughes, Dianne. Race and Ethnicity in Chicago Politics: A Reexamination of Pluralist Theory. Urbana: University of Illinois Press, 1987.

Portes, Alejandro and Robert Bach. Latin Journey: Cuban and Mexican Immigrants in the United States. Los Angeles: University of California Press, 1985.

_____ and Rubén Rumbaut. Legacies: The Story of the Immigrant Second Generation. Berkeley: University of California Press, 2001.

Prieto, Jorge. Harvest of Hope: The Pilgrimage of a Mexican-American Physician. Notre Dame, IN: University of Notre Dame Press, 1989.

Public Aid and Illinois Immigrants: Serving Non-Citizens in the Welfare Reform Era. Chicago: IIPP, 1996.

Puente, Sylvia. Race, Ethnicity, and Working Poverty: A Statistical Analysis for Metropolitan Chicago. Chicago: Chicago Urban League, Latino Institute, Northern Illinois University, 1997.

_____. Latinas in Chicago: A Portrait. Chicago: Latino Institute, October 1996.

Rakove, Milton. Don't Make No Waves, Don't Back No Losers: An Insider's Analysis of the Daley Machine. Bloomington: Indiana University Press, 1975.

Ramírez-Salazar, Blanca. Omaha, Nebraska Block Maps: Geographic Distribution of Racial/Ethnic Minorities—Census 2000. Lincoln, NE: Nebraska Equal Employment Opportunity Commission, 2002.

Rivlin, Gary. Fire on the Prairie: Chicago's Harold Washington and the Politics of Race. New York: Henry Holt, 1992.

Rogal, Brian. Latinos Emerge as a Force in Politics, Economy. Chicago, IL: Community News Project, Community Media Workshop, 2002.

Rosales, Francisco A., and Daniel T. Simon. "Mexican Immigration Experience in Urban Midwest; East Chicago, Indiana, 1919–1945." Indiana Magazine of History (December 1981): 333–57.

Rumbaut, Rubén G., and Alejandro Portes. "Introduction—Ethnogenesis: Coming of Age in Immigrant America." Ethnicities: Children of Immigrants in America. Berkeley: University of California Press, 2001.

Samora, Julián. *La Raza: Forgotten Americans and Mexican Americans.* Notre Dame, IN: University of Notre Dame Press, 1966.

_____. *A History of the Mexican American People.* Notre Dame, IN: University of Notre Dame Press, 1977.

San Juan Cafferty, Pastora, and David W. Ergstrom. *Hispanics in the United States: AnAgenda for the Twenty-First Century.* New Brunswick: Transaction Publishers, 2000.

Santillán, Richard. "Latino Politics in the Midwestern United States: 1915–1986." *Latinos and the Political System.* Ed. F. Chris García. Notre Dame, IN: University of Notre Dame Press, 1988.

_____. "Mexican Baseball Teams in the Midwest, 1916-1965: The Politics of Cultural Survival and Civil Rights." *Perspectives in Mexican American Studies, Mexican American Studies and Research Center.* Vol. 7. Tucson: The University of Arizona, 2000.

_____. "Rosita the Riveter: Midwest Mexican American Women during World War II, 9141–1945." *Perspectives in Mexican American Studies: Mexicans in the Midwest.* Vol. 2. Tucson: Mexican American Studies and Research Center, University of Arizona, 1989.

_____. "Saving Private José: Midwestern Mexican American Men during World War II, 1941–1945." *The Journal of Interdisciplinary Studies: A Journal of Research and Innovative Activities.* Vol. 14. Pomona, CA: California Polytechnic Institute, 2001.

_____. "Latino Political Development in the Southwest and Midwest Regions: A Comparative Overview, 1915–1989." *Latinos and Political Coalitions, Political Empowerment for the 1990s.* Eds. Roberto E. Villarreal and Norma G. Hernández. Westport, CN: Greenwood Press, 1991.

_____. "Midwestern Mexican American Women and the Struggle for Gender Equality: A Historical Overview, 1920s–1960s." *Perspectives in Mexican American Studies: Mexican American Women, Changing Image.* Vol. 5. Tucson: Mexican American Studies and Research Center, The University of Arizona, 1995.

_____. "Latinos in the Midwestersn United States." Ed. Chris García. *Latinos in the Political System.* Notre Dame, IN: University of Notre Dame Press, 1988. 99–118.

Sepulveda, Ciro. "La Colonia de Harbor: A History of Mexicanos in East Chicago, Indiana 1919–1932." Ph.D Diss., University of Notre Dame, 1976.

Suro, Roberto. *Strangers among Us: Latino Lives in a Changing America.* New York: Vintage Books, 1998.

Taller de Estudios Comunitarios. *Rudy Lozano: His life, His people.* Chicago, IL: Taller de Estudios Comunitarios, 1991.

Taylor, Paul S. *Mexican Labor in the United States: Chicago and the Calumet.* Berkeley: University of California Publications in Economics, 1932.

The Urban Institute. *Taxes Paid by Illinois Immigrants: A technical paper produced for the Illinois Immigrant Policy Project*. Chicago: IIPP, May 1996.

Valadez, John. "Latino Politics in Chicago: Pilsen in the 1990 General Election." Eds. Rodolfo de la Garza, Martha Menchaca and Louis DeSipio. *Barrio Ballots: Latino Politics in the 1990 Elections*. Boulder: Westview Press, 1994. 115–136.

Valle, Victor, and Rodolfo Torres. *Latino Metropolis*. Minneapolis: University of Minnesota Press, 2000.

Wilson, James Q. *Negro Politicians: The Rise of Negro Politics in Chicago*. Chicago: University of Chicago, 1935.

Young, Iris Marion. "Structure, Difference, and Hispanics." *Hispanics/Latino Ethnicity, Race, and Rights*. New York: Routledge, 2000.

Contributors

David A. Badillo, Ph.D. Visiting Fellow at the University of Notre Dame's Institute for Latino Studies (and Visiting Associate Professor in the Department of History), recently completed a book on Latinos and the Catholic Church. Several of his articles on Mexican-American religious identity have appeared in scholarly journals, and Michigan State University Press published his monograph, *Latinos in Michigan in 2003*. He is presently writing a history of MALDEF (the Mexican American Legal Defense and Educational Fund), a national civil rights organization.

Gilberto Cárdenas, Ph.D. has served as Assistant Provost and Director of the Institute for Latino Studies at the University of Notre Dame since 1999, where he also holds the Julián Samora Chair in Latino Studies and is Professor of Sociology. He has worked in the area of immigration for over thirty years, gaining international recognition as a scholar in Mexican immigration. Dr. Cárdenas has authored or edited numerous books, articles and reports on immigration, race and ethnic relations, historical and comparative sociology, and visual sociology. His publications include *Los Mojados 1971: The Wetback Story* (co-authored with Julián Samora and Jorge Bustamante) as well as recent articles and chapters on Latinos in the Midwest, Chicano art, formation of a national Chicano population, and Mexican migration to Texas.

Miguel A. Carranza, Ph.D. is a tenured Associate Professor of Sociology & Ethnic Studies and Coordinator of Latino and Latin American Studies in the

Department of Sociology and the Institute for Ethnic Studies, respectively, at the University of Nebraska-Lincoln (UNL). Dr. Carranza was co-editor of a special issue of *Great Plains Research* (Fall 2000) on "The Latino Experience in the Great Plains" (UNL Center for Great Plains Studies). He is also co-author of *Ethnic Studies in the United States: A Guide to Research* (Garland Publishing 1996). Dr. Carranza is a founding member of the Latino Research Initiative (LRI) and has also been a co-investigator on a statewide study of the "Integration of the Hispanic/Latino Immigrant Workforce," and a "Neighbors Working Together Project" focusing on the core neighborhoods encompassing the downtown and UNL areas of Lincoln.

Patricia Mendoza, Esq. is Chief of the Civil Rights Bureau of the Illinois Attorney General's office, where she enforces laws prohibiting discrimination on the basis of race, color, national origin, sex, religion or disability. Using federal and state civil rights laws, she investigates and litigates complaints alleging a pattern and practice or policy of unlawful discrimination in employment, housing, credit and places of public accommodation. From 1995 until June of 2003, she was the Regional Counsel of the Chicago office of the Mexican American Legal Defense and Educational Fund (MALDEF), a national litigation and advocacy organization that uses the law, community education and research to protect the civil rights of the nation's more than 37 million Latinos. She has spoken extensively on affirmative action, immigrant rights and education equity issues.

Judith Murphy, O.S.B. is a Benedictine sister and an educator who lives in Chicago. She taught in elementary and high schools in Chicago and Colorado, and served as Dean of Students, Principal, and then President of St. Scholastica High School in Chicago. In 1996, she became the founding Principal of Cristo Rey Jesuit High School in Chicago, and served there until 2001. She continues to consult with groups beginning new schools through the Cristo Rey Network and in the Chicago High School Redesign Initiative

Víctor Ortiz González, Ph.D. is a native of El Paso, Texas. He is an anthropologist who received his Ph.D. from Stanford University. Currently, he is the Coordinator for the Mexican and Caribbean Studies Program at Northeastern Illinois University in Chicago, Illinois. The University of Minnesota Press will publish his forthcoming book, *El Paso: Local Frontiers at a Global Crossroad*, in 2004.

Ricardo Parra is a Midwest writer and community activist residing in Indianapolis. Active in civil rights activities for many years, he is the past director of the Midwest Council of La Raza. He also is a past member of the Indiana Advisory Committee to the U.S. Commission on Civil Rights. In 2000 through 2001, Parra served as a member of the first Mayor's Commission on Latino Affairs for the City of Indianapolis. His articles and writings on Latino civil rights, economics, immigration, labor, farm labor, health, education, demographics, globalization, community studies, language and culture have appeared in various publications including the *Indianapolis Star, Latino Link, The Criterion, Revista Maryknoll, La Ola Latino-Americana, El Puente,* and *Mundo Latino Magazine, Hispanic Online, Catalyst, Aztlán Journal of Social Science* and other publications. He is a member of the National Association of Hispanic Journalists.

Sylvia Puente, M. A. is Director of the Metropolitan Chicago Initiative, Institute for Latino Studies (ILS) at the University of Notre Dame. She has spent her career in service to the Latino community, conducting community research, analyzing public policy, and building strong communities. She served as project director for "Bordering the Mainstream" in Berwyn and Cicero, Illinois. Before joining ILS, Puente served as New Community Initiatives Director for The Resurrection Project and prior to that as Director of Research and of Public Policy and Advocacy for the Latino Institute. In 2003, she was one of 25 Chicago area women named a "Pioneer for Social Justice." She is frequently asked to report on issues that impact Latinos in the Chicago metropolitan area. Puente has an M.A. in Public Policy Studies from the University of Chicago.

Refugio I Rochín, Ph.D. is an accomplished administrator, educator, author, fundraiser, social scientist, and leader in higher education. Since September 2003, Rochín has been the Executive Director of the Society for Advancement of Chicanos/Latinos and Native Americans in Science, headquartered in Santa Cruz, California. Prior to that, he was a senior fellow of the Institute for Latino Studies at the University of Notre Dame and the Institute's associate director for the Inter-University Program for Latino Research (IUPLR). Rochín was the founding director of the Smithsonian Center for Latino Initiatives in Washington, DC. From 1994 to 1998, he was Professor of Sociology and Agricultural Economics and the first permanent director of the Julian Samora Research Institute (JSRI) at Michigan State University (MSU). Prior to his appointment at MSU, Rochín was principal investigator and Professor of Agricultural Economics and Chicano Studies at the University of California, Davis.

Alex Santana, originally from Pico Rivera, CA, is currently an undergraduate at the University of Notre Dame. As a student of Political Science and Economics, he spent a semester in Washington, DC, where he had the opportunity to work with Refugio I. Rochín, Ph.D. at the Inter-University Program for Latino Research. Santana is interested in tax policy and immigration policy, particularly, its effects on local and national economies. He plans to attend law school in the fall of 2004.

María de los Ángeles Torres, Ph.D. Associate Professor of Political Science at DePaul University in Chicago, holds a doctorate in political science from the University of Michigan. Active in community service in Chicago for several years, Torres was Executive Director of the Mayor's Advisory Commission on Latino Affairs from 1983 to 1987. She has served on the Board of Directors of the Cuban American Committee Research and Education Fund (1979–94) and on the Board of Advisors of Cátedra de Cultura Cubana of the Pablo Milanés Foundation in Havana (1993–95). A member of the American Political Science Association's President's Task Force on the Status of Latinos from 1991 to 1994, she was a founding member of the Latino Studies section of the Latin American Studies Association, and served as co-chair from 2000 to 2002. Torres is the author of numerous publications on contemporary political and social relations between Cuba and the United States, as well as on Latino immigration and communities in the United States. Her books include *In the Land of Mirrors: Cuban Exile Politics in the U.S.*, *The Lost Apple: Operation Pedro Pan, Cuban Children in the U.S.* and *The Promise of a Better Future*. She co-edited *Borderless Borders: Latinos, Latin Americans and the Paradoxes of Interdependence* and edited *By Heart/De Memoria: Cuban Women Journeys In and out of Exile*.

Martha Zurita, Ph.D. received her PhD in Educational Policy Studies from the University of Illinois at Urbana-Champaign with an emphasis on the Sociology of Education. Her research focuses on Latino education at all levels. Prior to joining the Institute for Latino Studies at the University of Notre Dame as senior Latino Studies Research Analyst, she was the Director of Policy and Research for the Latino Education Alliance in Chicago, Illinois.

Additional titles in our
Hispanic Civil Rights Series

Message to Aztlán
Rodolfo "Corky" Gonzales
ISBN 1-55885-331-6

**A Gringo Manual on How
to Handle Mexicans**
José Angel Gutiérrez
ISBN 1-55885-326-X

**Eyewitness: A Filmmaker's
Memoir of the Chicano
Movement**
Jesús Salvador Treviño
ISBN 1-55885-349-9

**Pioneros puertorriqueños en
Nueva York, 1917–1947**
Joaquín Colón
ISBN 1-55885-335-9

**The American GI Forum: In
Pursuit of the Dream, 1948–1983**
Henry A. J. Ramos
Clothbound, ISBN 1-55885-261-1
Trade Paperback, ISBN 1-55885-262-X

**Chicano! The History of the
Mexican American Civil Rights
Movement**
F. Arturo Rosales
ISBN 1-55885-201-8

**Testimonio: A Documentary
History of the Mexican-American
Struggle for Civil Rights**
F. Arturo Rosales
ISBN 1-55885-299-9

**They Called Me "King Tiger":
My Struggle for the Land
and Our Rights**
Reies López Tijerina
ISBN 1-55885-302-2

**Julian Nava: My Mexican-
American Journey**
Julian Nava
Clothbound, ISBN 1-55885-364-2
Trade Paperback, ISBN 1-55885-351-0

César Chávez: A Struggle for Justice / César Chávez: La lucha por la justicia
Richard Griswold del Castillo
ISBN 1-55885-364-2

Memoir of a Visionary: Antonia Pantoja
Antonia Pantoja
2002, 384 pages, Clothbound
ISBN 1-55885-365-0, $26.95

Black Cuban, Black American
Evelio Grillo
2000, 134 pages, Trade Paperback
ISBN 1-55885-293-X, $13.95

Hector P. García: In Relentless Pursuit of Justice
Ignacio M. García
2002, 256 pages, Clothbound
ISBN 1-55885-387-1, $26.95

The Life and Times of Willie Velásquez: Su voto es su voz
Juan A. Sepúlveda, Jr.
2003, 384 Pages, Clothbound
ISBN 1-55885-419-3, $27.95

The Struggle for the Health and Legal Protection of Farm Workers: El Cortito
Maurice Jourdane
2004, 208 Pages, Clothbound
ISBN 1-55885-426-6, $34.95